John Bulloch and Harvey Morris

NO FRIENDS BUT THE MOUNTAINS

The Tragic History of the Kurds

OXFORD UNIVERSITY PRESS
New York   Oxford

Oxford University Press

Oxford   New York   Toronto
Delhi   Bombay   Calcutta   Madras   Karachi
Kuala Lumpur   Singapore   Hong Kong   Tokyo
Nairobi   Dar es Salaam   Cape Town
Melbourne   Auckland

and associated companies in
Berlin   Ibadan

Copyright © 1992 by John Bulloch, Harvey Morris

First published in England by the Penguin Group (Viking), London
First published in the United States by Oxford University Press, Inc.,
200 Madison Avenue, New York, New York 10016

Oxford is a registered trademark of Oxford University Press

Library of Congress Cataloging-in-Publication Data
Bulloch, John.
No friends but the mountains : the tragic history of the Kurds /
John Bulloch. Harvey Morris.
p. cm.   Includes index.
ISBN 0-19-508075-0
1. Kurds—History.   2. Middle East—Ethnic relations.
I. Morris, Harvey.   II. Title.
DS59.K86B85   1992
956'.0049159—dc20   92-36877

9 8 7 6 5 4 3 2 1

Printed in the United States of America
on acid-free paper

Contents

List of Illustrations

Author's Note

No attempt has been made in this book to give a scholarly
transliteration of Kurdish, Arabic, or Persian names for people
or places. The style adopted is the one generally used in British
or French newspapers, which it is thought would be most familiar
to readers of this work in the English language.

Acknowledgements

Our thanks are due to many people who have helped us with this book, but particularly to Ali Hassan, deputy head of the KDP office in Qamishli, Syria, who made it possible for us to travel into Kurdistan, and to see at first hand what was happening in those desperate days at the end of the Kurdish uprising in northern Iraq.

We are also most grateful to Siyamend Othman for allowing us to draw on the deep knowledge and research shown in his thesis *Contribution Historique à l'Étude du Parti Dimokrat i Kurdistan i Iraq*, published by l'École des Hautes Études en Sciences Sociales, Paris, 1985, and to the staff of the Kurdish Institute in Paris for assistance in using its extensive library.

Hoshyar Zebari, a member of the Central Committee of the KDP and European representative of the party, was generous with his time and illuminating with his personal recollections of many of the great events of Iraqi Kurdistan in recent years.

In earlier times we were greatly helped by officials in Iran, Iraq and Turkey, where we always found Kurdish leaders in all those countries to be courteous, understanding and realistic about their own situation.

All these and many others have given us valuable information, or have helped us with explanations and forecasts. We emphasize, however, that the interpretations and judgements, and any mistakes, are entirely our own.

London and Oxford, 1991

BLACK SEA

●ANKARA

TURKEY

Euphrates

● Incirlik

Diyarbakir ●

Tigris

● Mardin

Malikiyeh

Quamishli

● Aleppo

Hassaka ●

Sinjar

Euphrates

MEDITERRANEAN SEA

LEBANON

SYRIA

● DAMASCUS

IRAQ

Kurdistan Regions

0   200 Km

0   120 Miles

ESTIMATED KURDISH POPULATION: 17,110,000

TURKEY	9m (20% of total)	SYRIA	750,000 (8% of total)
IRAN	4m (11% of total)	USSR	300,000
IRAQ	3m (23% of total)	LEBANON	60,000

U S S R

• Yerevan

LAKE VAN

• Van

• Tabriz

CASPIAN SEA

Hakkari •

LAKE ORUMIYEH

Silopi •

Orumiyeh •

• Zakho

Barzan

Oshnaviyeh •

• Dahuk

Haj Omran •

Mahabad •

Rawanduz

Zab

• Mosul

Qaladiza •

• Saqqez

Arbil •

Ranya

Alton Kupry •

Baneh •

TEHRAN •

I R A N

Kirkuk •

Suleimaniyeh

Penjwin

Tigris

• Sanandaj

Halabja

Tikrit •

Kermanshah •

Khaneqin •

• BAGHDAD

Chapter One

THE UPRISING

Shortly before five on the afternoon of 29 March 1991 Massoud Barzani, fourth son of the legendary Mullah Mustafa and commander-in-chief of the Kurdish insurgent forces in northern Iraq, emerged from the guest house at Salahuddin which he had so recently commandeered from Saddam Hussein, posed briefly for a final photograph, climbed into his white super-saloon Toyota and drove away from the hill resort for a council of war with his rebel commanders.

Kirkuk, the chief town of southern Kurdistan and the biggest prize that had been won in seven decades of almost uninterrupted Kurdish rebellion against Baghdad, had fallen to government troops the previous night after little more than a week in rebel hands. Arbil, at the edge of the plain 10 miles below Salahuddin, was surrounded by Saddam's forces on two sides. The first refugees, travelling in trucks, cars and even in the buckets of bulldozers, were beginning to clog the roads to the mountains and the relative safety of the Turkish and Iranian borders. The Kurdish uprising, which in barely three weeks had succeeded in routing the Iraqi leader's forces from one fifth of Iraqi territory, was virtually at an end.

Barzani and his commanders were contemplating the collapse of the most dramatic, though short-lived, victory in modern Kurdish history. Yet even when the Kurds were forced to accept a formal ceasefire on 11 April, Barzani's forces still controlled more territory than his father had managed to secure at the height of his powers in the early 1970s. What was more, the vast exodus of up to three million Kurds fleeing the anticipated reprisals of Saddam's forces brought the Kurdish question to world attention more than at any time since the Kurds were cheated of a sovereign state in the aftermath of World War I.

Barzani had returned from exile in Iran at the beginning of March, a week after the victory of US-led coalition forces over Saddam Hussein's army of occupation in Kuwait and within days of a spontaneous uprising by the Kurds in the small town of Ranya against the apparatus of repression which enabled the Baath Arab Socialist Party to maintain control. Within the next ten days the uprising spread to all major towns, liberating 95 per cent of Iraqi Kurdistan. For the first time in most people's memory the ordinary Kurds of Iraq were enjoying a taste of freedom. After seven months of international sanctions against Iraq and almost two months of allied bombardment there was little food or petrol, no electricity or telephone service and only uncertain water supplies. But there was an atmosphere of euphoria in the streets of Arbil, Zakho and Dahuk and in the villages of the mountains, fed by the prospect that, this time, the insurgency might succeed in overthrowing the dictator in Baghdad and in establishing a regime of peace, democracy and national autonomy in the Kurdish homeland. It was a feeling that affected even the most sober members of the rebel leadership. For a while, it seemed, they forgot the mournful adage which has so accurately reflected their plight: 'The Kurds have no friends but the mountains.'

In the event the Kurds were abandoned in their hour of greatest need by the coalition forces which had been assembled in the Gulf to reverse the aggression against Kuwait. Only when news of the plight of Kurdish refugees, freezing and starving on the mountainsides, reached the outside world did the Western powers which had defeated Saddam Hussein respond to public opinion by setting up safe havens for the frightened refugees in the north of Iraq.

But it was not the Western powers but rather the Kurdish fighters themselves who halted the tide of the Iraqi counter-attack that Easter weekend. After meeting his commanders Barzani tried unsuccessfully to persuade tribal leaders to stand firm with him at Salahuddin to stop the Iraqis sweeping north along the main highway into the Kurdish heartland. As the Iraqi column headed towards the mountain resort, most believed that the war was already lost; with Barzani abandoned by his allies, all that lay between the Iraqi army and the liberated zone was Barzani himself and his 150-man *peshmerga* bodyguard. This small force made its stand in the Kore valley, just north of Salahaddin. In an encounter which rapidly entered Kurdish folklore, they held off an Iraqi division, backed by tanks and helicopter gunships. The battle of Kore halted the Iraqi offensive, protected the Kurdish territories further north, covered the retreat of the civilian refugees and, by denying Saddam an all-out victory, forced him to the negotiating table.

The 1991 uprising was a unique moment in the history of Kurdish nationalism. For the first time the world community was united in its opposition to the regime in Baghdad, with the US-led coalition actively calling for its overthrow. With the ending of the Cold War and the decline of Soviet power, there appeared to be nothing to stop the West from following up the victory in Kuwait by supporting the Kurds and other anti-regime forces fighting to escape Saddam's yoke. The Kurds believed what they heard; they were lured into a sense of false confidence by the apparently positive signals from Western capitals, and embarked on a rebellion which they assumed would have the backing of the West. The help they needed never came. Once more they were forced back on a policy of dialogue with their greatest enemy.

Throughout their long history, the Kurdish people have rarely enjoyed a period of peace and stability, and they have never been able to count on loyal allies. They have been the victims of their own divisions as well as of the rivalries of neighbouring and outside powers, and never more so than in the twentieth century. The bitter experience of March 1991 was no more than the latest of a series of near victories which turned to disasters. Yet despite the efforts of the outside world to deny their existence as a nation and to crush their separate identity, the Kurds have always persisted in challenging the status quo. They continue to do so today, struggling against the odds for their rightful place in the world.

The Kurds and their ancestors have lived in the land now called Kurdistan for 4,000 years, but in modern times they have only once had a mini-state of their own. In 1918 President Woodrow Wilson set out his Fourteen Points Declaration before Congress in which he spoke of a future Kurdish homeland emerging from the ruins of the Ottoman empire. But the machinations of post-World War I imperialism ensured that this vision never came to fruition. Within two years southern Kurdistan was annexed to the new British-run Arab state of Iraq. Modern Turkey swallowed up the Kurdish territories of the old Ottoman empire and set about a policy of cultural annihilation, while elsewhere Kurds were reduced to the status of a second-class minority.

Yet there still exists an unmarked frontier following the foothills of the Taurus and the Zagros mountains, running west into the Syrian Jezireh as far as the Euphrates, and to the north almost to the Black Sea. That boundary embraces the mountainous homeland of the Kurds, the largest nation on earth without a state of its own.

There are perhaps a million Kurds in the north-eastern corner of Syria, four million more in Iraq, five million in Iran and more than ten million in Turkey, as well as a smaller minority in the Soviet Union – more than twenty million people in an area the size of France, united by a common culture and a distinct language but divided by the frontiers of five states.

Since the end of World War I there have been revolts among Kurds demanding autonomy and independence in almost all the regions of Kurdistan. But these movements have invariably been isolated and unco-ordinated. For the first time, during the Iran–

Iraq war, there were rebellions among Kurds in the three principal states – Iraq, Iran and Turkey – against the central powers
in those countries, fuelling the pan-Kurdish feeling which had
already begun to emerge among ordinary Kurds.

The conditions of the Kurdish population in each state vary
widely, although all Kurds have suffered forms of repression
ranging from cultural assimilation to physical annihilation.
Ironically, it is in Iraq, where the treatment of the Kurds has
been the most brutal, that the Kurdish minority has for historical
reasons enjoyed the widest measure of autonomy. Perhaps as a
consequence of being able to retain a stronger sense of separate
identity than those of neighbouring states, the Kurds of Iraq
have also proved the most rebellious and recalcitrant. For this
reason the history of modern Kurdish nationalism is dominated
by the struggle of the Kurds of Iraq, who have had an influence
on the Kurdish movement much greater than their numerical
position within the Kurdish nation would suggest.

The Iraqi Kurds learned in the later stages of their long struggle
that there was no outside power on which they could depend. In
1975 the rebel leader Mullah Mustafa Barzani was cheated by
the combined forces of the CIA, Henry Kissinger and the Shah
of Iran – his supposed allies against the Baathist regime in Iraq –
and thrown aside in favour of a strategic settlement between
Baghdad and Tehran. When his successors resumed the struggle
during the Iran–Iraq war, they were answered with mass deportations, the destruction of Kurdish towns and villages, and a
scorched earth policy in the countryside; finally in 1988 they
suffered the unrestrained use by the Iraqi forces of chemical
weapons, leading to a mass exodus of civilian refugees, while the
international community looked on in virtual silence. It was
against this background that the Kurdish leadership had to plot
its strategy as the world moved towards war in the Gulf in the
autumn of 1990.

Back in the early summer of 1988 the Iraqi Kurdish leaders
had foreseen the campaign of vengeance that Saddam Hussein

would unleash against the Kurds once his war with Iran was over. So in June of that year they resolved to put aside sectarian differences within the nationalist movement and to form a unified Kurdistan Front to try to meet the challenge and to pursue their shared demands for autonomy. The parties which joined to form the Front were Barzani's Kurdistan Democratic Party (KDP), the Patriotic Union of Kurdistan (PUK), led by Jalal Talabani, the Kurdistan Socialist Party, Sami Abderrahman's Kurdistan People's Democratic Party, the small socialist PASOK Party and the Kurdish regional branch of the Iraqi Communist Party.

The formation of the Front represented a belated recognition that the chronic divisions within the Kurdish movement, which had often involved open warfare between rival parties, had done nothing except serve the enemy. Its founders acknowledged that their ideological differences were not irreconcilable, and they settled on a relatively modest political programme based on self-determination within Iraq. They did, however, commit themselves to co-operating with elements of the Iraqi Arab opposition – the nationalists, the Islamic parties and dissident Baathists – in seeking the overthrow of Saddam, something enthusiastically encouraged by Syria and Iran, which had their own quarrels with the Baghdad regime. Massoud Barzani spent three months in Damascus in early 1989 trying to work out a formula for a joint platform between the Kurds and the Arab parties, but the predominantly Shia Islamic parties baulked at the idea of putting their names to the essentially secular and democratic platform proposed by the other groups.

These tentative efforts at establishing a viable opposition to Saddam went almost entirely unnoticed in the West, where concern for human rights in Iraq took second place to concern for the lucrative trade opportunities arising from the end of the Iran–Iraq war. Guerrilla activity in Kurdistan had come to a halt, enabling the Iraqis to pursue unchecked a policy of destruction and forced deportations. The only option open to the Kurdish leaders appeared to be a new political initiative to bring the plight of their people to world attention. To do this, Barzani embarked on a frustrating tour of western Europe, visiting France, Sweden, Britain, West Germany and Switzerland; he told us he gained the impression that Saddam Hussein was regarded by the West as, at worst, a necessary evil whose continued existence would help to ensure stability in the Gulf, and, at best, as a useful addition to the moderate Arab bloc.

The Kurdish leader did win one significant victory when the British government turned down an export licence for the sale of British Aerospace Hawk trainers to Iraq, after he argued that they could be converted to offensive use against the Kurds. The deal had the support of the Defence Ministry and the Department of Trade but was opposed by the Foreign Office. The matter came up for decision at a Cabinet meeting attended for the first time in his brief role as foreign secretary by John Major, the future prime minister. Whether as a result of Barzani's persuasiveness or because it was felt that Major should not suffer a Cabinet defeat at the start of his tenure, the minority Foreign Office view won the day.

At the meeting of exiled Kurds in London in July 1989 Barzani said he had tried to warn the West that Saddam was not to be trusted, after having emerged from eight years of war against Iran with his armed forces virtually intact. He said the Iraqi dictator was likely to embark on some new military adventure and picked out Baghdad's border dispute with Kuwait as a possible flashpoint. If these arguments ever got as far as Western leaders, then they fell on deaf ears.

The tenth congress of Barzani's KDP, in December 1989, was held in an isolated village near Orumiyeh in Iran, the first such meeting in a decade. In view of the disaster of the poison gas attacks on Kurdish villages by the Iraqi army at the end of the first Gulf war in 1988, and the forced exodus that caused, Barzani offered his resignation as leader, but was prevailed upon to stay. In twelve days of talks delegates from Kurdistan and the Kurdish diaspora discussed how to revitalize the Kurdish movement after the savage Iraqi onslaught of 1988–9. The congress resolved to continue the struggle, despite the temptation to capitulate to Saddam, but not to rely entirely on developing a guerrilla army. In a move which was to have an important impact on the subsequent uprising, the congress decided to try to extend its influence in the cities of Kurdistan, and to contact the pro-regime units of the Kurdish Popular Army with a view to a future alliance against Saddam.

Throughout 1989 patrols of Kurdish *peshmerga* ('those who face death') began infiltrating back into Iraqi Kurdistan on reconnaissance missions. They found a country devastated by the army and emptied of people. Whole towns and villages had been forcibly moved to so-called Victory Cities, in fact virtual concentration camps for those who had been evicted from their land. Despite the difficulties, a group of senior commanders, including Dr Kamal Kirkuki, who was later to command the Zakho front in the uprising, were selected to reorganize guerrilla forces on the ground with a view to maintaining civilian Kurdish morale. Their orders were to keep the resistance going but to avoid direct confrontations with the army wherever possible.

Such was the situation when, on 2 August 1990, Saddam Hussein ordered his forces into Kuwait.

The Kurdish leaders were as uncertain as everyone about the ultimate intentions of the Americans and their allies in sending the expeditionary force to defend Saudi Arabia and to confront the Iraqis. Given their past experiences of Western betrayal, the Kurds opted for a position of neutrality in the dispute, condemning the invasion though not actively supporting the allied response to it. Given their relative military weakness, they did not want to give Saddam any excuse to launch a new wave of repression in the north on the grounds that the Kurds were siding with the enemy. A decision was even taken to suspend all military activities as a signal to Saddam that the Kurds were not preparing to stab him in the back if he were to be attacked by the allies.

The Kurds saw little prospect that the Western build-up in the Gulf would bring them any direct advantage. In the early months of the crisis there was certainly no thought in the West of a possible Kurdish role in an Iraqi post-war settlement, if indeed there was to be a war. The Kurds were also mindful of the fact that if they decided to strike at the regime but struck too soon and before it was sufficiently weakened, then Baghdad might respond as it had in the past, with bombardment by chemical weapons. Saddam's deputy, Izzat Ibrahim, had even gone to Suleimaniyeh to warn them: 'If you have forgotten Halabja, I would like to remind you that we are ready to repeat the operation.'

They learned from their Western contacts that there was no plan to topple Saddam, and they deduced from this that the coalition gathering its forces in Saudi Arabia had no commitment to political change in Iraq. But they reasoned that with Saddam facing a possible war, he might be prepared to make concessions to ensure Kurdish neutrality.

In October Iraqi intelligence officers did make indirect contact with Massoud Barzani through Kurdish middlemen. Barzani told them he was prepared to discuss any genuine peace proposals, but there was no further response. The leadership assumed that the contact had been merely an attempt by Saddam to gauge the mood in the Kurdish camp, and that the peace feelers were not genuine.

While continuing to remain open to any concessions Saddam might be prepared to make – for instance, the right of deported Kurdish peasants to return to their land – the leadership evolved a plan of what to do in the event of the collapse of the regime. This involved preparations for an immediate take-over of administration in the cities of Kurdistan, so as to be able to take control within just twenty-four hours. It was also during the Western military build-up that Barzani had a secret meeting with Mohamed Bakr al-Hakim, leader of Dawa, the anti-Saddam Shia group based in Tehran. Dawa claimed to represent the Shia population of southern Iraq, so Barzani was anxious to co-ordinate policy in the event of Saddam's fall.

In the last months of 1990 all the opposition groups met in Damascus to try to hammer out a policy to which all could subscribe. It proved a difficult task, with days spent discussing whether there should be the usual references to the Koran, demanded by the Shia groups and vigorously opposed by the communists and other secular organizations, with the Kurds trying to act as mediators. After three weeks of often acrimonious discussion a common position was worked out, with a modest programme drawn up to be ratified by another conference, held in Beirut in December. That conference saw the formation, in the last week of 1990, of a united front made up of the Kurdish and other Iraqi opposition parties, with the simple common intent of bringing about the overthrow of Saddam and the installation of a coalition government to lead the country towards democracy. Keeping to the even-handed approach, the meeting condemned not only Saddam's invasion of Kuwait but also the Western military build-up which followed it.

While maintaining a public posture of neutrality, the Kurds sought to strengthen the Iraqi opposition and to remind the world of its existence, as, until that moment, it had been largely ignored. With one in five members of the Iraqi armed forces and militia a Kurd, and with many sympathizers working within the regime, the Kurdish movement had excellent intelligence on Iraqi war preparations, but, given their cautious desire not to be seen directly helping Saddam's enemies, the Kurds chose to leak their information to the Western press rather than to deal with governments, a policy which considerably increased their profile as the crisis progressed.

Almost as soon as the air war against Iraq was launched by President Bush on 17 January, the allies began considering what kind of Iraq might emerge from the rubble. Key concerns were that the country should not be allowed to fall apart or fall under the domination of one or other local power. Yet the US administration produced no clear idea of what it foresaw, beyond a vague assumption that the successor to Saddam would probably come from within the armed forces. Given the terms of the Security Council resolutions permitting the use of force in the Gulf, the potential fragility of the coalition confronting Saddam and a suspicion of the motives and abilities of the Iraqi opposition, the Bush administration ruled out any attempt to involve itself directly in Iraq's internal politics. To make things more difficult all round, a policy of no contact with the Iraqi opposition had been in force since a visit to the State Department in 1988 by Jalal Talabani, head of the PUK, had provoked strong protests from the Iraqis and the Turks.

The British, much more than the Americans, appeared to recognize the possibility of promoting the opposition groups as a viable alternative. All of a sudden Kurdish representatives found doors opening to them which had previously been closed. From January onwards leaders of the rebel movements were invited to the Foreign Office for a series of meetings with senior officials. The British view put forward at these talks was that the Kurds might have a role to play in post-war Iraq, although not in the war itself. A senior British diplomat involved in these contacts said at the time: 'If Saddam is overthrown, and they stick together, the Iraqi opposition may be in with a chance.'

Among themselves, however, the same officials had concluded that the opposition stood little chance of taking over in the event of Saddam's fall, and regarded the Kurdish groups as irredeemably divided. This view persisted even after the combined opposition of Kurds, Shia and nationalists met in Beirut in March to discuss a common post-war strategy.

But the very fact of the London meetings encouraged the Kurds to believe they had Western support for an uprising. If the British were being so positive, this no doubt meant that they were also transmitting the views of the Americans. Had not George Bush called on 16 February for Iraqis to rise up against the dictator? 'There's another way for the bloodshed to stop,'

George Bush told an audience at the American Academy for the Advancement of Science. 'That is for the Iraqi military and the Iraqi people to take matters into their own hands, to force Saddam Hussein, the dictator, to step aside, and to comply with the UN, and then rejoin the family of peace-loving nations.'

That seemed clear enough to the people of Iraq, the Shia in the south of the country and the Kurds in the north. They rose up, as suggested, took matters into their own hands, and, with a little bit of help from the West, might well have forced Saddam Hussein to step aside, so that his successors could have complied with all UN resolutions. What the Shia did not know was that America's allies, the Saudi Arabians and the Kuwaitis in whose name the war had been fought, would not tolerate a state on their borders run by Shia, which might go the way of Iran. In the north the Turks vetoed an independent Kurdish state, which was equally abhorrent to the Iranians, whose goodwill the Americans wanted to free hostages in Beirut, and to the Syrians, who wanted no encouragement for their own Kurdish minority. What the president really meant, it emerged, was that the United States would like to see a compliant military regime in power in Baghdad. Kurds and Shia need not apply.

Of course no promises were made to the Shia or to the Kurds, but, as a diplomat not involved in the contacts bluntly put it: 'A climate was created which seemed to say: "If some of you people get together and rise up against Saddam, we won't dump you in the shit." Well, we did.' Encouraged by the signals from the West, the Kurds began to drop the cautious guard they had adopted throughout the crisis and started to plan for the final showdown with Saddam.

The turning-point came during the last hours of the Gulf war, when a large contingent of Kurdish officials, including Jalal Talabani, was in Washington to attend a conference at the Senate, ostensibly to discuss human rights in Iraq. In fact the meeting was designed as an opportunity for the Kurds to try to see US officials. Such was the air of optimism among the delegates on this final day of the war that Talabani was even discussing with some of his senior aides which ambassadorships they might like, once the opposition came to power.

Although the Kurdish side wanted desperately to know where the Americans stood before deciding how to act inside Iraq, US officials were still refusing to meet the Kurds directly. In an attempt to break the deadlock, Talabani, Sami Abderrahman and Hoshyar Zebari, the European spokesman of Barzani's KDP, had lunch with Madame Danielle Mitterrand, the wife of the French president and a long-standing supporter of the Kurdish cause, together with two American sympathizers, Claiborne Pell, the chairman of the Senate Foreign Relations Committee, and his chief aide, Peter Galbraith. The luncheon party decided that, as Madame Mitterrand was due to see Mrs Bush later that day, she should use the opportunity to get a personal message through to the president – that the administration should see the Kurds officially, just as the British and French had done. She returned from her White House engagement empty-handed. In their hour of victory the Americans were determined to remain unembroiled in the sectarian strife of the country they were in the process of defeating.

Talabani did not wait around for Bush to change his mind. The Syrians, one of America's nominal allies in the anti-Saddam coalition, and the Saudis, the main regional partner, were both jockeying for influence in the post-war settlement, and Talabani was being urged to return to the Middle East to help to set up a provisional government – a government in which the Kurds were already demanding seven Cabinet seats. Other Kurdish officials did stay on, but the only direct contact they had with the administration was a meeting with a junior official of the State Department in a coffee shop. They were told that as a meeting with a more senior official had not been cleared, they could not be allowed into the State Department building.

However, events in Iraq were outpacing the diplomatic manoeuvrings in Washington. On 2 March, forty-eight hours after

President Bush ordered a halt to the war, a disaffected Iraqi tank commander who had survived the retreat from Kuwait turned his gun on a 20-foot-high portrait of Saddam Hussein in the southern city of Basra. It was the first shot in a rebellion which spread among the Shia of the south and immediately threatened the regime of the defeated dictator.

The apparent success of the Shia rebels, who quickly captured most of the main towns of the south, alarmed the Americans, who feared that it signalled not only the break-up of Iraq but also the establishment of an Islamic republic in the south. These fears were fed by the exaggerated claims of Mohamed Bakr al-Hakim, the exiled Shia leader whom Barzani had met during the Kuwait crisis, that he was in control of the rebellion. In fact the movement was for the most part spontaneous and unco-ordinated, and took place within reach of concentrations of loyal troops – all factors in its swift collapse.

In the north it was a different matter. Internal security was largely in the hands of the Kurdish Popular Army, the pro-government Kurdish militia; many army units had been with-drawn to the south for the war, and the mountains, where the *peshmerga* had their bases, were virtually impregnable to a government counter-attack.

Ranya, a small town of 60,000, was the first to fall, on 4 March. After some minor incidents involving the Baath security forces, the townspeople attacked Baath Party headquarters, using weapons which the regime had distributed during the general mobilization caused by the Kuwait crisis. The Kurdistan Front coalition already had guerrillas in the town as part of the wartime plan to take power in the cities if Saddam fell. Barzani, who was in the Iranian border town of Sardasht when the rebellion began, crossed into Iraq to lead the uprising.

After Ranya, other towns and villages of Kurdistan rapidly fell to the forces of the uprising, the *intifada*, as the Kurds themselves called it. Suleimaniyeh followed Ranya, and then Arbil, Dahuk and Aqra fell within the next ten days. On

Newruz, the Kurdish new year's day (21 March), Kirkuk, the richest city in the north, was in rebel hands, and Mosul was under siege by guerrilla forces. Within two weeks of Saddam Hussein's defeat in the south by the coalition forces, almost the whole of Kurdistan was in revolt, and the dictator's troops were on the run.

The situation by mid-March was that most of Saddam Hussein's army was destroyed, the Shia south of Baghdad had risen against him, the Kurds were in control in most of the north, and the Americans and their allies were occupying a sixth of his territory. The remnants of his air force had been effectively grounded after Washington's blunt warning that 'If you fly, you die.' It seemed impossible that the regime could last for more than a few days.

One of the only ways into Iraqi Kurdistan was across the Tigris at the point where the borders of Syria, Turkey and Iran meet. We entered that way on 26 March, riding on a farm truck which slipped and slid down the mud track to the Tigris where wooden four-seater outboards were waiting to ferry us to the Iraqi bank 100 yards away. A group of vehicles and clusters of people stood in a field beyond a narrow spit of pebble shore. The local commander of the KDP in the Syrian town of Qamishli had entrusted us to the care of three tactiurn *peshmerga* – Ahmad, Nakmadi and Agid – who were to escort us the 10 miles to Zakho, the nearest liberated town. The rule seemed to be that no one crossed empty-handed, for food was running desperately short on the other side, so as we climbed into the boats Nakmadi heaved aboard a sack of carrots. Less than thirty seconds later we were across, and, as we neared the pebble shore, half a dozen guerrillas waded out into the shallow water to carry us to dry land and welcome us 'to free Kurdistan'.

For most of March the reports coming out of Kurdistan had been sketchy. The claims issued in Washington, London and Paris by representatives of the Kurdistan Front alliance, that virtually every town and village in northern Iraq had fallen to the rebels in the space of a few days, were almost impossible to believe. After all, Saddam had 100,000 troops stationed in the north, right up to the Turkish border, as well as many more pro-government Kurds in units of the Popular Army. Now, the insurgents claimed to control even Kirkuk, the northern oil town which had never, in seventy years of Kurdish struggle for autonomy, fallen into rebel hands. What we learnt at Zakho and towns further into the interior was that this vast army had collapsed virtually without a fight. At Arbil the 5th Army headquarters from which the regime had dominated Kurdistan was deserted. The troops had simply come out with their hands up at the first stirrings of the rebellion. It was a defeat even more ignominious than that suffered by the army in the south, where Saddam's troops had been beaten into submission by weeks of allied bombardment. In Kurdistan the army had fled in the face of spontaneous revolts by townspeople, backed only by small groups of guerrillas armed with little heavier than automatic rifles and rocket grenades. The role of the Popular Army units was vital. Drawn from Kurdish tribes whose leaders had supported Saddam against their fellow Kurds, these units defected en masse to the rebels as soon as the uprising began.

The narrowest stretch of liberated territory was at Zakho itself, wedged between a range of low hills and the Turkish border. To the south of the main road to Zakho from the Tigris crossing-point at Peshkhabur, the flatland stretched all the way to the nearest Iraqi artillery position, about 10 miles away.

The Iraqis had been shelling the main road since the fall of Zakho on 14 March, but the Kurds controlled a back road which ran past abandoned guard posts and barrack buildings, and the international customs shed at Ibrahim Khalil where Iraqi troops had blown the road bridge across the Khabur river to Turkey, and where Kurdish peasant women had now set up camp and were hanging out their washing.

At Zakho the KDP had commandeered a school as its headquarters, setting up two light anti-aircraft guns on the roof and plastering the façade with slogans and a portrait of the late Mullah Mustafa Barzani. Wood smoke was billowing from the kebab stall opposite; the stallholder was about the only man in the street without a rifle on his shoulder or a pistol on his hip. As we stepped down from our truck, the crowd in the street applauded. For a few heady, euphoric days, it was enough to be a Westerner, to be associated in some small way with that new hero of Kurdistan, President George Bush. 'Haji' Bush, they called him, using the term of respect reserved for elders who have made the pilgrimage to Mecca; 'Haji' Bush, after whom parents, it was said, were naming their new-born in recognition of his victory over the tyrant Saddam Hussein. It was a love affair which had barely a week more to run its course. Within a few days, as Saddam's army began its inexorable march north, people were asking with mounting anger, where was Bush? Why did he not come to save them?

The main schoolroom was full of armed guerrillas, burly middle-aged men with fat moustaches and chequered turbans and the obvious authority of tribal dignitaries. A younger man sat behind a desk, receiving an endless stream of people who handed him hand-written messages which he would either sign or put aside. It was government by scribbled chit, a rudimentary system of administration by which the rebels kept their territory running during the brief weeks of freedom. There were chits for food, chits for petrol – which was even scarcer – chits to order guerrilla patrols from one point to another. The only food the guerrillas had to offer was some flat bread, some apricot jam, a lump of crumbly sheep's cheese – all donated by brother Kurds in Syria. The Kurds had suffered, like the rest of Iraq, from the UN sanctions imposed in August 1990 after the invasion of Kuwait, and the rebellion now meant that no supplies were coming from the south.

Among the insurgents were many who had fled the southern front at the height of the allied assault. A small, thin man with sticking-out ears called Shehab Ahmed said he had been in the southern town of Basra at the start of the war. 'We were in our bunkers for twenty-four hours a day once the American bombing started,' he said. 'Anyone who could flee, Arab or Kurd, did so.'

The Kurds in the Iraqi army served mainly as frontline infantry conscripts, cannon fodder for Saddam's great pan-Arab enterprise. Their Arab comrades were scarcely better off. We met some of them towards sunset, part of a group of seventy piled into a high-sided orange truck and bound for Syria, which had said it would take them in. They were among the tens of thousands of Arab soldiers who had surrendered to, or been captured by, the Kurds in the first days of the uprising. They wore tattered uniforms and they stank, but they happily chanted: 'Long live the bloodless revolution, down with Saddam.' Private Ayad from Mosul said he had been in the army since 1981. 'Saddam Hussein is a tyrant and unjust,' he said, perhaps in part for the benefit of the Kurds who were gathered round. 'The Kurds gave us the choice of staying here or going to Syria. We chose Syria because we can't go back to our families until Saddam falls.'

Their officers had taught the Arab conscripts to fear the Kurds, but when the uprising came those who surrendered were well-treated. Some were camped in mosques, others were taken in by Kurdish families. But there was little enough to feed the Kurdish people, let alone the 40,000 to 50,000 prisoners who had fallen so easily into Kurdish hands, so they were told to fend for themselves. It was part of the Kurdistan Front plan that there should be no reprisals against army troops or ordinary members of the regime, nor indeed against the Popular Army, which played a vital role in the success of the rebellion. There were reprisals, however, against the secret police. At military intelligence headquarters at Arbil, the courtyard wall was riddled with bullets and stained with the blood of twenty-eight Baathist agents who had been summarily executed.

The KDP military command at Zakho was headquartered at the Baghdad Hotel, a fading two-storey building with cell-like rooms where *peshmerga* were camped out, sitting on the floor as they ate their rations. The regional commander was Dr Kamal Kirkuki, a quiet, intellectual man of thirty-seven with thick greying hair, a greying moustache and a withered hand, the result of one of two wounds he had received in almost twenty years of guerrilla fighting. Sitting in the light of a kerosene lamp in his baggy khaki fatigues, grenades hanging from his waist, a .45 poking out of his cummerbund and a Kalashnikov AK-47 resting in his lap, he still had the air of a country doctor or a small-town schoolmaster. At a time when the Kurdish side was still on the offensive, he spoke of his plans to move his forces southwards from Zakho across the plain, to establish a defensive position and knock out the guns that were hitting the main road.

His immediate problem was to ensure food and medical supplies, but the most convenient access-point, the Turkish road bridge, was closed. 'I went to the border at Ibrahim Khalil at the start of the uprising,' he said. 'Some Turkish officials came down from Diyarbakir and told us to bring our wounded there, but the bridge still hasn't been repaired. They said they'd raise the matter with Ankara, but we've had no response . . . We can expect nothing from the Iraqi government. The only thing they send us is death by chemical weapons and artillery. This is allowed by Saddam – to deal with the Kurds in such a way.'

In a dirt-stained ward of Zakho hospital lay the victims of fighting outside the town, guerrillas with horrific burns and little hope of survival in the absence of dressings, drugs and anaesthetics. 'That one was burnt by organo-phosphorus,' said Dr Hassan Sabry, pointing at a man who had lost all the skin on his face and who held his hands above his chest because it was too painful to put them down. 'A bomb dropped at his feet from a plane and exploded. There's maybe a 20 per cent chance he might live.' In other wards there were gaunt-eyed mothers bending over the cots of withered children with the yellow elastic skin that comes with malnutrition. 'We have lost children here already,' said Dr Sabry, 'because there simply isn't enough food.'

The Kurdish forces were a mixed bag of professionals, such as

Dr Kirkuki, enthusiastic amateurs who, even at the height of the war, would hitch-hike home to their families at sunset, and units of the formerly pro-Saddam militias which had so precipitately changed sides.

Among the professionals was our driver, Ali Hossein Aziz, a dark handsome man in his mid-thirties, of military bearing but with an incongruously high-pitched, hoarse voice. He shared the classic Kurdish characteristics of stubbornness and generosity, but the latter always overcame the former. He had two wives and nine children whom he left behind in Zakho as we headed off into the unknown. Ali Hossein had been a *peshmerga* for two decades, punctuated, as is not uncommon in the Kurdish guerrilla movement, by a spell in the Iraqi army. He was always immaculate in his tan uniform, and each morning he would refold the red and white chequered square of cloth which formed his turban and wind it carefully round a small white skullcap, tucking the end neatly in at the side. The material was red and white, which showed he was of the Barzani clan. His Landcruiser was one abandoned by the army and had been stencilled with the logo of the KDP. A portrait of the late, great Mullah Mustafa, the first modern leader of the Iraqi Kurds, was pasted on the windscreen. Although the fleeing troops had broken off the ignition block to try to prevent the rebels using the machine, Ali Hossein, with the help of a push, usually succeeded in hot-wiring the engine into life. If he needed to stop, he used the technique of leaning the barrel of his AK-47 on the accelerator pedal to prevent the motor stalling. He liked to drive fast, so that when he slowed and leaned forward in his seat we knew he had sensed some unseen danger ahead. One time, in the mountains, he slowed because he had seen a fox. He offered to shoot it, but, more out of superstition than anything else, we persuaded him to leave it be.

On the road to Dahuk, down the main highway with its signs to Mosul, Tikrit and Baghdad, lay the wreckage of burnt-out army trucks and abandoned tanks. On the outskirts of the town a white Chevrolet Malibu had mounted a kerb where its secret police occupants had been cornered and killed on the night of the uprising. Outside Mosul, from the Aqra crossroad, an Iraqi helicopter gunship could be seen hovering lazily in the distance over Mount Makloub. Several hundred guerrillas were mustering at the crossroads for what they believed would be the assault on Mosul, although Barzani said that night that there had never been any intention to attack this Arab city unless the Arabs themselves rose up and asked for help. The guerrilla forces often seemed in some confusion about what they were up to, the confusion made worse by the addition of volunteers and Popular Army units to the thousands of *peshmerga* who had held out in the mountains until the uprising. Despite the apparent chaos and disorganization, the fighters showed a remarkable discipline and cheerfulness. In Arbil, the capital of Iraqi Kurdistan, they queued patiently for hours in beaten-up trucks and mud-covered cars for the few precious drops of petrol that would take them to the front line, little more than 10 miles away. There, the Iraqi army had cut the road to Kirkuk – the start of Saddam Hussein's counter-attack which was to halt the uprising and prompt the mass exodus of refugees.

Barzani's guerrilla headquarters at Salahuddin was in one of Saddam Hussein's more modest residences, the terrace of which overlooked the Arbil plain. On the night of 27 March he was consulting with Kurdish leaders of the Popular Army who had defected to the rebel cause.

Later, with his foreign guests, he was particularly keen to stress the policy of the Kurdistan Front on the question of autonomy versus independence. 'Each Kurd belongs to his Kurdish nation, but, as the conditions are not ripe for a Kurdish state, the strategic goal is realistically for each to follow the state in which he lives: in other words, autonomy.' Barzani said he envisaged an Iraq in which Baghdad would control foreign affairs, defence, budgetary policy and oil production, while local matters in the north would be in the hands of Kurds.

He said he had been surprised by the speed and success of the uprising. 'We were expecting it might take two to three months, but the army almost didn't resist.' Barzani already feared that the uprising could not be sustained for ever without the help of the outside powers, and he appealed, without much conviction, for the United States, Britain and France to airlift supplies into the air bases held by the Kurds at Kirkuk, Arbil and Suleimaniyeh. Aid never came, at least not until the rebellion was lost and hundreds of thousands of Kurds had fled from the advancing army and were starving high in the mountains.

Although the Kurds were to be forced to retreat from the cities within less than a week, one significant effect of the rebellion was to uncouple the Popular Army forces from their allegiance to Saddam Hussein. The technique of divide-and-rule has traditionally been used to prevent the emergence of a unified independence movement in Iraq, and Saddam Hussein, like his predecessors, had attempted to use tribal and other rivalries to set the Kurds against each other. In the 1991 uprising, however, the pro-Baghdad Kurds, universally known throughout Kurdistan as the *jash* ('the little donkeys'), had not only been unreliable as allies but had taken a leading role in the rebellion against the central power.

During the build-up to the war in Kuwait, Saddam had committed the near-fatal error of handing over internal security in the north to the *jash*, in order to free troops for the southern front. The Kurdistan Front, which was aware of the changes, stepped up its campaign to make contact with *jash* commanders with a view to an alliance.

In Arbil the 56th Popular Army unit had been headed by Rifat Sherwani, a former friend, so he confessed, of Saddam Hussein himself. He was a striking man of forty-eight with a thin grey moustache who, in his immaculate Kurdish outfit and turban, bore a strong resemblance to Errol Flynn playing some mythical pirate king. He chain-smoked L & M cigarettes, which he insisted his guests smoke in preference to their own. 'The first goal of the Popular Army,' he said, 'was to let the Kurds kill the Kurds.' Sherwani confirmed that after the invasion of Kuwait, Saddam had pulled many of his best troops out of Kurdistan and relied on the Popular Army units to ensure internal security. But, according to Sherwani, these units were only waiting for an opportunity to turn against the dictator and support their fellow Kurds. 'I know Saddam Hussein personally. We have visited and eaten together. He is a sick man and his sickness is to show off in front of people. He wants everything done in his name. We had joined tactically with the government, waiting for the day when we could act. Now I see the whole nation, or at least 90 per cent, supporting the uprising. If the coalition doesn't lift the blockade against him or allow him to use planes, he is finished.' Earlier that evening the first government helicopter gunship had probed the outskirts of Arbil. Three days later the city fell.

Amidst the euphoria of revolution, there were ominous signs of its imminent collapse – confirmed when in Washington on 27 March the US State Department spokeswoman, Margaret Tutwiler, announced that Iraq was assembling a large force north of Baghdad to retake Kirkuk. The following morning, between Arbil and Kirkuk, the main four-lane highway, with its tourist roadsigns in English and Arabic and its defaced portraits of Saddam Hussein every mile or so, was blocked outside Alton Kupry, a village of 5,000 spanning the Lesser Zab river. There were two helicopter gunships hovering in the distance, occasionally darting off when the *peshmerga* put up anti-aircraft fire. A mixed force of some 10,000 Iraqi troops had attacked the road during the night, and, although the *peshmerga* were holding them off, the route to Kirkuk was effectively closed. Despite their numbers, the guerrillas, more used to fighting in the mountains than in the plains, did not have the equipment or the ability to counter the offensive.

It was the same story the next morning on the Arbil–Mosul road. Less than a mile from Arbil, near the abandoned headquarters of Saddam's 5th Army, the first of a growing column of trucks, cars and even bulldozers was heading towards Arbil, laden with refugees and their belongings. A mile further on, at a rise overlooking the town of Kalak, a group of *peshmerga* were hunkered down behind an earth embankment. Others were scattering across the surrounding fields as shellbursts hit the roadside further west. The Iraqis had appeared that morning with tanks and were being held off at the iron Bailey bridge over the Greater Zab at Kalak. It was clear that the government strategy was to cut the liberated zone in half, and that, given the meagre resouces of the Kurds and the unwillingness of the allied powers to come to their aid, the government counter-offensive could no longer be checked.

At Barzani's headquarters at Salahuddin, a senior KDP official, Fadhil Merwani, acknowledged that Kirkuk had already fallen to the government in an air and land assault involving 250 tanks. 'It was imposed on us to take these towns,' Merwani said. 'We aren't used to fighting in the towns. This was the first time.'

In the mountains beyond Salahuddin the mass exodus had already begun, slowly and almost casually at first, then turning to panic as the unstoppable Iraqi force moved north. The refugees headed off towards the Turkish and Iranian borders along dirt roads, past the ruins of some of the 4,500 villages destroyed by Saddam in a lust for revenge for the Kurds' supposed treachery in the Iran–Iraq war. The first refugees to flee were those nearest the fighting at Aqra and on the Mosul front. They intended to hold out in the mountains until the counter-offensive was repulsed or, if things went really bad, to head for the frontiers. They were the first of what became, within a week, a torrent of human suffering fleeing the advancing army, terrified that, as in 1988, Saddam would send his planes against them and gas them where they stood. 'Where is George Bush?' screamed a man near the ruins of Barzan. 'Tell him he must do something.'

But Washington failed to budge. In a highly critical account of administration policy during the rebellion, a staff report to the US Senate Foreign Relations Committee concluded: 'The public snub of Kurdish and other Iraqi opposition leaders was read as a clear indication that the United States did not want the popular rebellion to succeed. This was confirmed by background statements from Administration officials that they were looking for a military, not a popular, alternative to Saddam Hussein.'

By 30 March the Kurdish forces were on the run. The atmosphere at Zakho had changed dramatically; there were fewer guerrillas in town than just a few days earlier, and there was an air of unease on the streets. Within twenty-four hours the town would be in government hands.

Chapter Two

SAFE HAVEN

For those three heady weeks there was hope. From the first days of March in 1991 until the 25th of the month, the Kurds were the only forces in the north-east of Iraq able to exert any influence – to say they were in control of Iraqi Kurdistan would be stretching the point, as they did not have the men, the ability or the infrastructure to set up a civilian administration in such a wide area in so short a time. It was the *peshmerga* commanders who were the authority in the areas in which they operated, which was still more in the countryside and the villages than in the towns, though in the first days the Kurdish fighters took control of Zakho, Dahuk, and Suleimaniyeh without much difficulty. In Kirkuk they had to fight, and by 10 March, when the Republican Guard had finally crushed the revolt in the south, the Kurds had only part of Kirkuk, with army units which had not taken part in the war, and which were still loyal to Saddam Hussein, still holding much of the town.

On 25 March fixed-wing planes and helicopter gunships attacked Kurdish positions, and Republican Guard units swiftly and efficiently deployed from the south of the country went on the attack. Three days later it was all over; Kirkuk was back under government control and within days so too were Dahuk and Arbil, with Suleimaniyeh the last to fall.

In that desperate month the Kurdish leaders were back in their homeland, Jalal Talabani ostentatiously welcomed in the Barzan tribal lands, Massoud Barzani fêted when he travelled further south into what had been Talabani territory. True to the traditions established by each group, Barzani concentrated on trying to fight on, to mobilize his men to hold at least the north-east corner of Iraq, while Talabani worked on the complicated, often convoluted diplomacy which was always his forte – a private intelligence organization in London provided him with a satellite telephone so that he could keep in touch with the outside world from his makeshift headquarters on a hill overlooking Suleimaniyeh.

Almost as soon as the Iraqis regained control, the politicking began, with secret contacts between Baghdad and the Kurds leading to direct negotiations between the two sides as early as 20 April – the remarkable symbol of the new relationship was the televised embrace between a beaming Talabani and a poised and smiling Saddam Hussein. To many the kisses they exchanged seemed like betrayals, but to most Kurds they were merely expressions of a new reality: once again a Kurdish revolt had failed, so the time for talking had begun.

But this time the brief uprising had consequences far beyond Iraq. After all that had happened, the Kurds fled not in thousands or hundreds of thousands but in millions. Turgut Ozal, the Turkish president, rightly described it as the greatest mass migration of modern times; it had an immediate impact on his country and on Iran, but it also affected the peoples and governments of dozens of other states, as well as the United Nations and the relief agencies of the West.

The Kurds fled in such huge numbers because they had experience of what could happen. The memory of chemical weapons attacks in 1988 was still green in their minds – some 27,000 Kurds who fled Iraq at that time were still in camps in Turkey, and it was widely known that many of those who had accepted an offer of amnesty from Saddam Hussein and returned to their homes had quickly disappeared. On top of that were the daily reports from southern Iraq. The Kurds listened to the news broadcasts from Iran, which for its own purposes was reporting in detail – and often exaggerating – what was going on in the south of the country. Iranian radio gave accounts of the ruthlessness with which the Republican Guard had moved into Basra, of the brutality of the reprisals against the Shia fighters when they were captured, and of the disregard for the sanctity of the holy shrines when the troops moved into Kerbala and Najjaf. The final straw was the shelling of Kirkuk by the Iraqi army before it moved in to recapture the districts the Kurds had taken; if the Iraqis could do that to a town they considered part of Iraq, a place they had carefully 'Arabized' by moving in people from the south, what would they not do to totally Kurdish towns and cities? The Kurds believed they knew, and so they set off from every city, town and village of Iraqi Kurdistan for what they hoped would be the safety of neighbouring countries. In all, close to two million men, women and children left Kurdistan for Turkey and Iran – more women and children than men, as many heads of households stayed on to fight with the *peshmerga*, or to try to safeguard their homes and possessions.

It was still winter time, so that the mountains were snow-covered, the winds arctic; then, when the weather moderated, the roads turned into muddy slides, and sudden spates flooded the rivers. It was the worst of times for a mass exodus, across some of the most inhospitable terrain in the world. And when the Kurds reached the sanctuaries they sought, in one case – Turkey – they were prevented from entering, and in the other –Iran – found an administration which was willing to accept them but had neither the resources nor the ability to deal with such a crisis.

The world's attention was turned to Turkey, largely because the Turks allowed journalists in to see what was going on, while in the early days the Iranians maintained their policy of keeping correspondents out of their country. The result was a wave of criticism of Turkey which seriously damaged relations between that country and its Western allies; at one point a government newspaper in Ankara wrote: 'Countries which have not offered shelter to even one displaced Iraqi are now slandering Turkey and the Turkish people. What is most regrettable is that the accusations come from countries friendly to Turkey. May God protect us from such friends, for we can protect ourselves from our enemies.'

It was the Turkish policy decision to stop the refugees at the border which caused all the trouble. Just as mindful as the Kurds of what had happened in 1988, Turkey did not want to allow a situation to develop which might again lead to a permanent core of refugees in the country, nor would they allow the Kurds to attempt to join in the life of the people of the eastern provinces. With the campaign by the Partia Karkaris Kurdistan (PKK), or Kurdish Workers' Party, the violent, extreme Marxist Kurdish group waging an insurgent war in eastern Turkey, still going on (see p. 168), the Turkish leaders feared that the Kurds of Iraq, with the taste of freedom still fresh on their lips, might join forces with these Turkish insurgents to try to set up a Kurdistan there, rather than in Iraq, and would at the least seek to use Turkish territory from which to launch attacks against Saddam Hussein's forces – something that could embroil the Turks in a regional conflict they had long sought to avoid. A relaxation of the restrictions on the use of the Kurdish language and other concessions announced by President Ozal had come into effect, but the distrust of the Kurds still came over clearly in the Turkish press, which always referred to the fleeing Kurds as 'displaced Iraqis'. So the Turkish authorities decreed that the refugees should be stopped on the Iraqi side of the border, which meant keeping them on the mountain tops, not in the populated and accessible valleys on the Turkish side of the frontier, where they could have been fed and organized much more easily. Instead, the Turkish army was deployed to make sure that the Kurds did not get across the frontier, and were often seen on the world's television screens using clubs, rifle butts and live ammunition to make sure their orders were obeyed. Because trucks could not negotiate the steep mountain roads in the winter conditions, there were desperate shortages of everything needed, from tents to food, and the old, the sick and the very young were dying – in front of the cameras – at the rate of 1,000 a day.

By early April there were half a million people on the Turkish border, with 700,000 Kurds heading for Iran, which was already trying to look after many thousands of Shia refugees in the south. Not for the first time, world leaders misjudged the temper of their own people. They appeared to think that after the Gulf war, the only thought in people's minds would be 'to get the boys home'. That was certainly the attitude in Washington, where President Bush said on 5 April that 'American lives are too precious for us to be sucked into a civil war'. It was a theme he was to repeat several times, until public disgust with his attitude forced him to change it.

It was in Europe that public opinion first made itself felt, and in Britain most of all. Across the country there was general and genuine outrage at what was happening to the Kurds and the lack of response from the Western world. Prime Minister John Major responded by announcing an aid package of £20 million, as well as the dispatch of blankets and tents. But he otherwise washed his hands of the crisis when he was asked, outside his Downing Street residence, whether the Kurds had not been encouraged by the West to rebel. 'I do not recall asking them to mount this particular insurrection,' was his reply. He added: 'What is happening in Iraq is disturbing and malignant. But it is also within the borders of Iraq and we have no international authority to interfere.'

The prime minister's statement did nothing to allay public concern in Britain, and similar attitudes quickly spread to France and, to a slightly lesser extent, to Germany and other European countries as well. There was none of that sentiment which President Bush apparently anticipated, that now the war with Saddam was over, what happened in Iraq was no longer of any concern to the West. On the contrary, Bush's call to the people of Iraq to overthrow Saddam Hussein was seen as a direct cause of what was happening; the Kurds, like the Shia of the south, had believed Bush meant what he said, and that they could look to America if they acted. As late as the end of March a clandestine radio station called the Voice of Free Iraq was still calling on the Kurds to rise up and throw the Iraqis out of their homeland, and to depose 'the evil Saddam'. That station was subsidized by the CIA.

The Kurds were active propagandists in the West, with an efficient organization in Europe, and powerful voices were raised on their behalf in many countries. Unlike the Shia of southern Iraq, they had been fighting for years and realized the value of international support. The politicians got the message: something had to be done.

Their response was to try to get away with the minimum possible, so with much fanfare they dispatched food, medicine and tents to Turkey to be sent on to the refugees. Television pictures showed the Kurds mobbing the few lorries that got through to the border regions where they were camped, fighting with each other and with Turkish troops for the meagre rations available. There were reports of Turkish soldiers pilfering relief supplies – not unlikely, given their own low pay and poor standard of living – and of obstruction by Turkish officials intent on keeping the Kurds out of their country.

The next move was to organize air drops, with the crews of C130 transports pushing pallets of packages out through the open ramps of planes flying at 150 miles an hour. Experienced aid workers described it as about the worst possible solution in such terrain, and with the existing weather conditions, a point driven home by reports of a family sleeping in a make-shift shelter killed by one of the pallets dropping directly on them. The air drops, designed more for photographic effect than to help, were stopped.

Yet public opinion remained adamant, and was getting increasingly vocal. More was needed, but, far away in Washington, Bush and his advisers were reluctant to move. They remained determined not to be involved in what they saw as a civil war which had been going on for decades.

President Ozal finally gave the push which led to action –

though he did so not from any humanitarian motives, but in another attempt to keep the Kurds out of Turkey. Speaking on American television on Sunday, 7 April, Ozal suggested that the UN should take over territory in northern Iraq to provide a haven for the Kurds, and said that he would be ready to commit Turkish troops to any UN force sent to protect the area chosen. That set alarm bells ringing in New York and Washington; during the Gulf war, Ozal had made a series of remarks which seemed to show that he had ideas of reasserting Turkish domination in northern Iraq – he even raised the old claim to the city and district of Mosul in northern Iraq which had been advanced by the Ottoman empire after World War I. Britain, then the mandatory power in Iraq, was determined to hold on to the region because of the presence of oil, and, after complicated manoeuvring, the League of Nations in 1925 upheld the British claim. Yet Mosul had been the centre of an Ottoman *vilayet*, or district, and Ozal seemed to be opening the way to reviving this dispute as a means of asserting Turkish involvement in northern Iraq. Given this situation, the idea of Turkish troops moving into Iraq was clearly a non-starter – it would certainly have frightened the Kurds rather than reassured them, it would have worried every other regional power, and it would have been seen as blatant aggression by an Iraq which would one day have had to deal with the situation created. Yet the word 'haven' lingered in the minds of the politicians.

It was on the same day that US planes began air-dropping supplies to the refugees, with the immediate increase in television coverage causing public opinion in American to reinforce the pressure already being exerted in Europe. Brent Scowcroft, the national security adviser, was the first to become aware of the tide of popular opinion, and quickly announced that the US would not abandon the 40,000 refugees from Iraq under the protection of coalition forces in the south of the country. But he said the US did not have all the answers on what to do about the whole refugee problem, which encompassed the Kurds in the north as well as the Shia in the south. President Bush said he would urge the UN to take action – without suggesting what action, how it should be arranged or who would provide the funding. The defence secretary, Dick Cheney, said the US would work closely with Turkey, but he gave no specifics. The United States, apparently so powerful and decisive in time of war, seemed to be floundering once peace had broken out.

Next day, 8 April, Jim Baker, the secretary of state, was in Turkey on his way to the Middle East for an unsuccessful attempt to bring about Arab–Israeli peace talks. He made it all too painfully clear that his call in Ankara was strictly a courtesy visit to show US gratitude for President Ozal's help during the war. In response to public pressure Baker did visit the border area, spending just seven minutes at a refugee camp. He did not seem very interested in what was going on, but was anxious to stress that America was not going to get involved: 'We are not prepared to go down the slippery slope of being sucked into a civil war,' he said. 'We cannot police what goes on inside Iraq, and we cannot be arbiters of who shall govern Iraq.'

But within a week the Americans were indeed policing what went on inside Iraq, and by their insistence on maintaining sanctions they were doing their best to see that Saddam Hussein ceased to rule in Baghdad.

It was a surprise initiative from London which finally persuaded the Americans to act. John Major, the new British prime minister, had shown himself to be ill at ease with foreign affairs during his brief three-month spell as foreign secretary in 1989. But he had been taken aback by the adverse reaction to his apparent insensitivity towards the Kurds in his remarks at the door of 10 Downing Street. Comments by his predecessor may also have had an effect: Mrs Thatcher spoke out forcefully in favour of immediate help for the Kurds at a time when Major and his colleagues still appeared to be dithering, and the prospect of being upstaged by Mrs Thatcher may well have pushed Major into taking an initiative.

So, by-passing the diplomats and experts who usually surround politicians, he came up with his own idea, building on the vague mention of 'a haven' by President Ozal. As early as 5 April Major asked the Foreign Office in London to rough out ideas on how to help the Kurdish refugees, but when the Foreign Office, in desultory fashion, did not manage any concrete proposals, Major went ahead on his own. The foreign secretary, Douglas Hurd, was out of the country, and the civil servant in charge of the Kurdish issue, David Gore-Booth, was attending a weekend conference in Oxfordshire. He was swiftly recalled to London to try to formalize the prime minister's ideas.

Arriving in Luxembourg on Monday, 8 April, for an EC summit meeting, the British prime minister distributed the text of a proposal he would make that morning to his eleven fellow European leaders. He was going to suggest the creation of 'a Kurdish enclave' in northern Iraq which would be a protected by UN forces, where the refugees could be assured of safety and where they could be supplied with everything they needed.

John Weston, the political director of the Foreign Office, shuddered and went into action. He had travelled on an earlier plane to Luxembourg and so had not spoken to the prime minister before Major announced his idea; now, the diplomat set about repairing what he and his colleagues saw as a gaffe. To create an enclave inside the territory of a sovereign state, a member of the UN, and to protect it with UN troops, could set all kinds of precedents which would worry half the countries of the world. Even worse was the suggestion that it would be a specifically 'Kurdish' enclave. The immediate picture conjured up was of an embryonic Kurdish state protected by blue-helmeted troops, something which would certainly be vetoed by China or the Soviet Union, and which would spread horror among the Arab countries, each with its own minorities.

In a technique made familiar by White House aides during the Reagan years, John Weston and his team went about telling everyone who would listen that what the prime minister had really meant to say was that there should be 'safe havens' for the Kurds in northern Iraq. How that should be accomplished was left suitably vague, while in London, the Foreign Office spoke only of 'a safe environment' for the refugees, without specifying where, when, or how it should be made safe.

Whatever it was finally called, Major's plan was enthusiastically endorsed by the other European leaders, particularly by President Mitterrand, who was happy to be able to report to Madame Mitterrand that he had done something for her beloved Kurds, and equally happy that the British prime minister had chosen to launch his initiative at an EC summit without having previously consulted Washington – something that would never have happened under Major's predecessor. Yet the lack of consultation with Washington at first seemed likely to doom the enterprise. Without the approval of the US, the United Nations certainly would not give its authority for troops to be sent to northern Iraq; even with American backing it would be reluctant to do so.

In Luxembourg, John Major at last spoke for Britain: 'We cannot confine our efforts to mitigating this tragedy. We cannot just dress the wounds of the Kurdish people. We have to try to put a stop to the blood-letting of Saddam Hussein. If we cannot get rid of him, we can at least provide some protection for the most vulnerable of the Iraqi people.'

At the UN, Javier Pérez de Cuellar was at best non-committal about the idea of safe havens. 'I don't think it would be impossible,' he said, 'but of course it would be in Iraqi territory, which would raise problems of sovereignty. I don't know if we can impose a special area on Iraq. That would be complicated.' When the Americans adopted the idea two weeks later, Pérez de Cuellar was even more opposed: 'We would wish first of all to be in touch with the Iraqi authorities,' he said. 'We would need to see what their reaction would be to this sort of military presence on their territory. If this is to be a military presence under the aegis of the UN, consent would have to be obtained from the Security Council. If the countries concerned do not require the UN flag, then that is quite different.' The secretary-general was at least consistent. Faced with the Kurdish problem, he seemed to do all he could to avoid UN involvement, dragging the organization's heels in all possible ways, perhaps in retaliation for what many saw as the hijacking of the UN by the US and its allies during the Gulf war, perhaps anxious not to get involved in new difficulties in his last months in office. Pérez de Cuellar did appoint a special representative to go to Baghdad to investigate the refugee problem, but the man he chose, Erik Suy of Belgium, was not noted for his dynamism; even before leaving New York, he held that Iraqi consent for any safe haven for the Kurds being set up would have to be 'a fundamental principle', which rather weakened his own negotiating position. The secretary-general certainly seemed to think so, and therefore made a second appointment, putting Prince Sadruddin Aga Khan on the task as well.

As the diplomatic jockeying went on, conditions in the border regions got worse, with more and more people arriving there. In Tehran the deputy interior minister, Muhammad Atriyan, said that three times as many refugees had reached Iran as there were on the Turkish border – 750,000 at that time. But all attention was still being paid to Turkey, he complained, while the UN was being 'negligent and indifferent'.

As the politicians argued and squabbled, the refugees continued to flee their homes. They did so out of real fear, though some of the reports which made them go may well have been exaggerated. Rather like the Israelis in 1948, the Iraqis may have been quite happy to see this huge exodus from the north of their country – the final solution of the Kurdish problem which they had tried to bring about in 1988 but had not been able to follow through.

Certainly there was pressure on the Kurds. The Iraqis frequently used their artillery to strafe roads leading to the borders, though they were prevented from sending in their fixed-wing planes or helicopter gunships – in a quiet move which answered American concerns, President Bush warned that any flights north of the 36th parallel would not be permitted, and gave the USAF orders to shoot down planes violating that order. A couple of Iraqi planes were destroyed, and Iraq gave up any attempt to use its air force. There were also reports of atrocities by the Republican Guard and the Iraqi secret police as towns in the south were retaken by government forces. In one town 400 people were said to have been executed, dozens who had helped the Shia revolt in another were burnt alive, many disappeared, and others were taken away by police, according to the rumours among the refugees. It all added to the panic flight of a whole people.

In Washington the post-war euphoria showed no signs of abating, with the president and his officials all apparently content to let the Europeans take the lead in providing aid to the Kurds, and taking very little notice of John Major's idea of safe havens. It may not only have been euphoria and self-interest: just as China was afraid of the idea of a UN-protected enclave in a sovereign state because of its own situation in Tibet, and the Soviet Union was concerned about the Baltic states, so the US may have had in mind the situation in the Israeli-occupied territories. For years Palestinian leaders had been pressing for the UN to provide observers and troops to protect their people in the West Bank and Gaza against what they said were the brutalities of the Israelis; the plan for the Kurds in Iraq might have been seen as a trial run for what they had in mind.

The Kurds themselves were enthusiastically in favour of the safe haven plan: the desperate people on the ground because it would be an improvement on the dreadful conditions they were suffering in the camps and would also afford them a measure of protection, and the leaders because they too had a nightmare – that their people would become the new Palestinians, condemned to rot away in refugee camps along the borders of their homeland, striving to make themselves heard at the UN, always having to go cap in hand for help. Barzani called the plan 'a big humanitarian and political step forward' and urged all countries to support it.

By 10 April official figures showed that there were 800,000 refugees on the Turkish border and another one million in Iran – where, as the US Office of Foreign Disaster Assistance noted, relief operations conducted by the government of Iran and the Iranian Red Crescent were better organized than similar efforts in Turkey. The Iranian Red Crescent managed to find 6,000 staff and volunteers to send to help the Kurds on the border; the Turkish Red Crescent could find only 110. Yet still British and European efforts to establish the havens, to get the Kurds off the mountains and back down on to the Iraqi plain, were making no progress. The Kurds would not go back into Iraq unless there was protection for them there, and though John Major offered British troops and hinted that they would use force if Iraq tried to interfere in the safe haven plan, it was recognized that any international force would lack credibility without American participation.

Yet the Americans just did not seem to be interested, with President Bush going out of his way to say that he would not commit troops; privately, Administration officials admitted that the president and his advisers had in mind the disaster of Beirut in 1980, when US marines went in to oversee the evacuation of the PLO, sailed away with a 'mission accomplished' pennant flying, then had to go back to a civil war they did not understand and which eventually cost them more than 250 lives. 'I do not want one single soldier or airman shoved into a civil war in Iraq that has been going on for ages,' the president said in a speech at a military academy. 'I'm not going to have that.' That was on 13 April. Three days later George Bush reversed himself, ordering US troops into northern Iraq, adopting John Major's plan for safe havens as it if had been an American initiative all along, and brushing aside criticism from the UN. But President Bush still said he wanted all American troops home as soon as possible;

the whole affair was a classic example of Washington double-speak in which Bush and his aides finally bowed to allied pressure as they realized that their own public was swinging round to the European point of view. It was not so much a policy as an attempt to hold the line, and because it had not been thought out in advance, it soon created as many problems as it over-came.

Certainly the Americans could claim the credit for implement-ing the safe haven plan, as it could not have been put into effect without them, but they were ungenerous, at least, in failing to acknowledge the role of John Major in coming up with the idea in the first place, and that of European opinion for forcing the politicians to act. The White House spokesman, Marlin Fitz-water, agreed that when the proposal was first put forward, the administration did not think safe havens were necessary. 'We were hoping to be able to feed the Kurds in their locations. That obviously proved inadequate, there were just too many people crowding into the mountain areas. The problem just got too big and we had to go to this operation.'

President Bush spelt out the new American view:

If we cannot get adequate food, clothing and shelter to the Kurds living in the mountains, then we must encourage them to move to an area in northern Iraq where the geography facilitates such a large-scale relief effort.

I can well appreciate that many Kurds have good reason to fear for their safety if they return to Iraq. Let me reassure them that adequate security will be provided at these temporary sites by US, British and French air and ground forces. We'll have air power around there if needed. We'll be able not only to protect our own people but the people we are setting out to protect. Iraq has underestimated the United States before. They shouldn't do so again.

In the beginning the Americans seemed to think they would have no difficulty in going in for a few days or weeks, then handing over to the UN, and getting their own troops home by 4 July, the date privately set by General Colin Powell when he went on a tour of inspection and emphasized that the pull-out would be quick – something which did more to destabilize the situation than anything else.

Still, the Anglo-American plan worked. Allied troops on the ground persuaded the Kurds to go back; the use of air power alone would never have done so. In addition, relief efforts on the border were scaled down as supplies were sent to the camps set up in northern Iraq, so that the refugees had a direct inducement to leave the dreadful conditions on the Turkish and Iranian borders. The Iraqis bitterly denounced the whole affair at the beginning, and tried to hamper things. They sent Republican Guards disguised as police into Zakho, then, when the allies insisted they leave, the Iraqis infiltrated secret policemen into most of the towns; they also made sure they had informers everywhere, so that the Kurds who actively co-operated with the allies – 'the $8 a day interpreters' – were known to the Iraqis. It was an uncomfortable feeling for the Kurds who helped set up the camps, organized the administration and kept things working, but it did not become a problem until the allies wanted to go.

From the start it was obvious that setting up tented camps – a string of 'relief villages' – would not be enough; so many people had moved out that the only way to get things back to normal was to persuade them to go back to their homes. Dahuk, a city of 100,000 people, was vital, so the allies pushed forward and sent in troops to patrol the streets and to see that the Iraqi police who stayed there did not begin taking Saddam's revenge on the Kurds – a revenge the refugees still thought would come if they were abandoned. At the height of the relief effort there were almost 30,000 troops taking part in operation 'Provide Comfort' – unlike the British, the Americans went in for apposite code names, not just taking the next one in the book, as the British forces did.

The Americans remained determined to get their men out as soon as possible, and by June 1991 began winding down, though commanders on the ground from all the allied forces – French, Dutch and Italian as well as British and American – warned that the Iraqis would move in if the Kurds were left without protection. Washington's justification was that the Kurds and the Iraqis were reaching an agreement which would give the Kurds their own autonomous region once again, and would also allow them to keep the *peshmerga* in place as the protectors of Kurdish civilians.

The trouble was that the negotiations between the Kurdish leaders and the Baghdad government were not going as either the Kurds or the Americans had hoped. In the first flush of enthusiasm, Talabani announced 'an agreement in principle' and implied that within days everything would be settled. Then he went back to Suleimaniyeh to consult his colleagues, and it became clear that things were not so rosy. Talabani, the eternal optimist, always believed success was just around the corner; Barzani, brought up in an atmosphere of tribal warfare, was less trusting, though in the end he was the one advocating compromise by the Kurds, pinning his hopes on international guarantees to make Saddam Hussein keep his promises.

As in 1970, the main stumbling block in the negotiations appeared to be the status of Kirkuk, which the Kurds believed they had to have in order to exert pressure on Baghdad – Kirkuk remains the main Iraqi oil town despite the new finds in the south of the country. The Kurdish and Iraqi representatives canvassed all sorts of solutions for the city – a joint administration, a new census there, a special governor – but as time went on it gradually dawned on the Kurds that Saddam was merely playing for time: he wanted to spin things out until the allied troops left, in the reasonable belief that once that happened he could once again exert direct influence and force the Kurds to accept the terms he chose to dictate. Even with the allied troops still in northern Iraq, he demanded that the Kurds should hand over their heavy weapons, that they should close down their two radio stations, and that they should undertake to sever all ties with their allies inside or outside Iraq, an obviously impossible condition. Significantly, the hardening of the Iraqi attitude came just as the first of the 30,000 troops deployed in northern Iraq began to leave.

Not all the delay in reaching agreement was due to the Iraqis. As usual, the Kurds were less than united, and the leaders of the two main parties – Talabani and Barzani – and Sami Abderrahman of the Kurdistan People's Democratic Party, who was a senior negotiator, were quietly competing among themselves for positions of maximum power once an autonomy agreement was reached. The Iraqis encouraged this by holding out the prospect of seats in the cabinet in Baghdad for the Kurds, and by suggesting a regional assembly with real powers to run the affairs of the autonomous region. This would be based in Arbil and would be able to maintain open borders with both Turkey and Iran, a useful form of pressure given the state of relations between the countries. Ironically, Barzani, the tribal leader who had seen his father betrayed at the end, was the one most ready to do a deal with Saddam, believing that the Kurds had to capitalize on Western interest and support while it was available. Talking about the situation, he said: 'We have not defeated them, remember that. They haven't defeated us . . . we have got to live together.' Barzani's KDP emerged during the negotiations as a more tolerant group than Talabani's PUK. Its primary aim was to see 'democracy' established in Iraq, as the best means of ensuring the Kurds' own safety and well-being. If there was real democracy, would there be any need for Kurdish autonomy? 'I don't see that autonomy contradicts democracy,' Barzani said. And would democracy be possible with Saddam still in power? 'Things have changed a great deal. The world has changed. Why not?'

Talabani, always more a man of the left than the traditionalist feudal leader, was the first to embrace Saddam, the first to promise an agreement was near, and the first to voice the growing doubts of all Kurds as the talks dragged on and the allies began to lose interest. It was this which worried them most: 'I think if they leave before achieving democracy in Iraq or before final agreement between the Kurds and the Iraqi government, people will again leave their homes for the mountains,' Talabani warned.

He was wrong. On 15 July, only a couple of weeks later than the Americans had hoped, the allies finally pulled out of Iraq. Children waved and clapped as the soldiers rolled back across the Turkish border, and *peshmerga* leaders shook hands with officers whose positions they were taking. Much of the euphoria was because the allies were not moving far – the destination for the ground troops was Silopi, just across the border inside Turkey, while the air force units were kept at Incirlik and Batman, a few minutes flying time away from Iraq. In a determined attempt to avoid another exodus, the allies had set up, and widely publicized, a 'rapid response force' with the special mission of taking action if the Baghdad government sought to move against the Kurds. 'We'll be just a phone call away,' said General John Shalikashvili, the US commander. Many Kurds were less sanguine at the prospect of being left on their own once again. They accepted that there would be international intervention if Iraq tried to subjugate Kurdistan by force once more, but feared the kind of creeping revenge which Saddam Hussein and the Baathists might exact: that those who had 'collaborated' with the allies would be assassinated or abducted. An American-led strike force could do nothing to stop that, and the UN police left behind were there merely as symbols of international concern, with neither the authority nor the power to protect the Kurds. Aid workers stayed behind too, but they were given only thirty-day renewable visas by an Iraqi general brought specially to Shaklawa for the purpose. For all the smiles, the Kurds realized that, once again, they were on their own.

In Washington the aim had always been to do the job and get out as soon as possible. The administration was convinced that the main wish of the American people was 'to get the boys back home', and that for all the public pressure to help the Kurds earlier on, there was no longer much interest in the affair. Certainly the high level of publicity had been reduced, yet there was still a quiet groundswell of sympathy for the Kurds, both in the United States and Europe. It was a factor in the negotiations which were still going on in Baghdad, with the Kurdish leaders – whether they believed it or not – telling the Iraqi negotiators that if the worst came to the worst, they would not again be left on their own.

In London the Foreign Office seemed well aware of the doubts shared by the Kurds and by the British public. It issued, most unusually, a somewhat apologetic statement designed to show that all that could be done had been done, and that there was no alternative to a pull-out. 'Almost all of the 400,000 refugees who fled to the mountains in the area of the safe havens have returned home,' it said on 12 July. 'The refugee camps have closed and the transit stations are almost deserted. Towns and villages are returning to normal. With our help water and power supplies have been restored, food distribution and basic sanitation systems established and health care brought to those in need. Many lives have been saved. The aims of our deployment have been successfully achieved.'

The statement supported the use of an instrument earlier discarded: sanctions. The tough regime called for in Security Council Resolution 687 – the Gulf ceasefire resolution – would remain in force as a means of ensuring that Iraq obeyed all the conditions laid down: no planes or helicopters north of the 36th parallel, no Iraqi army, border guards or special forces inside the security zone area. Nothing was said about police of any kind.

The allies warned that they would be ready to go back in if necessary and, to show their intentions, would hold regular military talks inside Iraqi territory, while maintaining the multinational deterrent force in Turkey. 'These troops will be prepared, if circumstances so demand, to respond swiftly; to go back in, if necessary, to protect the safety of the refugees and UN personnel and to take any other action as may be required,' the Foreign Office said.

These were fine words which took no account of what was actually happening in the area, for on this eighth anniversary of the beginning of the PKK uprising President Ozal and his government seemed to have undergone a change of heart. The concessions to the Turkish Kurds announced during the Gulf war were forgotten, and instead there was a sudden and brutal return to the hardline tactics which had in the past encouraged the counter-violence of the PKK. Extreme right-wing vigilantes, generally believed to be connected, at least, with the Turkish political police or intelligence service, became active for the first time since they had battled left-wing activists in the near civil war of the 1970s. The Diyarbakir office of a human rights organization was bombed, as well as a magazine supporting the Kurds. Other bombs exploded in the cars of officials of the People's Labour Party (HEP), the officially sanctioned Kurdish parliamentary group which was increasingly becoming the legal arm of the PKK, much as Sinn Féin in Ireland speaks for the IRA.

At least eight Kurds were mysteriously murdered, culminating in the torture and killing of Bedat Aydin, a 36-year-old Kurdish activist. He was taken from his home in the middle of the night by men identified as members of the political police, and his tortured and mutilated body was found next day. Aydin's funeral was turned into a massive demonstration by the Kurds who make up the overwhelming majority in Diyarbakir, but instead of allowing it to go ahead peacefully, the authorities sent in paratroopers. There was a confrontation which quickly ended with the soldiers firing into the crowd. Three people were killed and thirty-six wounded, and just to underline their attitude, the troops waylaid and beat up Fehmi Iseklar, the HEP deputy, as well as his three companions. All four ended up in hospital.

To match their new tough stance in their own Kurdish areas, the Turkish government launched an offensive against PKK bases inside Iraq, and at the same time warned the allies that it might not permit the continued presence of the deterrent force at Silopi. The new prime minister, Mesut Yilmaz, said the allied group was there as a temporary measure and could be used only with Turkish permission. The situation would be reviewed after a few months.

The new Turkish attitude was largely a response to public opinion. With his Motherland Party rapidly losing popularity, Mr Ozal clearly felt he had to be more sensitive than usual to what was being said, and took to heart criticism of the deployment of allied forces on Turkish soil – one of Ataturk's legacies was a firm belief that only Turks should defend Turkey, and that no foreign presence should be allowed. This nationalist pressure from the right was matched by deep disquiet on the left, which saw Turkey being used as an American base for further action in the Middle East, or the promotion of Turkey as America's surrogate in the region. On all sides there was opposition to anything likely to lead to the establishment of an independent Kurdish state; allied support for the Iraqi Kurds was seen as leading in that direction.

As a result of all these pressures, in August the Turks launched their biggest operation ever against the PKK, bombing guerrilla camps and villages inside Iraq and setting up a 10-mile wide buffer zone inside Iraq which would be patrolled by Turkish troops and which, it was made clear, would be a free-fire zone, a concept borrowed from the Iraqis. Kurdish civilians as well as some PKK members were killed, though the scale of the casualties – thirty-five killed according to the Turks, 'very few' according to the PKK – seemed to show that the repeated massive air raids were less than a total success.

There was some evidence that they were politically motivated rather than being planned by the military. The immediate trigger for the attacks was the presence of Osman Ocalan, brother of the PKK leader Abdullah Ocalan, in a village on the Iraqi side of the border; in fact, he escaped. A deeper aim was to demonstrate to the allies that it was Turkey which would dictate the course of events in northern Iraq, and to show the leaders of the Kurdish Front in Iraq that Turkey was in a position to determine their fate.

It was a message which the Kurds understood, and responded to with the kind of cynical co-operation with Ankara which they had practised in the past with Baghdad. Mohsen Dizai of the KDP, a constituent of the Front, said that if the PKK insisted on fighting Turkey from within Iraq, then the Iraqi Kurds would push them out. 'We will say to them, either go to your region or stop your attacks,' he said. Talabani was equally plain. 'When the Turkish troops withdraw, control of the region will belong to us,' he said. 'The Kurdistan Front will be in control. We do not want anybody to operate from this region. If there are to be operations, they should go and operate from their own country.'

The deal behind it all became clear the following day: Turkey announced it was sending 10,000 tonnes of food and medical supplies to the Iraqi Kurds. And to twist the knife and ensure there would never be any possibility of an alliance between the Iraqi Kurds and the PKK, Turkish military intelligence let it be known that many of the camps and villages targeted by the air force had been chosen on the basis of information supplied by Iraqi Kurds.

One unexpected result of it all was to widen the growing rift between Talabani and Barzani, who issued a statement calling on the Turks to end their attacks 'on our people'. Barzani claimed that the air raids were killing Kurdish civilians. 'We condemn any attacks on innocent Kurdish refugees from Iraq,' he said. 'These raids have increased tension and undermined the relative peace prevailing in the region. We call on the Turkish government to end immediately its attacks against our people. It is our natural duty to protect our people and our areas.'

This was obviously at variance with Talabani's attitude, and underlined the differences within the Kurdish Front and between the traditional rivals, Barzani and Talabani – something, no doubt, that the Turks were happy to see. They could live with an autonomous region on their border, but divisions among its leaders would mean it would never grow towards independence, and would never be in a position to help the Kurds in Turkey. All in all, the Turks congratulated themselves on the way they had marked the anniversary of the uprising – even though the judgement of the allies was that their offensive was chaotic and their intervention deeply unhelpful.

The Iraqis too were pleased with the way things were going, and began giving quiet help to the PKK as a means of embarrassing their real opponents, the mainstream Kurdish political parties led by Barzani and Talabani. From the beginning, Saddam Hussein's policy had been to appear conciliatory while giving nothing away, to prevaricate and procrastinate in the sure knowledge that the victorious allies would soon lose interest. Gradually the Iraqi plan was succeeding: first the troops pulled out of northern Iraq, and when that did not provoke the frightened exodus Talabani had predicted, moves went ahead to run down the reaction force. Soon there were only aircraft available in case the Iraqis took any further action, with all pretence abandoned that there might be a new ground offensive.

Barzani and Talabani managed to contain the old rivalries between the KDP and the PUK, but some of the smaller groups in the Kurdistan Front were less accommodating. They argued that only direct action would produce results while the West still had half an eye, at least, on northern Iraq, and wanted to launch a new guerrilla war. Encouraged by Iran, eager to weaken still further the Iraqi forces, some Kurdish *peshmerga* did provoke violence on a number of occasions, but they were given no support by Barzani or Talabani, and failed in their attempt to involve the outside powers. With negotiating sessions in Baghdad interspersed with acrimonious tribal gatherings in Shaklawa, as the leaders tried to find an acceptable compromise, Saddam Hussein was able to spin things out, confident that the internal Kurdish rivalries would eventually make his task easier. As summer turned to the harsh winter of the Kurdish uplands, with many refugees still in the tented camps and thousands of others in unfamiliar cities or villages, time was certainly on Saddam Hussein's side. Once again the Kurds were on their own, with few cards to play, divisions appearing in their ranks, and Iran and Turkey seeking to exploit the new situation as they had the old. The huge drama of the revolt, followed by the tragedy of the exodus, was ending on a dying fall.

Chapter Three

THE ORIGINS OF THE KURDS

The rebellion against Saddam Hussein in the spring of 1991 reached its height at Newruz, the Kurdish new year on 21 March, which marks the anniversary of the overthrow of the tyrant Zahhak a thousand years before the coming of Islam. By the Kurdish calendar it was the year 2603.

The Newruz festival and the legends of Zahhak, although closely linked to Persian tradition, contain one of several folk myths of the origins of the Kurds, myths which set them apart from their neighbours and help to establish their identity as a separate people. Historically, the Kurdish calendar dates from the defeat of the Assyrian empire at Niniveh, north of Mosul, by the forces of the Medes.

The legend of Zahhak is colourful. According to Kurdish folklore, the tyrant had snakes growing from his shoulders, a deformity which the court physicians were unable to cure. Satan came to the tyrant and told him that he would be cured if he fed the snakes each day with the brains of two young people. The executioner appointed to the task of providing the brains took pity on his victims, and each day spared one of them and substituted the brains of a sheep. The survivors were smuggled to the safety of the mountains, where they became the founders of a new people, the forefathers of the Kurds. Zahhak himself was overthrown when one of the tyrant's intended victims rebelled against his fate and killed him.

In their myths and in their written history the Kurds consistently emerge as a separate entity, despite the efforts of the states which now rule over them to deny them a special identity. Even ıow Turkey denies their existence as a distinct people, calling them Mountain Turks, banning their written language and seeking to assimilate their culture. In Iran they are regarded essentially as an integral part of the Iranian nation with no right to be considered as a distinct people. In Iraq the word 'Kurd' can be used as a term of abuse to evoke the idea of the primitive, untutored nomad.

Yet for all these attempts at cultural annihilation the Kurds persist in seeing themselves as a separate nation with a right to autonomy and, ultimately, to independence. They have their own language, their own customs and their own territory – the high mountains which formed a natural barrier against their encroaching neighbours, the Arabs, the Turks and the Persians. They have a rich cultural history which saw its greatest flowering in the Middle Ages with the foundations of powerful Kurdish dynasties, including that of Saladin, who defeated Richard the Lionheart's crusaders and reconquered Palestine for the Muslims. What they have not had, except for one brief exception in modern times, is their own state.

If there were to be a Kurdish state, it is open to argument what territory it would cover and who would be its inhabitants. Divided, as they are, among the states of Iraq, Iran, Turkey, Syria and the Soviet Union, the Kurds have no centralized political structure and no forum in which to establish their own political identity. The host states, although they pursue different policies towards their Kurdish minorities, share an interest in suppressing the idea of a common Kurdish identity spanning national borders. As a consequence even the most elementary statistics – for instance, on population – are little more than informed speculation. Present estimates of the population of Kurdistan vary from fifteen to twenty-five million, representing an enormous disparity in relation to population estimates elsewhere in the world. As might be expected, the host states tend towards the lower estimate, while Kurdish nationalists favour the higher. A 1987 estimate of population published by the

British-based Minority Rights Group, described by the MRG as 'cautious', gave the following figures: Turkey, 9.6 million Kurds (or 19 per cent of the population); Iran, 5 million (10 per cent); Iraq, 3.9 million (23 per cent); Syria, 900,000 (8 per cent); the Soviet Union, 300,000 (negligible). In other words, the Kurds constitute a nation of at least twenty million people, larger (in terms of their Middle Eastern neighbours) than all the twenty-one countries of the Arab League except Egypt, and as big as Sudan and Algeria.

Similarly, the geographical area of a putative Kurdish state is open to question. An ethnic map of Kurdistan, based on areas in which Kurds predominate, would cover the south-eastern corner of Turkey, including the towns of Diyarbakir, Mardin and Hakkari, and taking in Lake Van and Mount Ararat; it would cross into the border areas of Syria – the Kurd Dagh ('Mountain of the Kurds') and the area east of the Euphrates called the Jezireh; then move into Iraq, where the Kurds inhabit the mountain areas north-east in a line running from Zakho in the far north-west to the towns of Mosul, Arbil, Kirkuk and Khaneqin. In Iran the Kurds inhabit the western border region which runs south from the Soviet–Iranian–Turkish frontier triangle to the city of Kermanshah, almost due east of Baghdad. In all, Kurdistan covers an area roughly the size of France. Even so, much of the present population of this theoretical Kurdistan would not consider themselves to be Kurds; in the lowland areas there are large Arab and Turkish populations, either indigenous or deliberately moved in by central governments to alter the ethnic composition of Kurdistan, while in parts of Iraqi Kurdistan the Kurds live alongside sizeable Turkoman and oriental Christian populations who have inhabited the region for centuries. In south-eastern Kurdistan, around the Iranian town of Kermanshah, the local population has traditionally regarded itself as more Persian than Kurdish, and in language and religion it is indeed closer to the Persians than it is to, say, the Syrian Kurds of the Kurd Dagh. Nevertheless, Kurdish nationalists have sought to expand the ethnic map to take in much of south-western Iran, including the majority Arab-populated province of Khuzestan, and some even lay claim to the Gulf seaboard facing the coastline of Kuwait. At the San Francisco Conference in 1945 at which forty-eight states gathered to sign the founding charter of the United Nations, a Kurdish delegation submitted a map which staked a claim to a Kurdish state stretching from Alexandretta, on the Mediterranean coast of Syria, to Bushire, 150 miles along the Iranian coast from the Shatt al-Arab.

Although such maximalist claims tend to ignore the historical rights of other minorities in the region, it is clearly the case that much of the whole area described above is inhabited in its over-whelming majority by people speaking Kurdish dialects, and who define themselves not as Turks, Arabs or Persians, Assyrians or Armenians, but as Kurds.

The heartland of Kurdistan is predominantly mountainous, rising to 15,000 feet, and centres on the Taurus and Zagros mountain ranges, which have served both as a barrier to invaders and as a refuge for bandits and rebels. The Armenian plateau has only been Kurdish in recent centuries, since Kurdish tribes were transferred there by the Ottomans to safeguard the frontier of the empire. Similarly, Kurdish claims to the cities of northern Iraq, which the *peshmerga* fought to defend in 1991, are histori-cally tenuous. Kirkuk had a Kurdish majority but was not or-iginally a Kurdish city, while Arbil, the capital of Iraqi Kurdistan, was until this century a small and predominantly Turkish citadel surrounded by Kurdish tribes. The first governor of Arbil, a Kurd appointed in the 1930s by the newly independent Iraqi monarchy, was the first person to build outside the medieval cita-del.

But by conquest and occupation the Kurds have extended their territory over the centuries, so that an independent Kurdis-tan, comprising all majority-Kurdish areas, would cover both plains and mountains, and would have a rich agricultural econ-omy based on wheat, barley, lentils and livestock – the plains of Iraqi and Syrian Kurdistan are the granaries of their respective states. An independent Kurdistan would control the headwaters of the Tigris and Euphrates as well as much of the oil reserves of Iraq, Turkey and Syria. There are important reserves of chrome, copper, iron and coal, and the strategic importance of Kurdistan is confirmed by the fact that the main road and rail links between Europe and Asia pass through Kurdish land.

It is a fallacy promoted by the host states that the Kurds are an essentially nomadic people. The nomadic and semi-nomadic tribes traditionally formed the dominant group in Kurdish society, but even before this century most Kurds were settled or else migrated seasonally from settled communities to the countryside to graze their flocks. With movement into the towns most Kurds have been detribalized.

Before the division of Kurdistan among five modern states, it was far from being a homogeneous territory. Differences of dialect and custom as well as religion combined with tribal rivalries to ensure that the Kurdish nation remained divided. These contrasts have been heightened by the differing natures of the modern host states, which have still not prevented the Kurds from maintaining a sense of their Kurdishness even, as is the case of many Turkish Kurds, where they have lost the knowledge of their own language. Family and clan attachments cross national borders, and modern frontiers are considered little more than an unwanted inconvenience that should be disregarded whenever possible.

The host states have invariably kept their Kurdish provinces in a state of underdevelopment and impoverishment for fear of an increase in Kurdish power. There are few indigenous industries, apart from tobacco manufacture, to exploit local Kurdish resources. Local craftsmanship, which was traditionally the preserve of Christians and Jews within the Kurdish towns and villages, has died out as a result of the emigration of these communities and the introduction of cheap manufactured items into Kurdistan. The isolation of Kurdish communities from each other has not been eradicated by the introduction of roads and communications, since these tend to serve the needs of the modern national states. Thus, it is easier to travel from Turkish Kurdistan to Ankara or from Iraqi Kurdistan to Baghdad than it is to travel within Kurdistan itself.

But who are these people who so doggedly refuse to accept the verdict of history – that they have no separate place in the world? One negative result of state policies of assimilation and denial of Kurdish nationhood is that there has been relatively little modern research on the Kurds' ethnic and cultural origins. This means that there is no definitive answer to the question of their origins, except to say that an identifiable Kurdish people has inhabited the mountainous regions north of Mesopotamia for up to four millennia.

The first historical reference to the forefathers of the Kurds (although even this is disputed) appears in Xenophon's *Anabasis*, the contemporary account of the epic journey of the Greek 10,000 as they fled the Persian empire in 401 BC after the defeat of Cyrus, and of their encounters with the barbarians. As they head north from Mesopotamia to the Black Sea, Xenophon and his fellow Greeks enter the territory of the Carduchi, or Kardoukhoi. After twenty-four centuries the identity of these ancient barbarians may still be obscure, but their name and their location – north of modern-day Mosul – link them to today's Kurds, as does their attitude to central authority. 'These people,' according to Xenophon, 'lived in the mountains and were very war-like and not subject to the [Persian] king. Indeed a royal army of 120,000 had once invaded their country, and not a man of them had got back, because of the terrible conditions of the ground they had to go through.' The Greeks fought their way through the territory of the Carduchi in seven days, but Xenophon acknowledged that they suffered more against these proto-Kurds than they had against the armies of the Persian empire.

Xenophon tells us little about the Carduchi beyond their war-like qualities and their skill with the bow. Although the Greeks spoke to them through interpreters, there is no description of the language they spoke.

The language of the modern Kurds is closely related to Persian, and belongs to the north-western Iranian group alongside the languages of Afghanistan, Baluchistan and Tajikistan. According to Herodotus, the Greek historian, Kurdish and Persian were mutually comprehensible in ancient times. By extension Kurdish is related to Sanskrit and to many of the languages of modern Europe, including English. The relationship can be seen in many basic words: *erd* ('earth'), *new* ('new'), *bru* ('eyebrow'), *ruber* ('river'), *dlop* ('drop of water').

The modern Kurdish dialects are in some cases mutually incomprehensible, with wide variations in both vocabulary and grammar. The two main dialect groups are Kurmanji, spoken in Turkey and north-western Iraq and as far as Lake Orumiyeh in Iran, and Sorani, spoken in southern Iraqi Kurdistan and south-western Iranian Kurdistan. A separate dialect, Zaza, is spoken among many Turkish Kurds, existing alongside Kurmanji, while the Shia Kurds of southern Iranian Kurdistan speak dialects which are closer to modern Persian than they are to the languages of their fellow Kurds. The lack of a unified language has been used as an argument for claiming that the Kurds are not one nation; but the dialects are essentially as close as, say, Portuguese and Spanish, and closer than the languages of modern China or of nineteenth-century Italy.

From linguistic and classical historical evidence, it has generally been concluded that the Kurds are descended from the ancient Medes, an Iranian people who moved down from central Asia and settled in the twelfth century BC in the Zagros mountains and around Lake Orumiyeh in what is now Azerbaijan. The Medes conquered the Assyrian empire and the great cities of Nimrod and Niniveh, near present-day Mosul, but they were in turn defeated by the Persians. The Kurds themselves have traditionally favoured the theory of their Median ancestry – Meda is a name given to girl children.

Another strand of the Kurdish heritage can be traced back to the Scythians, an Indo-European people who moved down from what is now the Ukraine and established a kingdom in Iranian Kurdistan in the eighth century BC.

The Kurds were probably but one ancient tribe which in the end gave its name to the mixed population of the region. History does show that the name was established by the third century AD when the Persian king Ardeshir founded the Sassanid dynasty, for among the rivals he had to subdue at the beginning of his reign was Kurdan Shahi Madrig – Madrig, King of the Kurds.

Modern-day Kurds are almost certainly descended from a much more complex racial mixture than the Indo-European origin of their language would imply. Modern anthropological theory has largely discredited the idea that ancient indigenous peoples were completely supplanted by the mass migration of more sophisticated or war-like newcomers. Rather, it is now believed that newcomers brought their language and culture to regions they conquered and contributed to a richer racial mix. In this context modern Kurds probably owe their origins as much to the pre-Iranian inhabitants of the region as to the Indo-European tribes who came to dominate them. This process, whereby the ancient inhabitants of the region were culturally and linguistically Indo-Europeanized, is reflected in another traditional myth about the origins of the Kurds. It relates how Noah's ark came to rest after the flood on the peak of Mount Cudi in Iraq, 4,490 years before the birth of the Prophet Mohamed, and that a great city was built there which was ruled by Melik Kurdim of the tribe of Noah. When Melik Kurdim reached the age of 600, he invented a new language which his people called Kurdim, the language of the Kurds.

Another legend in Middle Eastern folklore which may also reflect this ancient racial mixing relates how King Solomon reigned over a supernatural world of demons and djinns. He sent 500 of his most faithful subjects to Europe to abduct the 500 most beautiful young women they could find. On their return they found that the king had died, and so they kept the women for themselves; the product of this forced union was the Kurds.

A similar account is to be found in Jewish folklore, in which the Kurds are said to be the descendants of devils who raped 400 virgins.

Before the arrival of Indo-European tribes in the third millennium BC, the region now called Kurdistan was inhabited by indigenous peoples related to the tribes of Armenia and the Caucasus, and speaking languages distantly related to modern Georgian. Among these pre-Aryan tribes were the Lullubi, the Kassites, the Elamites and the Guti, the latter considered to be among the ancestors of the Kurds. These ancient tribes were in a state of constant warfare with the peoples of the Mesopotamian plain, who raided the mountains for timber, minerals, slaves and the blonde and fair-skinned Guti women who were renowned for their beauty. Even today the people of the plains tend to be shorter and darker than the people of the mountains, where it is not uncommon to come across people with fair or reddish hair and blue eyes.

The mountain tribes became gradually Indo-Europeanized from the third millennium onwards as fresh waves of conquerors moved south. But it was a process which was probably not completed until the fifth century BC, at around the time of Xenophon, when the peoples of the mountain had been racially and culturally amalgamated into the identifiable forerunners of the modern Kurds.

The racial mix became even more complex over subsequent centuries, as Turkish and Arab tribes pressed in on the Kurdish heartland. In early medieval times some ethnically Turkish tribes became Kurdified, while Kurdish tribes became Turkified. Kurds became vassals of Arab chieftains and vice versa, and Arab and Turkish words entered the vocabularies of the Kurdish dialects.

The theories cited here of the Kurds' mixed racial origins in no way undermine their claim to be a separate nation; the idea that racial purity is a necessary basis for nationhood or statehood has long since been discredited. On the contrary, the argument is that the Kurds represent a unique racial and cultural mix which has led to their being recognized, by themselves and others, as an identifiable nation.

Before the coming of Islam in the seventh century AD, the people of Kurdistan predominantly followed the Zoroastrian religion of their Persian neighbours, although there are still cultural echoes in Kurdish folklore and customs of earlier pre-Aryan pagan beliefs. Christianity made some incursions into Kurdistan in the centuries before Islam, and entire tribes were converted. For instance, the formerly nomadic Herki tribe, now settled in the Arbil district of Iraq, used to carry with it a wooden ark which was said to contain the head of St George.

The Kurds were relatively slow to adopt the new religion which emerged from the Arabian peninsula in the seventh century and swept into the Levant, central Asia and across north Africa to southern Europe. The Kurds' first contact with the Muslim armies was in 637, when the invaders captured Tikrit, 100 miles north of Baghdad, on the fringes of Kurdish territory. Two years later Kurds fought on the side of the Persian governor of Ahwaz, as the fading Zoroastrian empire struggled ineffectively to hold back the tide of the new religion. The Arabs established their first foothold in Kurdistan itself in 643, after defeating the Kurdish armies at a bloody battle in what is now the Iraqi province of Suleimaniyeh.

The Kurds fought more vigorously than most against the domination of the Arabs, taking part in numerous uprisings. This may reflect competition for grazing land between the Kurds and the Arabs of the plains, which long pre-dated the coming of Islam. The close tribal structure of Kurdish society and the natural isolation of their mountain homeland may also have been factors in their resistance to the new religion. That they eventually succumbed to it may have more to do, as it did elsewhere, with the fact that Muslims escaped the tax on unbelievers than with any particularly strong adherence to the spiritual tenets of the new religion.

As elsewhere the Muslim armies cemented new alliances by

intermarriage; the mother of the last Ommayed caliph, Merwan Hakim, was a Kurd. Even so, the more isolated Kurdish tribes held out against the newcomers and were mounting raids on Muslim territory as late as the thirteenth century. This spirit of independence and resistance to Arab domination is reflected in another legend from Kurdish folklore. It tells how, when the Prophet called on the princes of the world to embrace the new religion, all hurried to submit to him. Oguz Khan, the prince of Turkestan, sent a Kurd, Zemin, to represent him. The Prophet was said to have been so impressed by this giant of a man with piercing eyes that he asked about his origins. On learning that Zemin was a Kurd, Mohamed prayed to God that such a terrifying people should never unite as a single nation.

Once converted, the majority of the Kurdish tribes became the most vigorous and devoted defenders of the new faith, although the spiritual element of their religious fervour was always open to question; as the Turkish proverb puts it: 'Compared to an infidel, the Kurd is a good Muslim.' Their war-like abilities, which over the centuries had been variously harnessed to the service of the Roman, Byzantine and Sassanid empires, were now dedicated to the service of Islam.

For almost twelve hundred years after the coming of Islam, religion was the most important factor linking the peoples of the Middle East; whether ruled by Arab or Turkish dynasties, each Muslim of whatever race saw his first duty as being towards Islam. This pan-Islamism lasted until the nineteenth century, when it came to be gradually supplanted by European ideas of nationalism. Notwithstanding this unity of purpose, there was a conscious awareness among the Kurds that others were taking advantage of their divisions and that the Kurdish nation, by allowing itself to be exploited as a mercenary force, was losing out. In the seventeenth century Ahmedi e-Hani lamented the fate that God had reserved for the Kurds in the epic poem *Mem-u-Zin*:

These Kurds who have gained glory by their sword;
How is it that they are denied the empire of the world and are subject
to others?
The Turks and the Persians are surrounded by Kurdish walls. (But)
each time the Arabs and the Turks act, it is the Kurds who bathe in
blood.
Ever disunited, ever discordant, they refuse to obey each other.
If we would only unite, the Turk, the Arab and the Persian would be
our servants.

Ahmedi e-Hani was not writing as the representative of a subject people in the traditional sense. The Kurdish tribes, whether nomadic, semi-nomadic or settled, were not the slaves or serfs of other nations; indeed, Kurdish chieftains more often than not ruled over non-Kurdish peasantry, usually Armenians or other Christians. Rather, he was lamenting the fact that other races appeared to have the ability to act according to a common purpose, while the Kurds were more often than not confronting each other in the service of the rival powers.

The coming of Islam had an overall positive effect on Kurdish society and brought civilization to a previously primitive and isolated corner of the Middle East. The early Middle Ages saw the first flowering of a distinctive Kurdish culture and the establishment of powerful independent principalities and dynasties. As the proselytizing fervour of the Arabs declined after the first centuries of Islam and the power of the Arab dynasties decayed, so the Kurds and Turkish tribes moving into the Levant from central Asia brought new blood and new vigour to the Islamic cause.

Among the earliest and most glorious of the independent Kurdish dynasties were those of the Chaddadites, founded in 951 by Mohamed Chaddad ben Kartan of the Rawadi – the tribe which was to produce Saladin – and the Merwanids, which lasted for a hundred years from 985, after its foundation by Kurd Bad, a former shepherd turned warrior-prince. He made himself master of Nuseibin and Diyarbakir, the main city of what is now south-western Turkey, and his armies even threatened Baghdad before his death in battle near Mosul. The eastern half of Kurdistan was ruled in the same century by two other great dynasties, the Hassanwahid (959–1015) and the Banu Annaz (990–1116).

It was an era in which, as so often before and since, Kurdistan served as the battlefield between rival empires. In the west the Christian Byzantine empire was trying to extend its control towards Lake Van, while in the south the Seljuk Turks were emerging as the dominant military dynasty in the Muslim cali-phate centred on Baghdad. Kurd Bad's nephew, Abu Nasr, who ruled from 1010 to 1061, took the precaution of maintaining good relations with all the great powers, and as a result reigned over the most prosperous and splendid flowering of Merwanid civilization, establishing a Kurdish court at Diyarbakir which rivalled those of Damascus or Cairo. When he took over the dynasty, he received messages of goodwill from the caliph, from Emperor Basil of Byzantium and from the ruler of Fatimid Egypt, Abu Ali Mansour. The caliph granted him a charter which made Abu Nasr master of all the towns and fortifications of the province of Diyarbakir. It was a society in which a Kurdish aristocracy and tribal soldiery ruled over a predominantly Christian peasantry, and in which the court officials were mainly Arabs or Syrian Christians.

This era of glory and prosperity was not to last. In 1055 the Seljuks entered Baghdad and assumed the role of protectors of the politically powerless caliph, the nominal ruler of the Islamic world, from the Buyid dynasty. The Seljuks then moved north to confront the Byzantines, defeating Emperor Romanos IV near Malazgird, north of Lake Van, and in Merwanid territory, in 1071. The Seljuks went on to seize most of Asia Minor – modern Turkey – from the Greek-speaking Byzantines, and were soon in control of the entire eastern Muslim world, except for Egypt. They took the precaution of suppressing the independent Kurdish principality on the frontier, until in 1085 the Merwanids were defeated, and the prince's former subjects were henceforth obliged to pay taxes to their new Turkish rulers.

It was in the following century that the name Kurdistan was first used, having been adopted by the Seljuks to describe a *sanjak*, or province, stretching from Hamadan and Kermanshah in the east to Sinjar in the west. The province was divided into sixteen districts, bordered by Arab Iraq in the south, Khuzestan in the south-east and Azerbaijan in the north, an area which Arab geographers had previously termed the Jebel ('the Mountain'). Although the province was nominally part of the expanding Seljuk empire, in practice the Turks distributed fiefs to Kurdish chieftains who administered their tribal areas as semi-independent vassals of the Seljuks.

It was a time of significant racial and cultural mixing among the peoples of the region, particularly between Turks and Kurds. Many Turkish family names appear in Kurdistan from this era, such as that of the Kokburi, the hereditary governors of Arbil. Kurdish influence also spread northwards to Armenia and, according to Armenian tradition, the two great warrior princes Zacharie and Ivan were of Kurdish origin.

Twenty-five years after the Seljuk victory at Malazgird, the first news arrived in the Levant of the movement of huge forces from the west en route for Constantinople. These were the Frankish Christian troops of the first crusade. Asia Minor had only been superficially Turkified and the Byzantine emperor Alexius Comnenus was seeking to regain his lost territory with the help of his fellow Christians from western Europe. Those who responded were a rag-tag army of tens of thousands of religious fanatics, and a relatively small company of knights. It was not the first appearance of Frankish knights in the orient; they had travelled there earlier as mercenaries. At about the time of the battle of Malazgird, a Frankish knight named Roussel of Bailleul had even carved out a state for himself in Byzantine territory, and the emperor had appealed to none other than the Seljuks to help evict the intruder.

Such unlikely alliances were the hallmark of an era in which the boundaries of empires were shifting; they were typical of the next two centuries of Christian crusader rule in the Levant. Over the course of the next 200 years Christian would join with Muslim to fight Christian and vice versa. The Muslim rulers of Egypt welcomed the arrival of the Europeans because they saw them as a potential counterweight to the expansion of Seljuk power. Christian Constantinople, which had appealed for crusader help in the first place, was to be sacked in 1204 by the crusaders themselves. And almost as important as the conflict which, for two centuries, set Muslim against Christian was the conflict between orthodox Sunni Islam, of which the Kurds and the Turks were among the most ardent defenders, and the Shia sect which at that time predominated in Egypt.

The crusader era is remembered in the Middle East as a time of massacre and plunder, comparable only to the invasions of the Mongols which were to follow shortly afterwards. Some of the Christian knights who settled in the Levant, where independent crusader kingdoms were established, benefited from exposure to Muslim culture, but the mass of Christians who flocked to the crusades were looked upon, and acted, as barbarians.

The Muslim world was ill-prepared to confront this scourge, and within three years of landing in the East the crusaders took Jerusalem, and Baldwin, Count of Edessa, proclaimed himself king. It was almost a hundred years before the holy city was reconquered for Islam by the great Kurdish leader Saladin.

By the eleventh century the Kurdish dynasties were already an important force outside the confines of the Jebel, and were a substantial presence as far as the Mediterranean coast of Syria. One of the most important Muslim fortifications of the coastal region was the Hisn al-Akrad, the Citadel of the Kurds, which the crusaders captured and made their headquarters in 1099. On this site they built the Crak des Chevaliers – *crak* being a corruption of the Arabic word for Kurd – which still dominates the Syrian plain and is considered to be the supreme example of early medieval military architecture.   .

Salah al-Din Yusuf, or Saladin, as he was known to his crusader foes, was born in 1138 in the northern Mesopotamian town
of Tikrit, which 800 years later was to become the birthplace of
Saddam Hussein. The Iraqi dictator, a devoted amateur student
of Arab history, was not averse to promoting comparisons between
himself and Saladin. But, like most Arab historians, he glossed
over the fact that the saviour of Islam was not an Arab but a
Kurd.

Saladin was the nephew of Shirkuh – the Lion – a Kurdish
officer in the service of Nur al-Din Mahmud, the Turkish-born
ruler of Muslim Syria and the man who began to turn the tide
against the Christian interlopers. Saladin accompanied his uncle
on the conquest of Fatimid Egypt, an enterprise undertaken to
prevent Egypt falling into the hands of the crusaders.

Shirkuh was a rough and ready Kurdish war-lord, a one-eyed,
ill-tempered brute of a man, given to excessive drinking and
bouts of uncontrollable temper. He was nevertheless a brilliant
strategist and much loved by his followers, both Turks and
Kurds. In the spring of 1164 Shirkuh's cavalry headed down the
eastern bank of the Jordan river and entered Egypt across the
Sinai, avoiding the forces of the crusader king Amalric and
reaching the walls of Cairo in less than a month. The Kurdish
general was ostensibly acting to protect the Fatimid ruler of
Egypt, the grand vizier Shawar, but Shawar turned against his
saviour and appealed to the crusaders in Syria to help oust the
Kurdish-led forces. Shirkuh moved out of Cairo but was besieged
by the Christians at Bilbays in the Nile delta. Relief came when
Nur al-Din destroyed the crusader forces who had remained in
Syria under Prince Baldwin, thereby obliging the Christians to
abandon Egypt and head back north.

In October 1164 Shirkuh and Amalric reached an agreement
whereby both would lead their forces out of Egypt simultane-
ously, leaving it in the hands of the treacherous Shawar. The
Christians went north to Jerusalem along the coast, while Shirkuh's forces returned to Damascus. But Shirkuh refused to accept

that he had been duped by Shawar and constantly pressured Nur al-Din to be allowed to launch a new Egyptian campaign. Fearing Shirkuh's vengeance, Shawar signed a pact with the crusaders, who once again in 1167 sent troops south into Egypt.

The Christian forces of Amalric and the Muslim forces of Shirkuh and his nephew, Saladin, arrived in Egypt at the same time. But Shirkuh refused to take up the challenge to confront the Christians and their Egyptian allies outside the walls of Cairo. Instead he took his troops across the Nile and camped near the pyramids at Giza. The decisive battle came on 18 March 1167 near al-Babayn on the west bank of the Nile. Shirkuh gave Saladin command of the centre, ordering him to feign a retreat as soon as he came under attack by Amalric's crusaders. This he did, thus luring the Christians into a trap in which they were encircled by the flanks of Shirkuh's army. Amalric escaped from the scene of the Christian defeat and fled to Cairo, but there he received news that Shirkuh had gone north immediately after the battle of al-Babayn and seized the city of Alexandria. Amalric marched north to besiege Alexandria, an enterprise which once more ended in stalemate, with him and the Kurdish general once again agreeing to leave Egypt at the same time. Amalric left a small army of occupation in Cairo in the form of a detachment of Frankish knights – their presence helped to turn the Egyptian people against the foreigners and their ally, the grand vizier Shawar.

In the end Shawar, who had changed sides so often, was ambushed and killed by Saladin himself, and Shirkuh was made grand vizier – the first Kurdish ruler of Muslim Egypt – a post he enjoyed for just two months before his untimely death from overeating. The caliph al-Adid appointed Saladin as his successor and gave him the title of *al-malik al-nasir* ('the victorious king').

Saladin dismantled the old Fatimid bureaucracy and put his own men in charge; he dissuaded the Byzantine empire from a half-hearted plan to intervene in Egypt, and he rejected an offer from Amalric to ally himself with the Christians against his nominal master, Nur al-Din. Reluctantly, on the orders of Nur al-Din, he abolished the 200-year-old Shia Fatimid dynasty, replacing it with Sunni rule.

Although he was a Kurd, Saladin did not accentuate his Kurdishness; Saladin was not himself a Kurdish tribal leader, as were many of his generals, and the armies he commanded were predominantly Turkish. Among his officers, however, were a significant number of Kurdish war-lords in the style of his uncle, Shirkuh. For him, the defence of Islam was a more important cause than the furtherance of his own race. As a consequence Saladin is more often revered publicly as the hero of Arab nationalists such as Saddam Hussein, while only his own people remember him first and foremost as a Kurd.

In 1174 Nur al-Din and Amalric died, both leaving successors who were still children. Saladin's only other potential rival, Emperor Manuel of Byzantium, was defeated two years later by the Turks and died soon afterwards. Saladin sent troops into Syria, ostensibly to protect the throne of Nur al-Din's successor but in fact to make himself king of Egypt and Syria, a position he consolidated in 1181, after a series of campaigns against his rivals, by seizing the city of Aleppo. Nur al-Din's successor died prematurely, and Saladin the Kurd became sultan of a new dynasty, the Abbuyids, which posed a powerful threat to the crusader kingdoms of the East.

Initially, Saladin was happy to coexist with the Christians, and he signed a truce with the Kingdom of Jerusalem, which the Christians rather than the Muslims were the first to break. In response he sent for thousands of Kurdish, Turkish and Arab reinforcements to come to Damascus to prepare for a holy war against the infidels. On 4 July 1187 the Muslim army defeated the crusaders at a hill in Galilee known as the Horns of Hittin. Within a month Saladin had conquered most of the cities of Palestine and by September had encircled Jerusalem. The following month the crusader defenders of the holy city surrendered, and on 2 October the Kurdish sultan entered its gates. Unlike the crusader capture of Jerusalem in 1099 when its inhabitants, Muslim and oriental Christians alike, had been put to the sword, there was no massacre or pillage, and the inhabitants were allowed to go in peace.

The loss of Jerusalem prompted renewed efforts on the part of Western Christendom to subdue the Holy Land, and the German emperor Frederick Barbarossa set sail for the East to confront Saladin, who responded by raising fresh armies from among his own Kurdish people in the provinces of Sinjar, the Jezireh, Mosul and Arbil. Philip of France followed in 1191, the year which also saw the arrival of Richard the Lionheart of England. But, while Saladin remained alive, the Europeans never succeeded in regaining Jerusalem.

The sultan died in 1193 at the age of fifty-five and was buried in Damascus, where his tomb can today be visited in a small stone building in a quiet garden near the Grand Bazaar. There is no acknowledgement there that the saviour of the Muslim orient was a Kurd. The Kurdish dynasty which he founded lasted a few more decades, but its decline dated from his death, as his followers descended into fratricidal strife for the succession. The dynasty fell in 1250, when the Mamluk slaves who had been brought from Asia to defend it took power in Egypt.

Saladin's rise illustrates the importance of Kurdish power in the early Middle Ages, an era in which the Kurds rivalled the Turks, the Persians and the Arabs in terms of culture and military prowess in the Muslim world. The development and expansion of Kurdish power might have been greater had it not been for the next scourge which was to afflict the Middle East, and in which Kurdistan was once again a battleground – the Mongol invasions.

In the thirteenth century Mongol tribes raided and conquered as far afield as China, Japan, Burma, India and Armenia and, within a decade of the fall of the Abbuyid dynasty, began the conquests of Persia, Iraq and the Levant. At this time Kurdish territory extended into the plains of Persia and reached almost to

Rey, near present-day Tehran, where the Mongols slaughtered the local population and built a mound of human eyeballs. Some Kurdish tribes took the pragmatic option of fighting on the side of the invaders.

In Iraq, Kurdish tribes took part in the defence of Mesopotamia against the Mongol hordes, confronting the cavalry of Hulegu, the grandson of Genghis Khan, who sacked Baghdad in 1258, and, in the following century, the forces of Tamerlane, the great Mongol emperor who conquered Damascus. But the invasions had the effect of pushing the Kurds back into their mountains, and northwards and westwards into Armenian territory.

The thirteenth century also saw the foundation of the Ottoman empire by the Emir Osman, who declared himself Sultan of the Turks in 1290. As Mongol power declined, the Ottomans expanded north of the Black Sea and into south-eastern Europe, encircling the vestigial Byzantine empire, which eventually fell with the capture of Constantinople in 1453. The power of the Ottoman empire eclipsed that of all its rivals in the Middle East and for 500 years was to dominate the fate of Kurdistan. After the collapse in 1404 of Tamerlane's empire, which had been centred on Samarkand, the Ottoman and Persian empires began to emerge as the two rival powers in the region, and to develop into something approaching modern multinational states, with an ill-defined frontier running through Kurdistan.

The Ottomans moved eastwards into the Kurdish mountains, massacring the leading Kurdish families as a means of curbing independent Kurdish power. The Turkish ruler, Uzun Hassan, used Kurdistan as a base to move into Persia and Azerbaijan. Under Sultan Mehmed II, 'the Conqueror', the Ottoman empire expanded further, bringing it into open conflict with the Safavid dynasty which had been founded by Shah Ismael in Persia at the turn of the sixteenth century. Under the Safavids, 'heretical' Shiism became the state religion of Persia, which created an additional cause of conflict with the Sunni Ottomans and their majority Sunni Kurdish vassals.

Ismael used primitive and war-like Turkish tribes from the Asian hinterland – the so-called Qizilbash, or Redheads – to extend Safavid power into Kurdistan. Diyarbakir fell to Ismael's brother-in-law, Mohammad Beg Ustajlu, who had the old noble families slaughtered. The untutored Qizilbash were put in charge of Kurdish lands, pillaging the country as far as Cizre, stealing flocks, killing the inhabitants and burning down Christian churches. For the majority Christian peasantry there was little to choose between Ustajlu's Qizilbash levies and the rule of the Kurdish tribal chieftains. It is not surprising, however, that in view of the depredations of the shah's armies, the Kurds themselves should have opted to seek the protection of the Ottomans.

Rivalry between the two empires soon led to open warfare, which was settled on Kurdish territory at Chaldiran, north-east of Lake Van, in 1514, when the forces of Sultan Selim the Cruel defeated Ismael's army and advanced to take Tabriz. Not for the first or last time, Kurds fought on both sides in a decisive encounter. But, with Selim's victory, the leading Kurdish emirs flocked to pledge loyalty to the Ottoman cause; twenty emirs had declared in his favour even before the campaign was under way, and after Chaldiran, under the guidance of Idris Bitlis, a Kurdish nobleman who was later to become the first historian of the Ottoman empire, they united to expel the Qizilbash, forcing them to flee to Persia.

The battle of Chaldiran established a frontier between the Ottoman and Persian empires which, although it continued to be disputed, remained more or less in place for 400 years, until the conclusion of World War I. Most of Kurdish territory, in what is now Turkey, Iraq and Syria, was in Ottoman hands, while a minority of Kurdish tribes remained under Persian domination.

The Ottomans acknowledged the importance of Kurdish support in the war against Persia as well as their strategic location on the edge of the empire by making the loyal emirs hereditary governors, an anomaly in the Ottoman empire. The old feudal lords were restored to their traditional powers and privileges, and were essentially left to run their own affairs as long as they collected and transferred taxes to the Sublime Porte, the Ottoman court of Constantinople. Some areas – the so-called Kurd *huku-meti*, or autonomous regions – enjoyed complete independence, with the right to strike their own coinage and have Friday prayers said in the name of their emirs, while the bulk of Kurdistan was divided into three Ottoman *vilayets*, or governorates. It was a situation which was to remain virtually unchanged until the nineteenth century, when the decay of the Ottoman empire and the advent of European nationalist ideas began to change the old patterns of rule in the Middle East.

After 1514 the role of the Kurds as Ottoman lords of the frontier encouraged Selim to settle Kurdish tribes in southern Armenia, where they displaced or subjugated the local Christian population, forcing many deeper into the Caucasus. Other Kurdish tribes acted as frontier guards for the Persians. The Persian Shah Abbas transferred many Kurds to the eastern province of Khorasan to control his eastern border, and almost half a million still inhabit that region, more than 600 miles from Kurdistan proper. Although the Kurds were now the subjects of rival empires, they continued to preserve their own language, traditions and literary culture, and, although they were split among sixteen principalities, they were less divided than were the peoples of Germany and Italy in the same era.

Much of the medieval history of Kurdistan has only been preserved thanks to the efforts of the Kurds themselves, above all the monumental history by Sharafedin Khan of Bitlis, the Sharif-nameh, written in Persian and published in 1596, which records the history of the Kurdish nobility from the time of the legend of Zahhak. It is an aristocratic history, concerned principally with the fate of the noble families rather than with that of the entire Kurdish nation. Until the early twentieth century the narrow definition of a Kurd still applied only to the noble tribes, while other Kurdish-speaking subclasses, whether Christian, Muslim or Jewish, were dismissed by their masters as non-Kurds.

Noble Kurds enjoyed substantial power at the centre of both Ottoman and Persian empires. In 1760 Kerim Khan Zend, a Kurd, even had himself declared Shah of Persia, although he was overthrown within two decades by the Turkish-speaking Qajars with help — such is the legacy of division in Kurdish history — from an alliance of Kurdish tribes.

A description of Kurdistan under Ottoman rule and as it was to remain until World War I was given by the Turkish traveller, Evliya Celebi, who visited this isolated region of the empire extensively in the mid-seventeenth century. He describes the almost total independence of the Kurdish khans, the multiplicity of dialects of the population, the sophistication of their towns and villages, and the strength of their military. He ascribes a vast area to Kurdistan, including much of Syria and Iraq, as the Kurdish nationalists were to do three centuries later, and appears to include all provinces where there was a Kurdish presence, even a minority one. 'In these vast territories,' wrote Evliya, 'live 500,000 men carrying guns, faithful Muslims of the Shafite school. And there are 776 fortresses, all inhabited. Pray God that these districts of Kurdistan will remain for eternity as a barrier between the greatest of all dynasties, the House of Osman, and the Shahs of Persia.' Such was to be the fate of the Kurds, if not for eternity, then at least for another 250 years.

Chapter Four

THE GREAT BETRAYAL

In 1880, at about the time he gathered the tribes together in the Kurdish tribal league to launch a revolt against the Ottoman oppressors, Sheikh Ubaidullah of Shamdinan wrote for support to the British consul at Bashkal, outlining the motives of his uprising.

The Kurdish nation is a nation apart. Its religion is different from that of others, also its laws and customs. The chiefs of Kurdistan, whether they be Turkish or Persian subjects, and the people of Kurdistan, whether Muslim or Christian, are all united and agreed that things cannot proceed as they are with the two governments. It is imperative that the European governments should do something, once they understand the situation . . . We want to take matters into our own hands. We can no longer put up with the oppression which the governments [of Persia and the Ottoman empire] impose upon us.

Sheikh Ubaidullah's revolt was among dozens of greater or lesser Kurdish rebellions against the two empires in the nineteenth century, all of them ultimately defeated by a combination of the superior force of arms of their opponents and the endemic divisions within Kurdish society.

Although Sheikh Ubaidullah was defeated, his letter survives as the first clear statement of modern Kurdish nationalism. But Kurdish nationalism is a movement which is still far from achieving statehood or even autonomy for the twenty million people who regard themselves as Kurds. In the aftermath of World War I promises were made to the Kurds by the British and others on which the world powers quickly reneged. The Kurds were denied a state because of prevailing geopolitical conditions and the rivalries of competing world powers. But it is also true to say that the Kurds were their own worst enemies, constantly putting tribal and sectarian interests above those of the Kurdish nation and ever willing to side with foreigners against fellow Kurds. Although leaders emerged, like Sheikh Ubaidullah, who could understand the plight of the Kurds in a nationalist context, too often the Kurds owed allegiance to men in whom gullibility and avarice were the chief characteristics.

Until the nineteenth century the Asian subjects of the Sublime Porte – Turks, Kurds, Arabs, Greeks, Armenians and Jews – slumbered in the Ottoman twilight. The Muslims among them paid allegiance to the sultan as the caliph of Islam, and national identity was less important than the shared religion. Kurdistan had fallen from its early glory as a result of the frequent wars fought on Kurdish land between Turks and Persians, and because of intertribal warfare among the Kurds themselves. Towns and cities fell into decline, castles were abandoned, and irrigation canals silted up. Fierce mountain tribes preyed on the settled populations of the valleys and the plains.

The Ottoman empire had been in slow decline since 1683, when, ostensibly at the height of its powers, its armies had been pushed back from Vienna. By the nineteenth century this decline had become self-evident. The medieval Ottoman court was unable to cope with the task of administering and defending a far-flung empire. The Sublime Porte's grip on its European territories slackened as ideas of nationalism and independence inspired by the French Revolution spread from Europe to the East. Newer, more vibrant imperialist powers, those of Britain and Tsarist Russia, were pressing in on Ottoman territory. In the Asian areas there were wars against the Persians and against the Russians in which Kurds fought on all sides; the Kurdish minority in the Soviet Union includes descendants of those who fought on the Tsarist side in the wars against the sultan.

The Ottoman response to the internal decay of the empire was to centralize power and extend direct rule to regions such as Kurdistan, which previously had largely been allowed to run their own affairs as long as they paid their taxes. Among the Kurds the Ottomans successfully used a policy of divide and rule to prevent the tribes uniting to cast off the imperial yoke. Those chieftains, or *aghas*, who rebelled were part of a fundamentally reactionary movement against centralizing reforms which threatened their position as feudal lords.

But before examining the reasons for the failure of the nineteenth-century rebellions, it is important to examine the nature of tribalism in Kurdistan and its role in the failure of the Kurds to gain a state of their own.

Traditional Kurdish society was divided into members of tribes – a nomadic or semi-nomadic warrior class pledging total allegiance to powerful, landowning chieftains; and a non-tribal subclass, usually landless peasants or sharecroppers, who were in effect the serfs of the tribes. The first duty of the tribesman was to his tribe and its chief, and his second to his religion. The concept of a national duty towards fellow Kurds was practically non-existent. If a chief decreed that it was in the interests of the tribe to fight on the side of the non-Kurdish state authorities against other Kurds, then his followers would obey. Even to this day, in Turkey and Iraq, there are Kurds who side with Ankara and Baghdad against their fellow Kurds without any sense that they are betraying some higher national Kurdish cause. In the rebellion conducted in the mid-1970s by Mullah Mustafa Barzani against the Baathist government of Iraq, his 50,000 *peshmerga* were pitted against a far higher number of pro-government Kurdish irregulars. The logic of opposing the nationalist cause was not entirely mercenary; victory for the nationalists would automatically have enhanced the standing of the tribe which led the rebellion, in this case the Barzanis; rival tribes therefore had a sectarian interest in helping to ensure that victory was denied them.

The blood ties which bind the members of a tribe are often

more mythical than real, and tribesmen can rarely trace their ancestors back more than a few generations. Rather, tribes represent alliances of convenience which shift according to circumstance. At times whole sections of a particular tribe would break away and seek the protection of a more powerful tribe and eventually become integrated with it. Some tribes would thus grow more powerful, while others would decline. Tribes were generally associated with a particular region, to which they often gave their name. A number of traditions and practices were adhered to which were designed to ensure the integrity of the tribe; among these the most important were marriage within the tribe and the tireless pursuit of blood feuds.

Within Kurdish tribal society there is a tradition of marriage between cousins which does not exist among the non-tribals. A girl's male first cousin is generally accepted to have an automatic right to her hand in marriage and therefore to enjoy a theoretical veto on her marrying anyone else. Failing a marriage between cousins, parents will always prefer to find a partner from among other close rather than distant relatives, and any relative is considered preferable to someone from outside the tribe.

The tradition of the blood feud, particularly prevalent in what is now Turkish Kurdistan, also set tribal loyalty above all other considerations. If a Kurd were killed, his relatives would seek out the first member of the tribe responsible they could find and kill him. It was not thought necessary to pursue the actual killer. This would prompt a cycle of revenge and counter-revenge which could last for generations and was one of the main causes of tribal rivalry.

The principal benefit of belonging to a tribe is that it provides mutual protection and security for which, in return, the tribesman gives absolute loyalty and obedience to his tribal chief. Tribalism is therefore more important in times of conflict, the norm in Kurdistan, than in times of peace. Where necessary, tribes would join together in larger confederations out of mutual self-interest, usually warfare and brigandage against rival tribes.

Tribalism is not unique to Kurdistan nor indeed to the immediate region. Even in this century tribalism has been a powerful force in Iraqi Arab society – Saddam Hussein's reliance on his Takriti clan to run the modern nation state of Iraq is a classic example of tribalism in action. Kurdish nationalists are the first to acknowledge that Saddam Hussein, whatever his weaknesses in dealing with the outside world, acted as a shrewd and skilful manipulator of tribal politics within his own country.

The weakness of the tribal system, in nationalistic terms, is that it has, until this day, divided the Kurdish nation. For the Kurdish chieftains and tribesmen, the Ottoman and Persian empires, and their successor national states, were sources of power and influence. Loyalty to the empire or to the nation state brought benefits, position and the prospect of outdoing one's rivals. Tribes which, for whatever reason, found themselves in conflict with those loyal to central government automatically cast themselves in the role of rebels and outlaws. Antagonism among the Kurdish tribes was therefore a mixed blessing for central governments in that it offered an opportunity to divide and rule the Kurdish nation, but it also meant that for every loyal chief there was likely to be one in rebellion.

Leadership among the tribes is not hereditary except among some larger princely houses dating back to the Middle Ages. The great Iraqi guerrilla leader, Mullah Mustafa Barzani, drew his power from being chieftain of the Barzani clan but his fourth son, Massoud, who helped to keep the flame of Kurdish nationalism alive after his father's death, and led the *peshmerga* forces in the 1991 uprising against Saddam Hussein, is not the head of the Barzani clan.

He is the offspring of a political marriage between Mullah Mustafa and a prominent daughter of the Zebari tribe. The Barzanis are a clan of the Zebari, but relations between them have often been strained. A Zebari fired the first shots in the uprising against the British occupation after World War I, and Zebari *peshmerga* fought alongside Barzanis in the revolt of the

1940s. But the two sides fell out over tribal politics, and many Zebari went over to the government side. The marriage was to have been part of a settlement between them, although many Zebaris were to continue their role as loyalists to whoever was in power in Baghdad.

The role of the tribal *aghas* towards central government could also affect the attitude of non-tribal peasants, who were regarded by the chieftains as assets with little more status than flocks of sheep, in some cases denied the right of free movement outside their villages unless they had the permission of their tribal land-lord. In the early twentieth century the non-tribal peasantry around Arbil in northern Iraq became ardent nationalists in reaction to the Dize tribe, which controlled the region and which based its power on collusion with the Ottomans and, later, with the Arab government in Baghdad. As late as 1953, in the final decade of the Iraqi monarchy, there was a serious peasant revolt against the Dize landlords.

Tribalism continues to be an important factor in Kurdish life and in Kurdish national politics, although the image of the Kurds as a nomadic tribal race has been overstated. Very few still follow the nomadic life and even in ancient times, among the Medes, the ancestors of the Kurds had both sedentary and no-madic populations. In this century, where tribes have opted to abandon their nomadic life or have been forcibly settled, many have continued to maintain their clan links. What is more, towns-people have chosen to align themselves to powerful tribes in their immediate vicinity in order to enjoy their protection. Else-where, however, Kurds have been detribalized by force of circum-stances, their traditional ties broken down by forced migration to areas of Turkey, Iraq and Iran outside Kurdistan.

Under the Ottomans the Kurds of the empire, whether tribal or non-tribal, lived for the most part under the relatively benign rule of the semi-autonomous princes who ruled the region on behalf of the Sublime Porte. From the start of the nineteenth century, however, the Turks began to interfere directly in the affairs of Kurdistan, as a consequence of reforms which were aimed at centralizing the administration of the empire and also because Kurdistan represented an untapped source of manpower for the sultan's colonial wars in Europe and elsewhere. This direct intervention in Kurdish affairs was a challenge to the powers of the feudal *aghas*, who had been happy enough to pay allegiance to Constantinople as long as they were left to their own devices.

In the first quarter of the nineteenth century Egypt broke away from Ottoman rule, Serbia revolted, and the Greeks launched their war of independence. To combat these uprisings the Sublime Porte forcibly raised levies from among the Kurdish tribes. If there was one thing that offended the Kurds more than taxes and customs dues, it was military conscription.

The first Kurdish revolt against Ottoman rule was launched in 1806 by Abdurrahman Pasha, the leader of the Baban principality which had built the city of Suleimaniyeh in southern Kurdistan as its capital. Abdurrahman declared war on the Sublime Porte when the Ottomans named a usurper from a rival tribe as emir. The Baban revolt lasted for three years but was finally defeated by an alliance of Turkish forces and Kurdish tribes who were traditional rivals of the Baban. Typically, in this first of many attempts to assert Kurdish independence, the rebels were betrayed by fellow Kurds. The subsequent military occupation of the region by Ottoman troops prompted further revolts, as did the 1828–9 Russo-Turkish war which was fought in southern Kurdistan.

A much more serious rebellion broke out in southern Kurdistan in 1826, led by Mir Mohamed of Rawanduz, the Prince of Soran and a descendant of Saladin. He declared independence from the Sublime Porte and opened diplomatic relations with Persia and the Egypt of Mehmet Ali, whose successful rebellion against Ottoman rule had inspired his own uprising. Mir Mohamed established an armaments industry at Rawanduz and set about turning his unruly tribal warriors into something approaching a regular army. His aim, as he set out in 1833 with 10,000 cavalry and 20,000 infantry, was nothing less than to unite the tribes, conquer all Kurdistan and establish an independent kingdom.

Mir Mohamed sought the aid of his neighbour, the Prince of Botan, who had his own aspirations to become king, and sent envoys to the Kurds of Iran to enlist their support in his war of liberation. In 1834 Mir Mohamed succeeded in fighting off a fierce counter-offensive by the sultan's forces, and the following year conquered Iranian Kurdistan. The shah was so alarmed that he called in the Russians to help contain the rebels. Fearing a joint offensive by the Ottomans and the Persians, Mir Mohamed withdrew his forces to Rawanduz to consolidate his position, at the same time attempting to play off the shah against the sultan by offering to recognize Persian sovereignty over the Iranian provinces of Kurdistan.

In July 1836 Kurdish forces once more routed the Ottoman armies and the sultan resorted to appealing to religious solidarity to defeat the rebels. A *fatwa* was issued which decreed that all who fought against the armies of the sultan-caliph were infidels. Mir Mohamed refused to bow to this blackmail, but the appeal to Islam lost him support among his followers. This time it was religion, the second duty of the Kurd after his tribe, which undermined the nationalist cause.

Mir Mohamed was forced to surrender and was taken into exile at Constantinople. He was given symbolic honours by Sultan Mahmoud II and six months later was released, ostensibly free to return to Kurdistan; but on the way home he was assassinated at Trebizond by the sultan's men.

The next major rebellion was led by Bedir Khan Beg, who succeeded his father in 1821 as Emir of Botan, an unruly collection of nomadic and other tribes centred on the Jezireh, where the modern frontiers of Turkey, Iraq and Syria meet. He first showed his independence towards Constantinople by refusing to send troops to the Russo-Turkish war in 1828. He appears to have had some of the attributes of a modern, if autocratic, leader, bringing security and prosperity to his principality by punishing lawlessness and brigandage with extreme severity.

Like Mir Mohamed, he organized the tribes along regimental lines and struck alliances with other tribal leaders, including the head of the powerful Hakkari tribe. When the Ottomans besieged his capital at Cizre in 1836, his allies responded by sending a mixed force of Kurds, Christian Assyrians and Armenians to relieve him. The Turks won the day by blowing up the bridges over the Botan river in order to keep these allies at bay.

Bedir Khan survived, and in 1840, after the defeat of the Ottomans by the Egyptian forces of Ibrahim Pasha, he saw his opportunity to liberate the whole of Kurdistan. He secured control of all of Ottoman Kurdistan, principally through alliances with his fellow princes and chieftains. Again the Sublime Porte used religion to undermine the revolt, this time calling on Western Christian missionaries in Kurdistan to persuade the Christian tribes not to fight for the Beg. Despite his renowned personal tolerance towards the Christians, there had been massacres of the Christian community in Kurdistan, and this contributed to the decision of the Christian tribes to withdraw their support from the rebellion.

The Kurdish–Ottoman war dragged on until 1847, when the Ottomans persuaded Bedir Khan's nephew, Yezdan Sher, a senior Kurdish commander, to change sides. This treachery spelled the end of the Beg's rebellion. He surrendered and died in exile, while his nephew was rewarded by being made Ottoman governor of Hakkari.

Yezdan Sher proved an unreliable vassal, for in 1853, when the Sublime Porte again went to war with Russia, he launched his own rebellion and had, by the end of 1855, raised an army of 100,000 men which threatened even Baghdad. This time the Kurds sought the support of outside powers, the Russians and the British, little realizing that neither side wanted to see the emergence of an independent Kurdistan under the auspices of

the rival empire. Yezdan Sher was lured into going to Constantinople with the promise that the British would mediate in negotiations with the Sublime Porte, only to be arrested and imprisoned
as soon as he arrived.

The rebellions of the first half of the nineteenth century represented the first stirrings of Kurdish nationalism, but, on the basis
of their immediate achievements, they were a disaster. The principalities were dismantled and put under direct Ottoman rule,
Turkish troops were allowed to pillage the country, tribe was set
against tribe by means of skilful Ottoman diplomacy, and Kurdistan entered an era of chaos, poverty and lawlessness. The
relationship of equality between Kurds and Turks which had
existed in the Middle Ages under the Seljuks had now been totally
destroyed, and Kurdistan reduced to colonial status. Even so,
Ottoman writ ran only in the towns, leaving the countryside
prey to the most ruthless of the tribes, who regularly descended
from the mountains upon their fellow Kurds in the valleys and
the plains in the manner of the Mongol hordes.

The uprisings had all been directed by the tribal nobility
within Kurdish society and were aimed at preserving the feudal
rights of the aristocracy against Ottoman encroachment. They
nevertheless had a strong nationalist tinge which appealed to a
wide spectrum of Kurds who shared the sufferings caused by
warfare and Turkish occupation.

The last great rebellion of the nineteenth century, equally as
quixotic and unsuccessful as those which preceded it, was that
launched in 1880 by Sheikh Ubaidullah and directed, in the first
instance, against the Shah of Persia. The Kurds of Iran regarded
the sheikh as their spiritual leader and, by agreement with the
shah, paid their taxes to him rather than Persia. The shah reneged
on the deal and sent in the army, at which point the sheikh
appealed to the Ottoman authorities for backing.

The unrest could have remained a Kurdish–Persian affair had
it not been for the outbreak of yet another Russo-Turkish war in
1877, which promoted the dispatch of more marauding Turkish

troops into Kurdistan. The hapless Kurds turned to their spiritual leader for help, and the sheikh was sucked into an unforeseen conflict with the Ottomans. He appealed unsuccessfully to the Russians, but his call to the British was answered with guns and ammunition. These weapons Ubaidullah turned firstly against Persia, where he had considerable success in wresting control of Kurdish territory from the shah's forces. But his advances alarmed the Ottomans, who sent troops to encircle him in the west. In 1882 the sheikh abandoned this uneven struggle.

Despite the failure of his revolt, he must be credited with the intelligence and perspicacity to foresee how the Kurds could be used by their imperial masters to serve their own rather than Kurdish interests. Urged by his followers in 1885 to order the massacre of the Christians of Orumiyeh as a reprisal for their lack of support for the Kurdish cause, he retorted: 'We Kurds are only useful to the Turks as a counterweight to the Christians. Once there are no more Christians, the Turks will turn on us.' And so, in the following decades, it was to be.

In 1876 Abdul Hamid II succeeded to the sultanate and brought in a series of reforms aimed at modernizing the Ottoman state administration. Constantinople had reduced the power of the Kurdish emirs in the previous decades and put Kurdistan under direct rule, but Abdul Hamid now proceeded to cultivate the Kurdish elite in order to use it against other internal enemies, those nationalist minorities such as the Armenians, Albanians and Arabs who threatened the security of the empire. What was more, loyal Kurds could always be used against other Kurds.

He bestowed honours and titles on the successors of the old tribal rebel leaders and even made the son of Bedir Khan, Bahri Bey, his personal aide-de-camp. In 1890 the sultan decreed the formation of a Kurdish cavalry force modelled on the Russian cossacks who would have the honour to bear his name – they would be known as the Hamidieh.

The Hamidieh regiments were set up as a regular force but on a tribal basis. Their principal *raison d'être* was as a frontier force to guard against Tsarist aggression, though they were also to be used to put down the Armenian population, whose nationalist sentiments were being encouraged by the Russians.

The tribal chiefs associated with the Hamidieh were well-rewarded by the Sublime Porte and given titles. Membership of the Hamidieh constituted a licence from the state to raid other tribes and suppress the peasantry in exchange for total loyalty to the sultan. But the force itself was firmly under the command of Turkish officers.

The Hamidieh first saw action in 1894–5, when they were called on to put down an Armenian revolt against double taxation by Kurdish and Ottoman overloads. Tens of thousands of Armenians were slaughtered in the process, either on the direct orders of the Ottoman authorities or on the initiative of the Hamidieh themselves. It was a foretaste of the massacres of 1915–16, in which Kurdish units also played a part in the killings and deportations of the Armenians. In later engagements the Hamidieh were used to suppress revolts by fellow Kurds and by Arab tribes to the south.

There were practical reasons for the growth of Kurdish-Christian antagonism in the late nineteenth century. The Armenians, together with the Jews, had traditionally controlled the small-scale manufacturing and craft industries of Kurdistan, apart from the production of carpets and weapons. They were the tradesmen in a society dominated by a feudal warrior elite. The Armenians and the Kurds had enjoyed a symbiotic relationship for centuries, in many cases sharing the same territory, and, aside from religion, similar cultural traditions. Both were nations divided by the same international frontiers, and some of the tribes which considered themselves Kurdish were, in fact, Armenians converted to Islam in an earlier age. The Armenian saying 'Armenian brains, Kurdish arms' fairly describes the nature of the relationship in times when the two nations co-operated.

With the introduction of a cash economy to Kurdistan, the Christians became useful as money-lenders to the tribes, a relationship which inevitably led to ill-feeling on the part of their debtors. The Ottomans also gave spiritual justification to the pogroms by appealing to the Muslim solidarity of the Kurds against the unbelievers. As a consequence of their religion, the Armenians tended to look towards the Christian West both as a model and for political support, while the Muslim Kurds more readily identified themselves with the Ottoman caliphate.

The Hamidieh were officially disbanded, although allowed to continue their activities under another name, when the Young Turk movement took power in the empire in a military coup in 1908. These young nationalist officers were disgusted by the depths to which the empire had sunk and by its dependence on the whims of the European powers. They represented the interest of a Turkish and Muslim bourgeoisie, which felt oppressed by both the Christian merchant class, which dominated the economy through its links with Europe, and the corrupt court officials of the sultanate.

They evolved a doctrine of Ottoman nationalism in which the various nations of the empire, be they Turks, Albanians, Arabs or Kurds, would unite to create a modern state. These lofty ideas quickly foundered as the Turkish element of the movement came to dominate the others. As the empire continued to disintegrate – Albania and Bulgaria won their freedom on the eve of World War I – Ottoman nationalism gave way to Turkish nationalism, the idea of a new empire embracing the Turkish-speaking world from Anatolia to Azerbaijan, Uzbekistan and the furthest regions of central Asia. The main barrier to this enterprise was that the heartland of the putative Turkish empire was occupied by non-Turks, the Armenians and the Kurds. What simpler solution then, according to the Turkish nationalists, than to use the Kurds to eliminate the Armenians, and then to turn against the Kurds?

The desire to establish a new Turkish empire was one of the prime motivations of the nationalists' decision to enter World War I on Germany's side and against Britain, France and imperial

Russia. It was a war in which, according to the Kurdish historian Kendal Nezan, not only were more than one million Armenians massacred but 700,000 Kurds were also killed.

The Kurds were encouraged to take part in the great *jihad* against the infidels and, for the most part, responded positively. Even Kurds living under the ostensibly neutral Persian empire flocked to the Ottoman cause, although others under Ottoman domination refused to fight, while some actively sided with the Russians. As usual tribal and personal self-interest tended to outweigh other considerations.

The more sophisticated of the Kurdish leadership saw that the Kurds had more to gain from the defeat of the Ottomans, and they actively sought the support of the allies. Kamil Beg of Botan went to Tiflis in 1916 to try to persuade Grand Duke Nicholas, the viceroy of the Caucasus and Russian commander of the Turkish front, to support the Kurdish cause.

In the second year of the war, with the Bolshevik revolution in Russia still two years away, the British, French and Russians began secret discussions on how they intended to divide the spoils of the Ottoman empire among themselves once it was defeated. Sir Mark Sykes, for Britain, and Georges Picot, for France, were the main protagonists. After three months of deliberations they travelled to Petrograd in March 1916 to secure Russian agreement to an accord under which Armenia and most of Ottoman Kurdistan was to come under the Russian sphere of influence. The Ottoman *vilayet* of Mosul (modern Iraqi Kurdistan) was, however, assigned to France. The Arab territories of the Ottoman empire were to be divided between Britain and France.

Subsequent events altered the balance of power within the allied camp in Britain's favour. Allenby's forces took Jerusalem and Damascus, and, after a costly campaign against the Turks in Mesopotamia, the British took Arab Iraq as well. Four days after the 1918 armistice which ended the war with the defeated Ottoman empire, the British entered Mosul.

In the meantime the Tsarist empire had fallen and its Bolshevik successors abandoned Russia's imperial pretensions in the Middle East. The British, who were to have had no role in Kurdistan under the terms of the Sykes–Picot agreement, emerged as the biggest power in the region once the war was over.

Broadly speaking, the townspeople of the Mosul *vilayet* welcomed the arrival of the British after years of debilitating warfare, while the tribal chiefs saw it as yet another threat to their personal prerogatives.

The Ottoman empire was in ruins, and British power was stretched. Allied troops occupied most of Anatolia, and it was left to the Indian Army Expeditionary force in Iraq and to the Royal Air Force to pacify southern Kurdistan. The first tribal revolts were not long in coming; tribesmen north of Mosul ambushed and killed a number of British officers in the spring of 1919, and the RAF responded by bombing rebel territory, the first of many punitive air raids against the Kurds. Later the same year heavy-handed British attempts to impose order on the unruly tribes achieved the seemingly impossible – a reconciliation between the warring Zebaris and Barzanis, the latter led by Sheikh Ahmad, the elder brother of Mullah Mustafa. The British responded by occupying the tribal homelands and forcing the rebels into the mountains.

The Kurdish nationalist movement emerged from World War I with its ranks depleted, and divided on the issue of whether to put its faith in the allied powers which now dominated the area, or to throw in its lot with the Turks with a view to building a bi-national state out of the ruins of the Ottoman empire.

As soon as the war was over, Kurdish organizations based in Constantinople and in exile approached the British and French governments, some demanding support for an independent Kurdistan. Two of the three organizations involved were dominated by members of the powerful Bedir Khan dynasty, while the third – Istikhlas i Kurdistan, or Kurdish Liberation – was run by the son of Sheikh Ubaidullah, Abdul Qadyr, who had been courted and honoured by the sultan and who as a consequence was vigorously opposed to the concept of an independent Kurdish state.

The Kurds were also in touch with the King–Crane Commission, which was dispatched by the United States to assess the post-war situation in the Ottoman empire. The commission was later to report that a Kurdish state covering about a quarter of Kurdistan should be established, as well as an Armenian state in that area which was to have gone to Tsarist Russia. It recommended that both these states, together with a Turkish state to be created in Anatolia, should be placed under US mandate.

America's concern about the future of the region had been set out by President Woodrow Wilson in his Fourteen Points Declaration to a joint session of Congress on 8 January 1918, in which he said, *inter alia*, that 'The Turkish portions of the present Ottoman empire should be assured a secure sovereignty, but the other nationalities which are now under Turkish rule should be assured an undoubted security of life and an absolutely unmolested opportunity of autonomous development.'

Despite Wilson's noble aspirations for creating a new international order after the war, US interest in Kurdistan was essentially no more high-minded than that of Britain or France: all three were aware of the vast oil potential of the Mosul *vilayet* and each was anxious to prevent such resources falling entirely into the hands of the others. But when the preliminaries of the Paris peace conference began in January 1919 it was Britain which held most of the cards. British forces were, however tenuously, in possession of the disputed region, and British diplomats had taken the trouble to establish contacts with the Kurds even before the war was over. Sir Percy Cox, the architect of modern Iraq, had been to Marseilles the previous year to discuss the future of the region with the man who was to be the Kurds' representative at Paris, General Sherif Pasha.

The defeated Turks had not been idle either. In order to try to scotch the allies' plans to dismember the empire, they promised the Kurds autonomy, a pledge which was accepted and actively promoted by Abdul Qadyr's organization. In May 1919 the British committed the error of persuading the sultan to send a representative to Kurdistan to try to counter the activities of Bolshevik organizations in the region.

The man chosen was an Ottoman war hero, General Mustafa Kemal, the future Ataturk. Mustafa Kemal seized the opportunity to launch his war of liberation by appealing to all Muslims to rally to the cause of the sultan-caliph, who was imprisoned at Constantinople by the infidel allies. By playing on Kurdish fears that the Armenians were about to annex Kurdish lands for their new state, he was able to rally the tribes to his side. Thus, the Turkish war of independence, which was to lead to the cultural suppression of the Kurds and the total secularization of Turkey, was launched in Kurdistan under the banner of Islam.

In Paris, meanwhile, Sherif Pasha, a former ambassador of the Sublime Porte to Stockholm, had been chosen by the pro-independence wing of the Kurdish movement to put the Kurdish case. He found himself representing a deeply divided movement which had very little influence among, or relevance to, most of the inhabitants of Kurdistan. In a briefing paper prepared by the Foreign Office for the Paris conference it was noted that the Kurds lacked any national policy and had only a tribal consciousness.

The British and the French made it clear from the outset that they were unwilling to surrender those parts of Iraqi and Syrian Kurdistan which fell under their control, and that an independent Kurdistan, if such an entity were to be created, would have to be in what was still Turkish territory.

Sherif Pasha's negotiating brief was further complicated by the fact that he had no real mandate from the Kurdish nation, and no one had any clear idea of what the Kurds as a whole wanted. Despite these limitations, such was the weakness of the decaying sultanate that the conference ended by formulating a treaty which did include provisions for a Kurdish state.

British-occupied Mosul *vilayet* until such time as Turkish Kurdistan had gained its independence.

But even this truncated and impoverished Kurdish state was not to be. The Treaty of Sèvres was never ratified. The Turkish nationalists established a national assembly at Ankara which, shortly before the Sèvres treaty was signed, announced that it would not recognize any agreement signed by the Ottoman government in occupied Constantinople. The nationalist ascendancy was confirmed when Mustafa Kemal succeeded in reversing the humiliations of the war by ousting the occupying Greek army from Anatolia and establishing a fiercely nationalistic regime. In November 1922 the Kemalist National Assembly deposed Sultan Mehmed VI and abolished the caliphate, severing the last pan-Islamic link uniting the empire's Muslim nationalities. Mustafa Kemal declared: 'The state which we have just created is a Turkish state.'

The Kurds who fought on the side of the Kemalists in the hope of securing their autonomy within a revitalized Ottoman union of Turks and Kurds had fought in vain. Those who had opted for allied promises of independence contained in the Treaty of Sèvres were equally deceived. Sèvres, which had been imposed on a defeated Ottoman empire, was dropped in favour of the Treaty of Lausanne, which, when published on 24 July 1923, duly recognized a new Turkish state incorporating most of the Kurdish territories. The treaty did not mention the Kurds and spoke only of the rights of non-Muslim minorities, a category which excluded most Kurds.

This left open the future of the Mosul *vilayet* and the question of who would control its oil reserves. Britain had been appointed in 1920 to exercise a League of Nations mandate over Iraq and the Mosul *vilayet*, but at the time that the Treaty of Lausanne was signed on 6 August 1924 Turkey had yet to abandon its own claim to Mosul. Britain had secured allied support for its claim by signing over 25 per cent of future oil revenues to the French and a 20 per cent stake in the British-owned Turkish Petroleum to the United States after Washington had complained about the colonial carve-up of the region. The main shareholder in Turkish Petroleum, the company which had the exclusive rights to exploit the Iraqi fields, was Lord Curzon, Britain's chief negotiator at Lausanne.

At the conference Curzon and his Turkish counterpart, Ismet Inonu, both professed concern for the Kurds of the Mosul *vilayet* and used this to justify their conflicting claims to the territory. Britain was acting nominally on behalf of the new Arab state of Iraq, where Faisal, the son of Sharif Hussein of Mecca, had been enthroned in 1921 as king of a country which embraced both the Mesopotamian provinces and the Kurdish *vilayet* of Mosul. The creation of the Iraqi monarchy followed a pledge made to Hussein by the British in 1915 that, in return for him raising a revolt against the Ottomans in the Arabian peninsula, he would receive the Ottoman *vilayats* of Baghdad and Basra once the war was over. Hussein did not stake a claim to the predominantly Kurdish Mosul region, nor was it offered by the British. In the event Hussein was denied the throne, which went instead to Faisal, who had fought alongside T. E. Lawrence in the Arab revolt and who had in 1920 been ousted from Damascus by the French after a short reign as King of Syria.

Once the war was over, the Kurds showed not the slightest willingness to be absorbed into the new Arab state, an attitude best illustrated by the success of the revolt organized by Sheikh Mahmoud Berezendji, the self-styled King of Kurdistan, who in 1919 managed to wrest control of the Suleimaniyeh region from the occupying British and extend his rebellion into Iran. This first revolt was put down, but, between serving time in prison, Sheikh Mahmoud continued to plague the Iraqis and their British protectors into the 1930s.

After the signing of the Treaty of Lausanne, the League of Nations sent an international commission of inquiry to the disputed Mosul *vilayet* to assess the situation and the wishes of its population. The commission reported an almost total lack of consciousness among the Kurds that they were part of an Iraqi state and said that, on ethnic grounds alone, the best solution would be the creation of an independent Kurdish state. The commission nevertheless accepted the British argument that, on economic grounds, the Kurdish territory should be attached to the Iraqi state. The one proviso was that the demands of the Kurds to carry out the administration of the territory, and to use Kurdish as the official language, should be taken into account. 'Regard must be paid,' the commission said, 'to the desires expressed by the Kurds that officials of the Kurdish race should be appointed for the administration of their country, the dispensation of justice and teaching in the schools, and that Kurdish should be the official language of all these services.'

The Council of the League of Nations accepted the report and on 16 December 1925 agreed to the attachment of the Mosul *vilayet* to Iraq. Britain was given a mandate of twenty-five years and enjoined to ensure that the Kurds enjoyed the type of local administration which the commission of inquiry had recommended. Lip-service was paid to this requirement by promulgation of the Local Languages Law the following year, but, in practical terms, there was no attempt by the Iraqi government or its British patrons to extend anything approaching autonomy to the people of Kurdistan.

Throughout the 1920s, and despite the repeated revolts raised by Sheikh Mahmoud and the Barzanis, the Kurds nevertheless put a touching faith in Britain's good intentions, which even the British officials involved sometimes found surprising. British documents of the time reveal not only a cynical manipulation of Kurdish nationalism but also a patronizing attitude to the Kurdish nation.

In a secret report to London from Air Headquarters Baghdad, dated 11 November 1924, it is noted that

It is to the British and to no other nation that the Kurds look for assistance as they are regarded as the givers of liberty, or a considerable degree of it, to smaller nations, as opposed to the policy of subjugation and absorption which is the habit of others . . . Up to date, in spite of an almost entire absence of practical help, the Kurds continue firmly to believe that in the end, when the opportunity comes, the British will take up their case and effect their salvation.

The report stemmed from the debriefing of four Kurdish officers who had deserted from the Turkish army and who were sympathizers of Amin Ali Badr Khan's Kurdish National Society. The report concludes that it would be a useful ploy to support and arm the uprising of Kurds in neighbouring Turkey, both as a potential weapon against the Turks and as a means of gaining popularity among the Kurds of Iraq. 'That the Turks are very nervous of the movement is undoubtedly true and, particularly at the moment, it would be a very powerful weapon against Turkey in case of war,' the report stressed.

This menace has been of considerable value to the British government during past years, the more so on account of the considerable Kurdish population within Iraqi borders . . . It is sufficiently clear that generous treatment of Iraqi and emigrant Kurds and encouragement of their national susceptibilities if they can be reduced to practical terms would repay themselves over and over again. Such a policy would go far towards providing a friendly population over the border along the whole Northern frontier and northern third of the Eastern frontier of Iraq, and would furnish the Iraq government with a weapon against the Turks both in diplomacy and in potential war.

Once again the Kurds were regarded as useful cat's-paws in interstate disputes; as for encouraging Kurdish 'national susceptibilities' for their own sake, however, the British proved to be less accommodating.

In a 1930 memorandum to the League of Nations, the British government failed to disguise its irritation that the Kurds should still be aspiring to an independent state. It refers to the widespread belief in Kurdistan

that there was in existence a special decision by the Council of the

League requiring the establishment of an independent state in southern Kurdistan upon the withdrawal of mandatory control from Iraq . . . It seems certain that unrest and discontent will continue in the Kurdish regions until this report as to the existence of a decision by the Council of the League promising an independent Kurdish state is authoritatively denied, and the Kurds themselves are brought to realize that Kurdish independence is outside the realm of practical politics.

The memorandum goes on to state that

On political grounds . . . the conception is almost fantastic. Although they admittedly possess many sterling qualities, the Kurds of Iraq are entirely lacking in those characteristics of political cohesion which are essential to self-government. Their organization and outlook are essentially tribal. They are without traditions of self-government or self-governing institutions. Their mode of life is primitive, and for the most part they are illiterate and untutored, resentful of authority and lacking in sense of discipline or responsibility.

In such circumstances, according to the memorandum, it would be 'unkind to the Kurds themselves to do anything which would lend encouragement to the sterile idea of Kurdish independence'.

Even the High Commission in Baghdad regarded some of this as unnecessarily high-handed and requested that the more negative aspects of the memorandum relating to the inability of the Kurds to govern themselves should be deleted, 'since we should be exposed to the retort that they are equally applicable to the greater part of Iraq and that in fact in Turkish times many Kurds rose to the highest offices of state'. This had no impact on the Colonial Office, which rejected the request; an anonymous official scribbled in the margin: 'Then you can counter-retort with, "that's why the place was in a mess".'

Nowhere, however, is the British cynicism and duplicity more exposed than in a letter to the Colonial Office from Acting High Commissioner S. H. Bourdillon in February 1926. Following the League of Nations acceptance of the incorporation of Kurdish territory into Iraq, London had asked to be reminded of the various and no doubt contradictory pledges which had been given to the Kurds in the past. Bourdillon recalled, among others, a statement issued in 1922, which ran as follows:

His Britannic Majesty's government and the government of Iraq recognize the rights of the Kurds living within the boundaries of Iraq to set up a Kurdish government within those boundaries and hope that the different Kurdish elements will, as soon as possible, arrive at an agreement between themselves as to the form which they wish that government should take and the boundaries within which they wish it to extend and will send responsible delegates to Baghdad to discuss their economic and political relations with His Britannic Majesty's government and the government of Iraq.

This remarkable statement amounts almost to an offer of full autonomy to the Kurds and was, in theory, as important to them as the 1917 Balfour Declaration was to the Jews. It was made at a time when the British were trying to harness moderate opinion to counter the rebellion of Sheikh Mahmoud, an uprising which was finally put down by a military expedition to Suleimaniyeh and Rawanduz. The statement was communicated to Sheikh Abdul Karim, a former supporter of Mahmoud who had parted company with him. It was published in a Kurdish newspaper in Suleimaniyeh, but, as Bourdillon noted, no doubt to the great relief of the Colonial Office, 'it was given publicity nowhere else'.

Abdul Karim had failed to act on the statement, though there was always a danger that it might be picked up on in the future. Again, Bourdillon sought to calm Colonial Office nerves.

Owing to the limited publicity which was given to the proclamation I doubt whether it will ever be mentioned again. Had it remained a living memory it is probable that the attention of the Frontier Commission would have been called to it. Should a Kurdish nationalist party again consolidate in Iraq and demand the autonomy conditionally promised in this proclamation, they can be answered by telling them that their right to demand autonomy has lapsed owing to their

failure to secure that right, when its recognition was offered, by coming
to the assistance of the government in its endeavour to restore law and
order in their country.

In the event, this particular piece of sophistry was not needed:
the issue of the 1922 proclamation was never raised, and Britain
was allowed to get away with its broken promise. In 1930 an
Anglo-Iraqi treaty was signed which ended the mandate twenty-
one years before it was due to expire, and Iraq was granted
nominal independence. There was no mention of the Kurds, an
oversight which prompted a fresh revolt by Sheikh Mahmoud in
Suleimaniyeh and the Barzanis in the Badinan.

With independence, Britain washed its hands of the Kurdish
question. The British may have admired the warrior qualities of
the Kurds and their fierce spirit of independence, but they had
no intention of helping them fulfil their aspirations if they conflicted with the higher purpose of maintaining the integrity of
the new Iraqi state. In essence, the British were contemptuous of
Kurdish nationalism and of its leaders. In a confidential report
written in 1946, the research department of the Foreign Office,
remarking on the rebellions led by Sheikh Mahmoud, and by
Ahmad and Mullah Mustafa Barzani, noted that:

Their hostility to the 'Arab' government of Baghdad is fundamental
and, in that sense, they may be regarded as champions of Kurdish
nationalism; but it is a nationalism limited to achieving their personal
ambitions rather than one inspired by a wider patriotism. Their primary aim is to be left alone to exercise their feudal tyranny over as
many of their countrymen as they can contrive to control.

Chapter Five

THE REPUBLIC OF MAHABAD

The Kurds in Iran have had to cope with two special conditions that their cousins escaped in neighbouring countries: they have the Soviet Union as a neighbour, and they are part of a state made up of minorities, and so determined to prevent any one of them achieving an autonomy which would set a precedent for others, which could thus lead to the break-up of the state. In Iran the desire of the Kurds for independence is matched by the separatist movements in Azerbaijan and Baluchistan, and even such groups as the Bakhtiars, the Georgians or the Arabs of Khuzestan could cause trouble for the central government. Thus the policy of successive administrations in Tehran has always been to centralize, to allow devolved government in the provinces only if the governors are loyal to Tehran, and to crack down on any separatist movements which might occur.

Equally, from the time of the Czars to the present day, Iran has always had to consider the wishes and likely actions of its northern neighbour, and to step carefully in its own dealings with its people in the border zone. From the nineteenth century onwards, it was always accepted that Russia had a sphere of influence in the northern half of the country, while the European powers vied for control of the south, until the US and Britain took over by invading in World War II.

None of this stopped the Kurds of Iran from acting as Kurds do in all countries in which they live – seeking to throw off the yoke of central government and to set up their own regime. But in Iran more than in other countries, pan-Kurdism had little place in politics – though the first cross-border Kurdish agreement was signed as a result of an initiative by Iranian Kurds. It happened in 1944 at the suggestion of the Komala (literally, 'Committee'), the Kurdish nationalist party founded by a group of Iranian Kurds from Mahabad and a representative of the Iraqi party Hewa ('Hope'). The Komala stemmed from a meeting in Iran in 1942 between a delegate from the Iraqi Kurds and a group of prominent men from Mahabad, the main town of Iranian Kurdistan. At the time the Khoybun, the exile party which was active in European capitals and had some influence in Turkey, was virtually unknown in Iraq and Iran, where tribal politics dominated Kurdish thinking, so that it was left to the urban Kurds to try to rise above the petty squabbles and jockeying for power of the tribal sheikhs. That was the origin of Hewa, a party established in northern Iraq during the mandate period, to oppose the British and to work for a greater Kurdistan.

Due partly to the difficulty of travel, partly to the need to evade official notice, Hewa was for years confined to the main cities of northern Iraq, Kirkuk, Mosul, Suleimaniyeh and Zakho, with membership limited to the educated Kurds, leaving the tribes to get on with their perennial battles, which even as late as the 1940s had more to do with grazing land and water than with political beliefs.

In 1942, with the upheaval of war forcing people to look ahead and to try to shape their own destinies, the decision was taken to extend the rudimentary contacts made by Hewa with a few Turkish and Iranian Kurdish leaders on the border into something more. Mir Haj, a captain in the Iraqi army as well as a Kurd and a member of Hewa, was dispatched to make contact with nationalists in Iran, and in particular in Mahabad, then in the Soviet zone of interest and known as the capital of Iranian Kurdistan. Mir Haj met about a dozen leading citizens of Mahabad who were also known as Kurdish nationalists – in the atmosphere of the time, there was no need to conceal their opposition to the domination of Tehran over local politics.

The Iraqi messenger was more than a fraternal delegate: from the experience of Hewa he could give practical advice on how a Kurdish nationalist group should be established and run, emphasizing that even if things were relatively easy at that time, conditions could change, and they should prepare themselves for official retribution. A cell system was advised, with new members knowing only two or three others joining with them or allocated to their small group. After hearing the lecture from Mir Haj, the Mahabad men decided to form themselves into a committee – the Komala i Zian i Kurdistan, or Committee for the Rebirth of Kurdistan.

The Komala flourished, with the original dozen or so recruiting many others, who at the initiation ceremony all swore on the Koran to work for self-government for all Kurds. The mixture of clandestine organization and semi-public acknowledgement of the Komala's existence gave it greater influence and attracted more followers, so that within a couple of years the Komala in northern Iran was a considerable force, able to repay the original help from Iraqi Kurds by sending delegates to visit Hewa officials, and to propose a further expansion of the movement. By 1944 many tribal chiefs had joined the educated urban elite in the Komala, seeing it as a potent nationalist force at a time of great power rivalry which could be exploited, particularly as the central government in Tehran was weak, unable to enforce its authority in the north of the country, while in Iraq all Kurds, like most Iraqis, were united in opposition to the British occupation of the country. So by 1944 visits were being made back and forth by the Kurds of Mahabad to Iraq and, in a new development, to Syria and Turkey as well. The Hewa Party began to recognize the Komala as the true voice of Kurdish nationalism, while the Khoybun had quietly disappeared, lost after the failure of the revolts in Turkey in the 1920s and 1930s.

In August 1944 came the first formalization of cross-border Kurdish nationalism, a written treaty between representatives from Turkey, Iraq and Iran. It was known as the Peman i Se

Senur, or the Pact of the Three Borders, and was signed at Mount Dalanpar, where Iran, Iraq and Turkey meet. It was no more than a symbolic gesture, but one which gave heart to the Kurds, already emboldened by the publication of the first map purporting to show the whole of Kurdistan, and also by the adoption of a Kurdish national flag – the Iranian tricolour turned over, red, white and green instead of green, red and white. At least it would be easy to change the symbols of power if ever there were to be a take-over in northern Iran.

Until World War II the Kurdish structure in Iran was always based on the tribe and the family, even more than in Iraq, and calls for cross-border co-operation, or for the setting up of a Kurdish federation, were no more than pretexts for persuading Iraqi or Turkish tribes to join in feuds inside Iran. Although the abortive Treaty of Sèvres had not held out any prospect of autonomy or independence for the Kurds of Iran, they shared in the general disappointment of the Kurds of the old Ottoman empire that its terms were never ratified. They were concerned more because it deprived local leaders of the possibility of enhanced power rather than because of any deep commitment to nationhood.

The outbreak of World War II formalized what had already taken place – the division of Iran into Soviet and western spheres, with the American and British forces taking Tehran and the south, and the Soviets occupying the northern provinces of Azerbaijan and Kurdistan. The main concern of the Soviets was to secure the supply line up from the Gulf to the border, so they were careful to do nothing which might antagonize the local tribes, and so jeopardize the route along which war material was being shipped in from the West. German agents based in Turkey were active among the Kurds, but the Russians were determined to avoid local conflict, and so resolved to keep the Kurds on their side by diplomacy rather than force of arms for as long as possible. No difficulty was made when Kurdish irregulars seized arms and ammunition from the retreating and disintegrating

Iranian army, and Kurdish leaders who had been exiled by the Iranian leader Reza Shah were treated with respect by the Russians as well as by the Kurds when they returned home. Iranian officials who remained at their posts had to rely on the Soviets for security, and so were thus unable to enforce the decrees of the Iranian government, now a weak committee of ineffectuals under the nominal leadership of Reza Shah's young and inexperienced son, Mohammad Reza – Reza Shah himself was deposed and exiled to South Africa.

Apart from a general policy of trying to keep the Kurdish and Azerbaijani regions quiet, the Soviets seemed to have little idea of how to deal with the area they occupied, with no evidence emerging that they had moved in with any plan to hold on to the north of Iran after the war. Yet there were Russian political officers at work who had the future in mind, and it was as a result of their influence that thirty leading Kurdish figures were invited to pay a visit to the Soviet Union in 1941. It was the first step on to the international stage of Qazi Mohammed, a man destined to become a hero of Kurds everywhere, as well as one of the first martyrs of Kurdistan.

Qazi Mohammed was a judge, in the Islamic sense, settling all cases according to sharia law. He came from what was acknowledged to be the first family of Mahabad, who had for generations provided the town's judges; he inherited his position from his father and grandfather. Educated at a mosque school, where reading and writing was supplemented only by learning the Koran by heart, Qazi Mohammed was fortunate in having a father who was able to enlarge his education, and to live in a house where many books were available, not only the Koran, the one book to be found in most homes. So Qazi Mohammed grew up not only learned in sharia law but also progressive in outlook, receptive to new ideas, with a knowledge of English and Russian gained from books given him by his father and by his contacts with visitors to the town, and an outgoing character which did not detract from the sense of public duty he felt as a result of his birth. Mohammed was one of a family of five and, marrying late in life, himself had one son and seven daughters – a sign of his free-thinking attitude was that he married a divorced woman, something looked at askance in such a society; there was also gossip when, as the head of Awaqf, the religious foundations which play an important part in the life of an Islamic city, he provided shelter and help for girls sent away by their husbands or thrown out by their fathers for some misdeed, as well as men seeking sanctuary after a clan vendetta.

Qazi Mohammed had one brother, Abol Qasim Sadr i Qazi, and a cousin, Muhammad Husain Saif i Qazi, who rose and fell with him; Abol Qasim as a deputy in the Majlis in Tehran, Muhammad Husain as a military commander in Mahabad. Qazi Mohammed himself became in effect the governor of Mahabad after the allied take-over of the country in August 1941. The Russians at first pushed as far south as Sanandaj, where the British linked up with them, but then by agreement each country withdrew its forces, the Russians to a line just north of Mahabad, while the British stayed at Kermanshah, acknowledged as the southern limit of Iranian Kurdistan. Between these two places political officers from both sides operated, as well as buying-missions and diplomats, but within a few months clear spheres of influence grew up, with Mahabad firmly within the Soviet zone. At the same time the influence of Tehran, where Mohammad Reza Shah had taken over from his deposed father, was growing less and less as the Iranian army fell apart. In the vacuum thus formed, powerful local leaders either set themselves up as governors or commanders, or were prevailed on by the citizens of towns or districts to represent them; in the case of Qazi Mohammed, there was never any doubt: he was the most prominent local citizen, and was also popular with the people. He became, in effect, the ruler of the Mahabad region, able, with the consent of the people, to keep the peace inside the city, though unable to control the tribes, who soon turned the countryside back fifty years, with the Kurds practising their old tribal ways – fighting each other, exacting tolls on all travellers and goods passing through, and battening on the poor peasants and farmers. The Iranian government, which still had its officials in all the towns of the north, could do nothing, as the Russians would not allow Iranian army units to enter the region.

So, as a leader on whom the Russians hoped to depend to maintain order, Qazi Mohammed was one of the group of about thirty invited to travel to Baku to sample the Soviet way of life, and perhaps to negotiate a formal relationship between the Kurds and the occupiers. The main Kurdish request – they were in no position to demand – was that they should be allowed to keep the light arms and ammunition they had seized from the retreating Iranian army; there was also some vague talk of 'freedom for Kurds in their national affairs', and the hope that the Kurdish language would be used in all education. The Russians concentrated on the need to restore security and peace in the region, and therefore to respect the authority of the Tehran government: more than anything else, they were still concerned to get their convoys through safely.

The generally ambivalent Soviet attitude towards the Kurds encouraged the growth of nationalist feeling, and the Komala intensified its recruiting efforts, in 1944 persuading Qazi Mohammed to give his seal of approval by joining at a ceremony witnessed by more than a hundred people. Events in neighbouring Azerbaijan were also pushing the Kurds to think of their own autonomy: all the indications were that the Russians intended to use the province to extend their influence into Iran if they were eventually forced to withdraw – the Tripartite Treaty legalizing the occupation, signed by Britain, the Soviet Union and Iran on 29 January 1942, provided for the allies to pull out within six months of the end of the war. In 1945 the Russians had reinforced local Azerbaijani sentiment by sending in experienced party workers and politicians from Soviet Azerbaijan who played on the local complaints that the province had been neglected by the Tehran government.

In September 1945 a Kurdish delegation was again invited to the Soviet Union, this time formally chosen and led by Qazi Mohammed, and plainly understanding that the object of the visit was to discuss the future of Iranian Kurdistan. In Baku the initial Soviet position was that Kurdistan should be a province of Azerbaijan, when and if that state came into being. Qazi Mohammed and his colleagues quickly rejected that plan, and the speed with which the Russians accepted the idea of an independent Kurdistan seemed to be an indication that they had expected that all along. They moved swiftly to the practicalities, defined by the Kurds as the means to defend their new state and to make it prosper – in other words, financial support and arms. The Russians promised in general terms that money would be forthcoming and were more specific about arms, but they seemed most concerned to get the Kurds to set up the kind of political system they wanted: a Democratic Party of Kurdistan, clearly intended as a front organization allowing Soviet control of a second Iranian province. The Kurds replied as vaguely as the Russians.

In the end there were concrete results: the Russians agreed to supply a printing press for the Kurds, as well as tanks, cannon, machine guns and rifles, and promised places would be found for Kurdish cadets in Soviet military academies. It was just enough to push the Kurds into their fateful decision: they would go for independence. Even then, the cautious Qazi Mohammed might have held back, but he was forced to act after crowds attacked a police station, one of the last surviving symbols of Iranian authority, and then set off to burn down the local court – eventually being persuaded merely to destroy the imperial coat of arms with which it was decorated. There was also the example of Azerbaijan, which declared itself an autonomous republic within Iran in December 1945, after Soviet troops had stopped two battalions of Iranian troops dispatched by Tehran to restore order in the area. On Soviet advice the Azerbaijanis never formally declared independence, thus legally only exercising rights bestowed by the Iranian constitution; but by a series of decrees nationalizing banks, ordering land distribution, and establishing Turki as the language for education and all official dealings, the Azerbaijanis were in practice going much further than the Kurds ever had. There was also more violence: police and gendarmerie posts were attacked, and by the end of the year all representatives of the central government had been forced to flee, and ties with Tehran completely severed.

Qazi Mohammed may well have wanted to avoid what seemed to the Kurds to be Soviet-inspired violence by proclaiming independence when he did. The formal proclamation of the Republic of Kurdistan was made on 22 January 1946 at the Chwar Chira circle in the centre of Mahabad, at the junction of the town's only two paved roads. Qazi Mohammed made a short speech to the crowd of townspeople and representatives of the tribes, speaking of the Kurds' separateness, their right to self-determination, and the help they had received from powerful friends. A Soviet liaison officer, Major Yermakov from Tabriz, watched from a parked jeep.

A month later Qazi Mohammed was sworn in as president of the republic, and ten members of the central committee of the Komala were named as ministers, including Muhammad Husain as minister of war, a self-trained chemist as minister of health, and a young man who had done a few years at an agricultural college as minister of agriculture. Representatives were sent to as many other parts of Iranian Kurdistan as could be reached to invite adherents to the nascent republic, but no effort was made to attract the interest of those in Greater Kurdistan, the Kurds of Iraq, Turkey or elsewhere. Nor was there any effort to extend the writ of the Mahabad government into the tribal lands; instead, Qazi Mohammed relied on the tribal leaders to keep order there, hoping that his own good relations with them would persuade them to do so.

It was not events in Azerbaijan or Kurdistan which were to determine the future, however, but what was going on in world capitals and at the newly formed United Nations. The situation in northern Iran was to become the first confrontation of the Cold War, and this time the Soviets put commercial advantage ahead of ideological interest. The clash began when, under the terms of the Tripartite Treaty, Iran complained to the United Nations that the Soviets were showing no signs of withdrawing in the stipulated period, but instead appeared to be consolidating their presence, particularly in Azerbaijan. The British, then the Americans, and then the UN Security Council all expressed their concern; notes were delivered to Moscow, until suddenly, on 26 March 1946, the Soviets backed down: Foreign Minister Andrei Gromyko announced that all Soviet forces would leave Iran by 6 May. A month later the Iranian prime minister, Qavam Sultaneh, and the Soviet ambassador, I. G. Sadchikov, signed an agreement in Tehran to form a joint Irano-Soviet oil company. Kurds and Azerbaijanis were being abandoned for the prospect of new oil supplies.

This was clear to all Iranians, but not yet to the Kurds, or even to the Azerbaijanis, who believed the Soviets would prevent government forces being sent against them – the Soviet government had warned Tehran that it would not tolerate disturbances on its border, which was taken in Azerbaijan and Kurdistan as an undertaking that force would be used to prevent the entrance of the Iranian army into either province. In Tehran the politicians had to weigh the relative merits of Western or Russian interference in their country, and came down firmly on the side of the West, while Russian agents in the Tudeh Party, the communist party of Iran, tried to organize active opposition by fomenting a strike directed against the Anglo-Iranian Oil company. To combat this, the devious government in Tehran stirred up old antagonisms, so that a 'spontaneous' tribal uprising took place against the Tudeh Party and its sympathizers, while Britain sent troops to Basra, just across the border in Iraq.

After months of haggling the Azerbaijanis gave in: Azerbaijan returned to the Iranian nation with its national assembly recognized as a provincial council; a governor-general was appointed by the central government from a list provided by Azerbaijan; and the Tehran government began to deploy police and gendarmerie to oversee elections for deputies to the Majlis in Tehran. On 13 June 1946 it was all over for Azerbaijan, and in August Qazi Mohammed went to Tehran – under a Soviet guarantee of safe-conduct – to see if he could negotiate something similar; he failed, and again when an Iranian representative travelled to the north, the Kurds remained adamant that they would not hand over weapons seized from the Iranian forces.

Left to themselves, the Kurds might have reached an accommodation with Tehran, but they were still beholden to the Russians, and the Soviet Union, deprived of Azerbaijan, had only the Kurdish card to play in Iran. It was a situation in which the Kurds found themselves driven on, no matter what their private inclinations.

On 13 December the first Iranian army units entered the Azerbaijani capital, Tabriz, while the mob turned against the communist sympathizers and agents who had been in the ascendancy for the previous year. In Mahabad a number of prominent officials prepared to flee north, but Qazi Mohammed announced that he would stay on: the Kurdish tradition is to fight if it looks possible, to submit if it does not. The next day a group of Mahabad citizens who had not been particularly enamoured of the independent republic drove to Miandoab to surrender to General Homayuni. They found him in a tolerant mood, and returned to Mahabad to advise others to submit to the Iranian commander. Two days later Qazi Mohammed did so, along with Saif i Qazi, Haji Baba Shaikh, who had been prime minister, and several others. It was the end of the only independent Kurdish state of modern times.

But not the end for those who had defended it, which in practice meant the fighters of the Barzani tribe under their legendary leader Mullah Mustafa. One of the ironies of the history of the Kurds is that it has always been the educated elite who have

The Treaty of Sèvres was signed on 10 August 1920 after a conference attended by the victorious allies, Turkey and former subject nations of the Ottoman empire. The Kurds had observer status in that part of the talks involving Kurdistan and Armenia.

Under Article 62 of the treaty, a commission appointed by Britain, France and Italy was to oversee the introduction of Kurdish autonomy in an area bounded in the west by the Euphrates, in the north by the future Armenian state and in the south by Turkey, Syria and Mesopotamia. Article 63 bound the Ottoman government to acceptance of the allied commission's decisions.

Article 64 merits quoting in full:

If, after one year has elapsed since the implementation of the present treaty, the Kurdish population of the areas designated in Article 62 calls on the council of the League of Nations and demonstrates that a majority of the population in these areas wishes to become independent of Turkey, and if the council then estimates that the population in question is capable of such independence and recommends that it be granted, then Turkey agrees, as of now, to comply with this recommendation and to renounce all rights and titles to the area. The details of this renunciation will be the subject of a special convention between Turkey and the main allied powers.

If and when the said renunciation is made, no objection shall be raised by the main allied powers should the Kurds living in that part of Kurdistan at present included in the Vilayet of Mosul seek to become citizens of the newly independent Kurdish state.

The putative state amounted to little more than a mountainous rump of geographical Kurdistan. The Kurdish subjects of the Persian shah were naturally excluded, as were those Kurds who lived within French-mandated Syria. Much of northern Kurdistan was assigned to the future Armenian state, to be placed under US protection. Furthermore, the creation of an independent state was hedged around with qualifications. It depended ultimately on the judgement of outside powers as to the Kurds' desire and capacity for independence, and it excluded the Kurds of the dreamt of freedom, of a state of their own, of a Kurdistan transcending borders; yet it has always been the tribes who have had real power, the ability to change things, and there has always been an antagonism between the two groups. That may be one more reason why there is still no Kurdistan. However that may be, through all the turbulent years of this century, men from the small area on the Greater Zab river north of Arbil have always played a major role: the Barzanis are not the biggest of the northern Iraqi tribes, nor the richest, yet they have wielded an influence greater than most others, not least because of their fighting qualities, commented on by many a rueful loser.

The Barzanis are the epitome of hardy hill people, shepherds moving their flocks up and down the mountains according to the seasons, isolated in their valley homeland, knowing only the river and the ranges around them, unwilling to turn themselves into farmers despite the good land, a tough and frugal people untouched for decades by the changes found in the cities. They were unquestioningly obedient to their leaders, not least because tribal authority had always been reinforced by religion: in the nineteenth century Sayyid Taha of Shemdinan to the north converted the Barzani sheikhs to the Naqshabandi Sufi order, one of the great dervish disciplines of Islam, an allegiance which has endured from generation to generation, so that all tribal sheikhs have their natural authority enhanced. To the other qualities – or defects – of the Barzanis was added a natural disinclination to accept outside authority, a fierce independence which led them to battle the central government, Ottoman, British or Iraqi, as well as the adjacent tribes, and which frequently led their leaders into revolt, exile or imprisonment.

Thus it was in 1931, when the Baghdad government, anticipating the end of the British mandate and anxious to extend its authority into tribal lands, sent an expeditionary column against the fractious Barzanis. As usual, the experienced tribal fighters ambushed and defeated the half-hearted soldiers from the plain, conscripts who had no quarrel with the Kurds and no stomach for a fight. But now the situation had changed, with air power available to the central government, something against which the tribesmen had no defence. So by 1932 the Barzanis had been bombed into submission, and a new Iraqi force was able to reach the small town of Barzan, compelling the tribal leader, Sheikh Ahmad, to flee to Turkey. There he was captured and handed back to the Iraqis, who put him under house arrest in the town of Suleimaniyeh. With him was his younger brother, Mullah Mustafa, a man destined to become the most famous Kurdish commander of modern times.

Mullah Mustafa, like everyone of his generation, had no education but the village school, with its emphasis on the Koran; and, perhaps because of this, throughout his life he had great respect for intellectuals, or indeed for anyone better educated than himself. Yet he had many qualities the educated did not possess: he was a fighter of almost foolhardy courage, yet he was a good tactician who did not persist in an impossible situation; he was always careful of his men's lives, thus making it easier to recruit when necessary; and he was a wily diplomat, well-practised in the arts of deception and dissimulation that were inseparable from the tribal feuding which was almost a hobby with the Kurdish leaders.

In exile in Suleimaniyeh, Mullah Mustafa was unable to lead the free and open life he was used to, and determined to escape. He did so in 1943, crossing into Iran and then back into Iraq to reach his home a mere 120 miles north-west of Suleimaniyeh. Back in Barzan, he was immediately the centre of attention, not only from his own people but also from the sheikhs of the smaller tribes near by, all eager to exploit the complicated international and regional situation to their own advantage. The government in Baghdad, humiliated by Mullah Mustafa's escape and by his open defiance of authority once he returned home, made the mistake of sending another punitive column against him; it was ignominiously defeated, and this time the British had neither the planes nor the inclination to back up the weak authority of Baghdad. Nuri al Said, the Iraqi prime minister, decided to negotiate, which merely served to strengthen Mullah Mustafa's position and to make him more intransigent. The talks failed, the government fell, while Mullah Mustafa became the ruler of much of Iraqi Kurdistan.

His position was further improved when in 1945 a general amnesty from the Baghdad government wiped the slate clean for those who had been in revolt before 1944. But this time Mullah Mustafa overplayed his hand: flushed with past success, and perhaps influenced too by the blandishments of the Kurdish nationalists who were increasingly active, and who were anxious to get such a famous leader on their side, Mullah Mustafa still refused to accept the authority of Baghdad, and when local raids again prompted a massive Iraqi response, he declared a general revolt. But times had changed: Iraq now had its own air force to send against the rebels, and a more sophisticated government in Baghdad exploited old Kurdish animosities by arming and supporting the many enemies of the Barzanis, so that Mullah Mustafa always had to fight on several fronts.

Coming under increasing pressure, the Barzanis were forced to retreat in the only direction open to them – towards Iran. As they moved further away from their own homelands, they heard more and more about a place which seemed to offer them safe haven, an area free of Iranian, Soviet or allied troops: Mahabad.

By October 1945 Mullah Mustafa had reached the town, and set up camp in the hills just to the north. With him was his elder brother Sheikh Ahmad, the spiritual guide of the Barzanis, who had been released from internment, and some 10,000 people, including the women and children. There were about 3,000 fighting men, of whom less than half were Barzanis, the rest from other tribes which had thrown in their lot with Mullah Mustafa as the Iraqis and their tribal allies pressed into Kurdistan. Mullah Mustafa himself went to see Qazi Mohammed, and was said to have been deeply impressed by the Mahabad leader's learning, nationalism and piety – not something which his own followers had particularly noticed. Mullah Mustafa pledged the support of himself and his men to the cause of Kurdish freedom, and in particular undertook the defence of Mahabad – no doubt believing that this would result in new arms for his men, perhaps with heavier weapons, and more money from the Soviets.

Despite the legends which have grown up since, it was a relationship of mutual suspicion, with the Mahabad government trying to keep the Barzanis out of the town, and to set up a force to balance them in case of need, while the Barzanis were deeply distrustful of the abilities and motives of the townspeople. The convoluted pattern was well shown when the Mahabad government did set up its own army, recruiting the unsuitable townspeople and those from the surrounding villages, while making no effort to enlist the hardened fighting men from the tribes. Yet the tribal leaders were all given ranks in this makeshift force, and, to his dying day, Mullah Mustafa himself proudly used the title of general bestowed on him.

South of Mahabad, the Iranian army still had small garrisons or police posts in a number of villages, notably at Sardasht, close to the border. Some of the tribal units, anxious for action – and for loot – moved south and attacked these Iranian outposts; they were beaten off, and the Tehran government immediately sent more troops to reinforce Sardasht. Yet for some months the Barzanis were kept north of Mahabad, as Azerbaijan was considered more of a threat than the Iranians: for all the talk of brotherly co-operation, the Kurds were more concerned about what would happen when the Soviets withdrew from Azerbaijan than about any offensive from the Iranians.

It was not until the spring of 1946 that the real danger was appreciated, when the Barzanis were given the best of the arms delivered by the Russians and sent south to face the nearest Iranian garrison at Saqqez. Almost immediately the tribesmen were given the opportunity to score a great victory, and they happily accepted the challenge: the Iranians, heavily reinforced, had announced that they would advance north from Saqqez to demonstrate the government's control of the region. With flags flying and a band playing, some 600 troops duly moved out along the road north to Miandoab; it was a gift to the Kurds, always happiest lying in ambush for unsuspecting enemies. At the village of Qahrawa the Kurds fell on the marching column, killing twenty-one men, wounding seventeen and taking forty prisoners; the rest fled back to Saqqez. It was more a hideous mistake by the Iranian commander, a Colonel Kasra, than a triumph for the Barzanis; but in tribal legend the small engagement quickly became an epic battle, and the tribesmen lorded it even more over the bureaucrats of the town. It also emboldened them to more action, and a plan was launched to move south in force to 'liberate' all of Kurdistan down as far as Kermanshah.

In the meantime the Barzanis occupied themselves by sniping at traffic on the road from Saqqez to Baneh and Sardasht, and making life difficult for the demoralized garrison in Saqqez; they did not realize that the Iranians had been further reinforced until the garrison once again moved out of the town. This time it was no propaganda march but a small-scale and well-executed offensive aimed at capturing the hill of Mamashah held by the Kurds, from which they could survey Saqqez and harass their enemies. In a day-long battle the Iranian troops took the hill and drove off the defenders, with each side claiming victory: the Iranians because they had reached their objective, the Kurds because they claimed to have lost only one man while inflicting some forty casualties on the attackers.

Emboldened by their two successes, as they saw them, the Barzanis and their allies prepared for their projected great offensive: to sweep south as far as Kermanshah, driving the Iranians before them, linking up with the southern tribes, and uniting the whole of Iranian Kurdistan under the leadership of Qazi Mohammed. Given the fighting spirit of the Kurds and the demoralized state of the Iranian troops, the Barzanis might well have been able to do so; but they were not allowed even to try. The Russians vetoed the idea because of their interest in securing the oil concession in Iran following Azerbaijan's compromise with Tehran; they warned that any Kurdish push might intrude into the British sphere of interest, leading to a confrontation with a much more effective force. Some of the Kurdish leaders wanted to ignore the Russian warning, others saw it as a useful excuse not to fight, and some even wanted to submit to the Iranian government. As it was, Qazi Mohammed agreed to a truce which opened the way for the various Iranian garrisons to be resupplied, while desultory negotiations went on for a more permanent settlement. With nothing to do, many of the Iranian Kurdish tribal fighters began to drift back north, though the Barzanis, far from their home territory, still held a line above Saqqez.

In August 1946 Qazi Mohammed made his trip to Tehran to try to negotiate some form of autonomy for his state within Iran. Denied Soviet support, no progress was made, and the way was clear for the final surrender. That did not come until December, with Iranian forces entering Mahabad from the north and east. By this time Mullah Mustafa and his men had concentrated near Naqadeh, north-west of the town. They took with them the best arms in the arsenal of the short-lived republic – 3,000 rifles, 120 machine guns, grenades and two field guns. The Iranian generals knew they could not hope to pacify the area and disarm the local tribes so long as the Barzanis remained there, but were equally conscious that available Iranian forces could not take on Mullah Mustafa. Again a truce was arranged, and Mullah Mustafa and his chief lieutenants went off to Tehran, where they were entertained in an officers' club for a month while they tried to work out a permanent solution. First they sought guarantees from the British that they would be allowed to return to their own tribal lands in Iraq, then they considered an Iranian plan to resettle them in the Hamadan area in the north-west corner of the country.

But back in Naqadeh, Sheikh Ahmad was determined to get back to his home, while Mullah Mustafa himself had no desire

1 Mullah Mustafa Barzani (front row, third from left)
with his aides.

2 Guerrillas of the PKK attend a lecture at their headquarters in the
Bekaa valley of eastern Lebanon.

3 International pressure and help persuaded the Turks to allow camps to be set up inside Turkey. This orderliness, for all the crowding and lack of facilities, was an improvement on what had gone before.

4 At the height of the exodus from Iraq in 1991, this was a common sight. In the worst times, babies were dying at the rate of 1,000 a day.

5 Two PKK guerrillas in training.

6 Massoud Barzani, who carried on the struggle for independence begun by his father, though he showed himself willing to compromise.

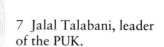

7 Jalal Talabani, leader of the PUK.

8 The Kurds showed their feelings as soon as they were sure the Iraqi army had gone. Everywhere pictures and murals of Saddam Hussein became targets for gunfire.

9 The Iranian Kurdish leader assassinated in Vienna, Abdolrahman Qassemlou.

10 One of the images that shocked the world: a father dies trying
to shield his child as the Iraqi airforce drop poison gas on the
Kurdish town of Halabja.

11 The long trek to safety: a column of refugees stretches for miles
as Kurds in their hundreds of thousands flee from Iraq in fear of
Saddam Hussein's vengeance.

to live among the hostile tribes of north-west Iran, denied his own local power base. At the same time he could not move in mid-winter, with the passes blocked by snow, and he was also worried about what the Iraqi forces would do if he returned – he had left Iraq as a rebel, forced to go by the improved Iraqi forces; he might be in just as bad a position in Iraq as he now was in Iran. Delay was the order of the day, so the tribal leaders spun things out until March, when the snows were beginning to melt. Then they began to move north, but a peaceful escape was denied to them when an altercation broke out after an advance party of Barzanis demanded that a tribe through whose area they had to pass should surrender their weapons. One of the Barzanis fired an automatic rifle, killing eleven of the local fighters. Then on 14 March 1947 the Iranian army, supported by some local Kurdish tribes, launched a general offensive against Mullah Mustafa's forces. Still the Iranians could not succeed; fighting on familiar terrain, the Barzanis constantly harried the Iranians, and even beat them in a few small set-piece battles. Yet the pressure was continuous, and gradually the Barzanis were forced back towards the Iraqi frontier, where troops dispatched by the Baghdad government were awaiting them. To add to the misery, a dozen planes of the Iranian air force regularly strafed Barzani positions, usually killing more women and children than fighters.

Sheikh Ahmad, tired of wandering far from home, constantly fighting and intriguing, arranged to return the prisoners the Barzanis had taken: then in early April 1947 he led the bulk of the tribe, with the women and children, across the frontier into Iraq. He and the leaders with him submitted to the Iraqi authorities, but Mullah Mustafa and a hard core of some 500 to 800 men took a different route, and remained at large. As Mullah Mustafa slowly moved into Iraq, news reached him that four Kurdish Iraqi army officers who had been with Sheikh Ahmad had been seized and hanged. He called a tribal meeting and warned that because of the blood shed in defending Mahabad there was no going back to Iran, that the news of the executions meant there would be no mercy in Iraq, and that Turkish efforts to detribalize and pacify the border regions meant there could be no refuge there. The Soviet Union was the only possible haven.

The tribesmen agreed, and on 27 May 1947 began the epic fighting retreat. With Mullah Mustafa and most of his men on foot – there were only enough pack animals for the wounded and the stores – the journey north was a slow one, with scouts constantly deployed to watch for Iraqi, Iranian or Turkish forces, as the column of men moved back and forth across the frontiers to escape capture. The Iraqis made no effort to stop them, and the Turks were ill-organized; but in Iran the shah and the chief of staff issued firm instructions that the Barzanis were to be halted, and dispatched two battalions of troops to the Qotur valley to cut off their march towards the Soviet Union. The Barzanis travelled along the mountain sides in darkness to evade the Iranian trap, and a few days later launched a surprise attack on the flanks of another column sent to catch them; then they crossed back into Turkey, and on 10 June were in sight of the Soviet frontier. There they stopped, as two envoys went into Soviet territory to negotiate a crossing, while the dispirited Iranian troops moved slowly up to attack them in the rear. It was too late: on 18 June the Iranians reached the Barzani position on the Aras river to find the Barzanis had crossed into the Soviet Union two days earlier, after securing permission from Moscow. They left behind a few broken rifles and the bodies of two men who had drowned while crossing the river. It was eleven years before Mullah Mustafa and his men saw Kurdistan again.

While the Barzanis were fighting their way to freedom in the Soviet Union, humiliating the Iranian army in the process, the Tehran government was taking its revenge on the men who had set up the first Kurdish republic. At 3 am on 31 March 1947 Qazi Mohammed, his brother Sadr i Qazi and his cousin Saif i Qazi were hanged on three makeshift gibbets in Chwar Chira, the site of the proclamation of the republic fourteen months earlier. This time there were no crowds, no speeches. Troops sealed off the area, nearby houses were cleared, and it was only in the morning that the people of Mahabad learned what had happened. It shocked them into submission. There had been talk of an uprising, wild plans to enlist the help of the tribes to free the leaders of the republic. Now there was only a cowed silence. Seeing the effect of their actions, the Iranians followed up their advantage. A few days after the first executions the makeshift courts which had been established sentenced twenty-eight Kurds to terms of imprisonment ranging from two years to life. And within the week five more were hanged. It was a bitter end to the Kurds' one sustained effort to establish their own state.

And the questions remained, questions posed but not answered by the American diplomat William Eagleton Jr, who wrote the definitive history of Mahabad: 'What did the Kurdish republic of 1946 really represent: a valiant national struggle or a treacherous separatist revolt? What had Barzani participation involved: a selfless contribution to a noble cause, or a self-seeking attempt to extend personal and tribal influence?' Eagleton gives no answers. However, he concludes that the people of northern Iran were still aware of Kurdish separateness within the Iranian family, though they were not attracted by Soviet communism. Instead, he wrote in 1963, the Iranian Kurds were united in sympathy with the Kurdish nationalist movement in Iraq.

Speaking of his own time, the 1960s, Eagleton says:

The present condition of Kurdistan recalls not so much the republic formed at Mahabad after that visit to Baku in 1945, which diverted the Kurdish movement towards Soviet goals, as the days of the Komala in Iran and the Hewa Party in Iraq, with tribesmen defiantly pursuing their own ideals of freedom in their traditional ways. Once again the tribes of a portion of Kurdistan have taken up arms in a struggle against heavy odds, possessed by mixed ambitions. In some cases they are sustained by little more than the old Kurdish tradition that *shar chaktira la bekariya*' ('fighting is better than idleness').

It can be predicted for the future, as we know from the past, that the Kurds in their distant mountains and separated valleys will at times be forgotten or ignored. Then, when moved by resolve or temerity, some of the characters of 1946, and others, younger and perhaps unknown in Mahabad, will be heard of once again.

Eagleton might well have been writing of 1991.

Chapter Six

THE STRUGGLE FOR AUTONOMY

Eleven years after his epic fighting retreat through three countries which took him to exile in the Soviet Union, Mullah Mustafa Barzani returned to a rapturous welcome in his homeland. He was able to go back not as a result of pressure by his own people, but as one of the consequences of the Free Officers coup of July 1958, led by Abdel Karim Qassem. The Kurds welcomed the July revolution, which overthrew the Iraqi monarchy, though they had played no part in bringing it about. They were heartened when the new constitution was published, which for the first time seemed to give formal recognition to Kurdish 'separateness', and to promise some degree of autonomy: 'Arabs and Kurds are partners in the Iraqi homeland and their national rights are recognized within the Iraqi state,' it said.

To underline the new relationship, only three months after the Qassem regime took over, the secretary of the KDP, Ibrahim Ahmad, was released from house arrest and sent off to Prague with Iraqi passports for Mullah Mustafa and the exiled leader's closest associates. Iraqi army officers watched benignly as thousands of Kurds flocked to the Baghdad airport to welcome home the man who was already a legend.

It was a brief honeymoon, lasting only long enough for a ship bringing 400 Barzani men back from the Soviet Union to dock at Basra and make their way north to join the fighters already oiling their rifles. The trouble was that while Qassem showed general benevolence to the Kurds in the first months of his rule – a Kurd, Khalid Naqshbandi, was included in the three-man sovereignty council – many of the Free Officers had spent their army

careers fighting in the north, and they had no intention of grant-
ing the Kurds in peacetime what they had denied them for so
long while the battles were going on. Equally there was a strong
Arab nationalist trend in the new government which was calling
for union with Nasser's United Arab Republic, and which as a
result could not permit any devolution in the country. Qassem's
own strategy played its part too: lacking any real power base of
his own, he sought to set off one group within the country
against another, at first relying on Mullah Mustafa to 'deliver'
the Kurds to him, using the Barzani tribal forces to deal with the
big landowners in Kurdistan who were alarmed at the Agrarian
Law which was passed, limiting land holdings and imposing new
taxes.

Mullah Mustafa was the president of the KDP, formed in
Mahabad during the brief independence of the republic there. A
group of Iraqi Kurds met Mullah Mustafa and other prominent
figures and decided to form a separate party for the Kurds of
Iraq rather than join in Qazi Mohammed's existing Kurdistan
Democratic Party. The secretary of the new party, Hamza Abdullah, was sent back to Iraqi Kurdistan to contact leaders there
and to muster support; but almost as soon as he started work,
splits developed, as Abdullah, though a communist, insisted on
involving the large landowners and tribal leaders, on the grounds
that it was only such feudal figures who could ensure the loyalty
of the tribesmen, who would have to provide the numbers – and
the fighting strength – of the new party. Few intellectuals or
urban political figures joined the movement, which they saw as
reactionary and backward, instead giving their loyalty to Ibrahim
Ahmad, the representative in Iraqi Kurdistan of the Iranian
branch of the party which gave its support to the Republic of
Mahabad. In 1950 the Iraqi government banned the KDP of Iraq
and imprisoned Abdullah. That left the way open for Ibrahim
Ahmad to take over. He did so through a secret, underground
congress, and then sacked Abdullah and took over himself.

These complicated machinations had results which powerfully

influenced the course of events and the development of Kurdish nationalism in Iraq: they made certain that Kurds in Iraq would seek to gain autonomy in isolation, rather than in partnership with the Kurdish population of neighbouring countries. Mullah Mustafa soon emerged as the one leader capable of uniting the tribes, and thus was able to put a credible force into the field, but he had little appeal to the urban elite which was Ahmad's power base. This split between the two strands of Kurdish society was a constant factor which succeeding governments were able to exploit.

While Mullah Mustafa was in exile in the Soviet Union, many of the Barzani tribal lands were expropriated by the pre-revolutionary governments and distributed among tribes which had been loyal to the central authority – notably the Herki, Zebari and Baradost. Eventually this was to make Mullah Mustafa less concerned than other tribal leaders at Iraqi attempts at agrarian reform, and to push him to a more nationalistic approach.

On his return to Baghdad, Mullah Mustafa immediately proclaimed his support for Qassem and called for Kurds in neighbouring countries to be given the same rights as those enjoyed in Iraq. He denounced imperialism, praised 'the anti-colonial struggle', and generally said all the things the regime wanted to hear; in return he was given a car and chauffeur, lodged in the house formerly occupied by Nuri al Said, with the government doing all it could to enhance his prestige, clearly hoping to co-opt him in any future struggle against internal opponents.

In the heady new political freedom allowed by the revolution, the Kurds were still split among themselves; in the north all the old tribal animosities were still in place, while within the KDP Ahmad tried to align the party with the Arab nationalists who were seeking union with Nasser's UAR. Others took the same view as the powerful Iraqi communist party, which saw the pan-Arabists as rivals.

The latter included the ex-communist Hamza Abdullah, sacked by Ahmad and subsequently reinstated by Mullah

Mustafa. His line and that of the communists prevailed on a national level, and the proposed union with Egypt, for which President Qassem himself had little enthusiasm, was blocked. Later, however, Qassem turned on his communist allies, as he tried to pick off his opponents one by one. Mullah Mustafa belatedly realized what was happening and invited Abdullah to a meeting at which he would have been required to stop his pro-communist activities; Abdullah refused to attend, so Mullah Mustafa resorted to the methods of his youth: he sent a group of Barzanis to storm the party headquarters and forcibly evict Abdullah and his supporters. What Mullah Mustafa did not see was that he himself was the next target, as it was now only the Kurds and the KDP who had an organized, legal, political structure capable of opposing the regime.

Qassem tried to show Mullah Mustafa that he no longer had his total support by bringing back a number of tribal leaders who had fled to Iran after attempting to defy the government's agrarian reforms; Mullah Mustafa's people, safe in the most inaccessible area of the far north and in any case little affected by expropriations, were used to quell this revolt by their traditional tribal enemies. By bringing these feudal leaders back, Qassem hoped to show Mullah Mustafa that the Barzanis were not the only tribesmen capable of putting forces in the field. Mullah Mustafa did not get the message. Instead he continued to act as the Kurdish elder statesman, seeing himself almost the equal of Qassem, who in turn regarded himself as the country's sole leader.

The attempted assassination of Qassem in October 1959 – in which Saddam Hussein took part – seemed to make the president feel he had been too soft on opposition elements, too conciliatory; Mullah Mustafa's offer at the time to provide him with Kurdish bodyguards was hardly tactful. Gradually, Qassem withdrew all the privileges he had bestowed on the returned hero and began cultivating the Barzanis' traditional opponents, the Zebari and Surchi. While Mullah Mustafa was on a return visit to the

Soviet Union in 1960, fighting broke out between the tribes, and it was clear that co-operation between Mullah Mustafa and the regime was at an end.

The Kurdish revolt which began in the summer of 1961, and was to last intermittently for the next fourteen years, started with this series of tribal clashes, only gradually escalating into a full-scale uprising against the government which commanded the support of almost all Kurds. As it became clear that Qassem had no intention of translating his general expressions of sympathy for the Kurds into practical steps, both Barzani and Ahmad had to step up their pressure on the government to keep the backing of their supporters and to show they would not accept the status quo. Mullah Mustafa and his men attacked Kurdish groups working with the government, but it was an apparently unplanned raid on an army column on manoeuvres on 11 September 1961 that finally led to all-out fighting. Qassem retaliated by sending the Iraqi air force to bomb Barzan and other towns, drawing a reluctant Barzani directly into the conflict. It was a pattern repeated many times over the years.

Mullah Mustafa inherited the mantle of Sheikh Mahmoud, who had led the struggle of the Iraqi Kurds from the establishment of the British mandate. At the time of his defeat and exile in the early 1930s, the Barzanis were taking over as the principal Kurdish leaders. Sheikh Ahmad Barzani was the acknowledged head of the tribe as well as a noted religious figure, but it was his younger brother Mullah Mustafa who became the popular leader, and by his tenacity, exploits, and military skill retained that position until he died in bitter exile in 1979. Today his son Massoud has taken on this role, and is proving himself a more realistic and pliant politician than his unbending father, who often lost at the conference table what he had won in battle.

When Mullah Mustafa returned to Iraq at the end of 1958, it was not only the Kurds who were dissatisfied with Qassem. The communists fell in and out of favour, while the Baathists were violently opposed to his policies, and in February 1963 took over in one of the bloodiest and most savage coups the Middle East has ever seen. Qassem was executed, and the Baath National Guard – party thugs formed into a militia – went on the rampage, hunting down and killing all the members of the communist party they could find. The Baath gunmen often seemed to know who they were looking for as they searched out communist activists; according to a number of sources, this was because they had been in contact with American intelligence, which was eager to break the back of the strongest communist party in the Middle East at that time. King Hussein said categorically that the February coup had the backing of America, and the historians Marion Farouk-Sluglett and Peter Sluglett report contacts between the Baath and the State Department in the late 1950s. At that time, they say, the Baath was regarded in Washington as 'the political force of the future', and therefore deserving of American support. It was an American attitude which was to linger, with disastrous consequences.

One basic tenet of Baathism which seemed to be overlooked was the party's commitment to pan-Arabism, which made it even more unlikely than its predecessors to make any concessions to the Kurds. Yet the Baath, like the Free Officers, realized very well that no conventional army could defeat the Kurds in their mountain retreats, just as the Kurds could not hope to win if they moved out of the mountains and down on to the plains. So there were attempts at negotiations, most of which were designed more to gain time than to reach any conclusion.

Today, Kurdish officials claim that their people were united, and that Mullah Mustafa was the undisputed leader of a mass movement. It was not like that; the Kurds spent almost as much time and energy fighting each other as they did the Iraqi government, though there could be no doubt that Mullah Mustafa's legendary career and military experience, as well as his domination of the most important tribal coalition, made him the supreme leader, the man with whom negotiations had to be conducted. According to Hoshyar Zebari, a central committee member close to Massoud Barzani and to Mullah Mustafa, the Kurds in Iraq always understood that their ultimate goal had to be autonomy, and their strategy was to pressurize the government in Baghdad to come to the conference table acknowledging that autonomy would have to be the conclusion of all negotiations. Fighting and political efforts were both deployed, but, given the nationalist feeling in the army, always an important consideration in Iraq, it was the armed struggle which became most important. 'We were always clear that democracy in Iraq had to come first, then Kurdish autonomy,' Zebari told us in what seemed to be a 1991 rationalization of 1970 strategy.

When the apparently uncoordinated series of tribal raids began to escalate in 1961, the urban-based section of the KDP led by Ahmad tried to stand apart, describing the uprising as 'reactionary, inspired by imperialists, and directed against the progressive Iraqi republic'. On one point both the KDP and the government agreed: in the throes of a dispute with Britain over Kuwait at this time, Qassem was convinced that it was the British who had inspired the Kurds to act. His first move when the fighting began was to expel the British ambassador.

Within the party, Ahmad favoured keeping the KDP out of the fighting, arguing that Iran was manipulating the tribes, and that the time for a revolt had not arrived. Jalal Talabani led the group in favour of an immediate declaration of war; he believed that if the party did not take part, then it would be the tribal leaders who would dominate the rebellion, and would perpetuate the old feudal system if they were successful. He wanted to declare it a national revolt, but in the end both groups agreed to consult Mullah Mustafa, who at that early stage was in favour of holding back. In the event it made no difference: Qassem himself pushed the KDP into open rebellion by announcing the party would be banned.

So in December 1961 the KDP joined in the fighting, and as one of its first acts established the *peshmerga*, designed as a Kurdish national army to ensure that all the fighting was not done by the tribes, and notably the Barzanis, who would then take all the credit. The KDP kept the *peshmerga* strictly under party control, with a headquarters at Mawat, north-west of Suleimaniyeh, while Talabani commanded the eastern sector; thus Kurdistan became divided into two regions, with Mullah Mustafa and his tribal allies in the north and the KDP in the south.

This first stage of the revolt lasted until the coup of February 1963 in which Qassem was deposed and executed, to be followed by Abdel Salam Aref. Though the Kurds were divided in their assessment of the coup, at Mullah Mustafa's urging they agreed to stop fighting and to try to negotiate. Jalal Talabani led a delegation to Baghdad for the negotiations, as he was to do thirty years later. He found that Arab unity, not Kurdish autonomy, was at the top of the agenda for the new administration, and was whisked off to Cairo to demonstrate Kurdish support for Iraq's membership of the UAR. On 17 April 1963 Egypt, Iraq and Syria did finally sign an agreement to form a Federal Arab Republic, but the only practical result as far as the Kurds were concerned was that four months later Syria sent a 5,000-man brigade to fight against them.

Talabani, impressed by all he had seen and heard in Cairo, believed the time had come for the Kurds to negotiate, while Mullah Mustafa, fretting and out of the picture in northern Iraq, was intent on resuming hostilities. Unsure of itself, the new government opted for talks, and dispatched Talabani to prepare the way. Mullah Mustafa was in a cantankerous mood: he refused to meet the Iraqi delegation, led by the chief of staff, General Tahir Yahya, in Rawanduz, and demanded they travel on to his remote headquarters at Kani Miran. It was not a good start, but as time went on things improved, and 'impossible' demands by Mullah Mustafa were watered down so that a compromise seemed possible. At the same time inter-Kurdish rivalries were becoming accentuated, as Mullah Mustafa'a domineering style of leadership and negotiation were contrasted with Jalal

Talabani's more reasonable and conciliatory manner as he spoke on behalf of the KDP. But by May 1963 all the talks broke down on the issue of Kirkuk, which, just as in 1991, the Kurds wanted to include in the autonomous region. Losing patience with the Kurds, the army launched a massive attack after a 24-hour ultimatum; two months later Barzan itself fell to government forces.

In November 1963 Abdel Salam Aref approached Mullah Mustafa directly, and a ceasefire was negotiated which went into effect on 10 February 1964. This move had the effect of bringing the latent splits within the Kurdish movement into the open, with Ahmad and Talabani denouncing the agreement made by Mullah Mustafa as 'a sell-out'. It was more a means of gaining time on both sides, with Aref eager to rebuild the Iraqi forces after the purges which had been carried out, and Barzani intent on crushing the opposition to his own authoritarian rule. The opportunity came on 16 July, when Ahmad and Talabani and their supporters in the KDP refused an order to hand over the Kurds' radio station to Barzani's forces. Mullah Mustafa's son Idriss led the tribal unit which seized the radio station and pushed Ahmad, Talabani and some 4,000 of their men into Iran. Having defeated his internal opposition, Mullah Mustafa now had to stifle criticism of his deal with Aref, and so once again he began making demands and sending ultimatums to Baghdad.

Another round of fighting seemed certain, and duly erupted in April 1965, after Kurds murdered three army officers. But after early gains, the army onslaught was halted unexpectedly: Abdel Salam Aref was killed in a helicopter accident, leading to a new power struggle in Baghdad. As a compromise, he was succeeded by his brother Abdel Rahman Aref, who appointed the civilian Abdel Rahman Bazzaz as prime minister. The brief premiership of Bazzaz brought the high spot of Kurdish diplomatic success prior to the 1970 agreement, which formed the basis for the 1991 talks in Baghdad. In June 1966, after Mullah Mustafa's forces had inflicted a heavy defeat on the army, Bazzaz announced that he was ready to recognize the national rights of the Kurds, and entered into negotiations which resulted in the declaration of 29 June – while applying pressure on Mullah Mustafa by holding simultaneous contacts with the dissidents led by Ahmad and Talabani.

The June declaration was the most important of all the many statements made about 'the Kurdish question' in Iraq, and led to the agreement with the Baath four years later. In the declaration the government committed itself to recognizing the 'bi-national character of the Iraqi state', a phrase which gave the Kurds the basis for everything they wanted to achieve. But Bazzaz could not deliver. His government was deposed, and the army, bitterly opposed to a settlement with the Kurds which might lead to a fragmentation of the country, made sure the autonomy talks went no further. At the same time the army was still too weak to resume the fighting, so instead the regime encouraged the Kurdish splits, forming what they called the Fursan forces from among Kurdish elements hostile to Barzani. The Ahmad–Talabani group was also armed and subsidized, but Mullah Mustafa remained in control. The Barzanis contemptuously dismissed the Kurds fighting for the government as the *jash* – 'little donkeys' that anyone can ride. It was one of the classic contradictions of Kurdish politics that, at this stage of the war, Talabani, one of the leading nationalists of the KDP, commanded pro-government *jash* forces fighting Barzani. Talabani's men earned the nickname Sixty-six – the year of their 'betrayal' – and were still being taunted with it twenty-five years later by Barzani's men when both found themselves fighting on the same side.

Despite the forces ranged against him, Mullah Mustafa was obviously in control and extending his influence, able to hold off the army and attack his opponents whenever he wished. His own position was strengthened, but Kurdish national aspirations had made little progress.

In Baghdad the political ferment continued until 1968, when the faction headed by General Ahmed Hassan al Bakr, in which

Saddam Hussein was the real strongman, finally won the day. But the Baath Party of 1968 was not the monolithic structure it was later to become; it was still riven by internal dissent and factionalism, and so had to do what it could to minimize the opposition, still mainly the communists and the Kurds. The way chosen was the usual one for the Baath – pleasant words and the prospect of negotiations in public, brutality on the streets. This time the Baath priority was to purge the army and to get their own men into positions of power, as it was the fear of a military coup against them which was their main worry; as far as the Kurds were concerned, it was at first enough to support the anti-Barzani groups led by Talabani and Ahmad. Mullah Mustafa saw all this as the weakness of the new regime and went on the offensive, inflicting significant defeats on the army and damaging oil installations in Kirkuk. That prompted the government to launch an offensive which was at first successful, but was then beaten back with heavy losses to the army.

Saddam Hussein, emerging as the tactician of the regime, decided to bring the fighting to an end, realizing very well that there was no hope of defeating the Kurds, particularly as the shah had earlier refused to withdraw his support or seal the border. Saddam went about things in the style he was to make his own, giving importance and drama to the occasion by decid-ing to go personally to Kurdistan to visit Mullah Mustafa, paying no attention to warnings of personal danger, and by sheer force of personality trying to succeed where so many had failed in the past. It was later to emerge that his attempt at a settlement was not a genuine one but a tactic, and that too was typical of the man.

In January 1970 Saddam travelled north with a small en-tourage, to be met by Massoud Barzani at Rawanduz. The two got into Massoud's car for the drive to Chomar, where Mullah Mustafa had his headquarters. Sitting in the back seat, Saddam put a briefcase between himself and Massoud. 'Do you know what I've got in this briefcase?' he asked. 'Plain paper, empty paper. I've come to see your father, and I've come to sign an agreement with him. He can write what he likes on this paper and we will sign it. I won't go back to Baghdad without an agreement. If we don't agree, then he should put me in Galala prison.' Galala was the place the Kurds kept their political opponents and those they considered to be government spies or collaborators, a neat demonstration of Saddam's knowledge of what was going on, and a hint that he was acting alone, so that his offer should be welcomed.

And an agreement was reached, though not on that day; this was perhaps as a result of Saddam's bold action in going to see Mullah Mustafa, the first time a leading government figure had gone to the Kurds. He went there several other times after that first visit, although the negotiations were carried on by other members of the government and by Mahmoud Uthman, Barzani's *chef de cabinet*. The 11 March agreement, officially a fifteen-point document, was actually in two parts, with only the first section published on 11 March, when Ahmed Hassan al Bakr read it over the radio and proclaimed the end of the conflict between the Kurds and the rest of the Iraqi people. The agreement paid lip-service to the ideal of Iraqi national unity, but it gave local self-government to the Kurds, allowed education in the Kurdish language, Kurdish participation in central government and Kurdish administration in Kurdish areas. It was the extent of these Kurdish areas which provided the main difficulty, just as it did in the 1991 talks, with no attempt to delimit the areas set out. Instead the agreement provided for a census to be held, promising that those parts in which the Kurds were found to be in the majority would be included in what came to be known as 'the autonomous region'.

In the meantime the secret protocols provided for autonomy to be applied on the basis of the 1957 census, and set out in detail how the agreement was to be applied. The *jash* were to be disarmed and disbanded, while Barzani's own *peshmerga* were to be made into frontier forces formally under the command of the Iraqi army, but in practice still owing their allegiance to their own commanders, thus providing some guarantee to the Kurds against government double-dealing. The Kurds were also to be allowed their own unions and professional associations; a Kurdish newspaper was licensed in Baghdad. In return the Kurds were to hand over some heavy weapons, and to break relations with Iran, which was always the main supply route, and often the actual provider of most of the arms used. All this was to be on a four-year trial basis, with full autonomy to go into effect in 1974, after the projected census had decided just which areas should be covered.

The announcement of the agreement was greeted with huge enthusiasm not only in Kurdistan but throughout Iraq. The long war in the north of the country, and in particular the 1969 army offensive, had taken a heavy toll of casualties, so that the families of the conscripts and of young men due to be called up were delighted at what they believed would be an end to the internal conflict. In Kurdistan it was widely appreciated that the agreement went further than anything which had been offered in the past, and also put an end to the divisions among the Kurds by forcing Talabani and his followers to return to the Kurdish national fold – they did so, and were sensibly given an amnesty by Barzani, a move which removed a weapon from the Baghdad government's hands, as they had hoped to exploit factional differences to undermine the agreement.

For it soon became clear that Saddam Hussein, at least, had no intention of carrying out either the letter or the spirit of the agreement. Instead he was intent on consolidating Baath Party power and needed a temporary halt to the destructive war in the north. He was merely playing for time, whereas Mullah Mustafa believed in the agreement reached, scaled down his relations with Iran, sent representatives to the committee established to oversee the transition to autonomy, and did his best to prevent incidents between his men and the Iraqi forces. The new census had been promised for 1971, but it soon became clear that

Baghdad not only had no intention of organizing it at that time, but that it was actively trying to change the demographic balance in fringe areas. In Kirkuk in particular the government began a programme of settling Arabs from the south almost before the ink on the agreement was dry, something the Kurds could see for themselves – though their bitter complaints had to be set against the fact that up until only a few years earlier the Turkomans had been in the majority in Kirkuk, and it was the Kurdish drift to the town which altered the demographic balance there.

For the rest of 1970 things went on reasonably well, though there were incidents, and it became increasingly plain that powerful sections of the Baath Party and the government were against the agreement. The way it was to be implemented was never announced because the pan-Arabists in the party feared the extent of the autonomy offered would draw criticism from other Arab states; because the army was unhappy at the freedom being given to a breakaway section of the population; and because the police, already emerging as the backbone of the regime, saw their authority eroded. In addition to the largely symbolic post of deputy president which was to go to the Kurds, they were also to have four ministers in the government, a means by which they believed they could exert real control.

Four years later they were to admit that their ministers had never been allowed any real power, and that they had been taken in by Saddam's promises. In 1970 it was the secret police under Nadim Kazzar, a notorious and ruthless man whose weapons were assassination, arbitrary arrest and torture, who showed the real intentions of the regime, while Saddam Hussein set the political framework for the erosion of the agreement. Saddam's line now was that autonomy was 'a gift' from the government, not a result of the war the Kurds had been waging or of their political negotiations. It was no more than part of the 'revolutionary restructuring' being undertaken by the Baath Party. Kazzar's method of showing the way things were going was more direct: he organized attacks on KDP offices in the hope of provoking retaliation which would be an excuse to scrap the agreement; and when that failed, he resorted to assassination.

The first, botched attempt was on the lives of Idriss and Massoud Barzani when they went to Baghdad for celebrations marking the end of Ramadan. Their driver was wounded, but they escaped when gunmen opened fire on their car, and though everyone knew quite well this was a police operation, the incident was blamed on 'brigands'.

Much more serious was a sophisticated attempt on the life of Mullah Mustafa himself in September 1971. Aware of the dangers, Kurdish security men always checked visitors to Barzani's headquarters, but these were the days before electronic screening methods, so the guards had to carry out body searches. When a group of Shia clerics from southern Iraq went to see Barzani to bring him greetings and discuss the situation, he would not allow his men to subject such visitors to the indignity of being 'frisked'. Knowing his respect for all religious leaders, the secret police had counted on this, and a number of those in the group, which included some well-known mullahs, had been persuaded to carry tape recorders strapped to their bodies. It was important for the government to know exactly what Mullah Mustafa was saying, they were told. As the meeting between Barzani and the mullahs went on, the two drivers who had taken the group to Haj Omran in government-supplied limousines, a Toyota and a Chevrolet, lounged outside by their cars. Then as the group inside settled in chairs facing Mullah Mustafa behind his desk, one of the drivers reached inside his car, pressed a switch, and the explosive-packed recorders strapped to some of the mullahs were activated. A number of those present were killed and wounded, and though Mullah Mustafa was hurt, he was saved because a servant was bending over his desk to put a glass of tea in front of him just as the explosion occurred. The unfortunate man took the full blast and was blown apart, but his presence saved Mullah Mustafa. Though the government disclaimed all knowledge of the incident and promised an investigation, there was never any doubt about who had organized the murder attempt, and it was equally well-known that Kazzar was under the protection of Saddam Hussein.

To the Kurds it was a plain signal that hopes of peace and autonomy were hollow, a realization reinforced by arrests of activists, harassment of *peshmerga* positions and more attacks on KDP offices. Hoshyar Zebari recalls his own experience of the atmosphere.

I had to go to Baghdad to make some arrangements for entering university, and while there I went with other Kurds to call on one of our ministers. When we got back to our hotel we were all arrested. The police said they were taking us in because we had guns, but we were able to produce permits from Kazzar to show we were allowed to be armed for our own protection. They took no notice of the permits, a sure sign that Kazzar himself had ordered our arrests. In fact, they thought we had been sent by Parastan, Kurdish intelligence, to mount a revenge killing in Baghdad for the attempt on Mullah Mustafa's life, perhaps against 'Mr Deputy', as Saddam Hussein was always known.

The deteriorating relations between Iraq and Iran, culminating in Iran's seizure of three islands in the Gulf just as Britain was withdrawing its troops, impelled the shah to give more support to the Kurds at a time when they were beginning to understand that their trust in Saddam Hussein was misplaced. An additional cause of the new conflict was Iraq's reaction to Iran's seizure of the islands. In a move to be repeated later, Iraq chose to deport thousands of people it said were of Iranian origin. Most of the 50,000 sent across the border were Shia Kurds whose families had emigrated from Iran many years earlier, a move interpreted by Barzani as a deliberate attempt to reduce the Kurdish population.

Then in 1972 Iraq signed its Treaty of Friendship and cooperation with the Soviet Union, causing the still-powerful communists to change sides and support the Baath, leaving the

Kurds more exposed. It also meant that the Kurds were being pushed more and more into dependence on the West, both because the Eastern bloc was supporting Baghdad, and because Iran was moving even closer to the United States. In 1973 Massoud and Idriss Barzani went on a secret mission to Washington, where they met Richard Helms, then head of the CIA, and Al Haig, the White House chief of staff. As a result of these meetings, Israeli advisers began operating in Kurdistan, and Israeli supplies were channelled to Barzani via Iran, which in the end had regular forces operating with the Kurds inside Iraq – two and a half battalions of artillery and anti-aircraft guns, according to David Kimche of the Israeli Foreign Ministry. The Americans also sent weapons and CIA operatives to advise the Kurds, so that as hostilities once again built up, Barzani's *peshmerga* were in a better condition than ever before to present a real challenge to the Iraqi forces.

The 1973 Arab–Israeli war brought a break in the growing hostilities between Iraq and the Kurds, used largely by Mullah Mustafa and the Iranians to improve Kurdish defences and push ahead with training – a number of Kurdish fighters went to Israel and Iran to learn how to use the increasingly sophisticated weapons being delivered. Yet right up to 1974, the year when full autonomy was supposed to come into force, desultory negotiations went on between the Kurds and the government, with meetings of the joint committee, visits by officials, and interminable discussions which never seemed to result in any practical improvements. It soon became clear that the Baghdad government was now determined to press ahead with its own version of autonomy, on its own terms, in the areas it chose. On 11 March 1974 the new autonomy law was duly announced, giving the Kurds far less than they wanted or believed they had already negotiated. They were given fifteen days to accept and join the National Front, the ruling coalition. Instead the raids, border skirmishes and localized actions by both sides escalated into full-scale war.

This time the *peshmerga* were not guerrilla fighters secure in their mountains and only occasionally launching hit-and-run attacks on the Iraqi army on the plain; the Kurds had been transformed by American, Israeli and, above all, Iranian support into an army able and willing to engage in set-piece battles with their enemy. It was a tragic error, putting the Kurds at the mercy of their backers, and beholden most of all to the cynical and self-seeking Shah of Iran. It was something of which Mullah Mustafa and his lieutenants were well aware, not least because the arms coming from Iran were mainly defensive, and whenever the *pesh-merga* went on the offensive, there was always a drying up of supplies. 'It was drop by drop from Iran, and no better from the United States,' according to Hoshyar Zebari.

The reason was plain: the shah had to tread a careful path between giving the Kurds enough to tie down the Iraqi army and supplying them so well that they could defeat Iraqi government forces. The shah had his own Kurdish minority; he had vivid memories of the trouble caused by the Mahabad Republic at the beginning of his reign; thus he had no wish to do anything which would again stir up Kurdish nationalist feeling inside his own country.

By 1975 the war had settled into its old stalemate, with neither side able to bring about a clear end; the Iraqis had to commit almost all their troops; they used their air force to bomb the towns and villages; yet still they could not subjugate the Kurds, now well-supplied with anti-aircraft defences, including batteries of Rapier surface-to-air missiles which knocked out some Iraqi planes. At this time, Saddam Hussein was threatened by the situation in the south of the country, where Iran was stirring up trouble among the Shia, smuggling in arms and propaganda through the marshes, and massing troops in Khuzestan in a threatening display of the new Iranian power.

With the atmosphere remaining unstable between the Arabs and Israel in the aftermath of the 1973 war and the Kissinger-arranged disengagement agreements, it was an explosive situation; this worried the other regional states, particularly Jordan, which depended on the goodwill of its neighbours for its survival. King Hussein, newly confident after his 1970 defeat of the Palestinians, arranged contacts between officials which led on to meetings in Turkey between Iraqi and Iranian ministers, and a mediating effort by President Houari Boumédienne of Algeria, who was particularly concerned at the effect the dispute was having inside OPEC.

It was the Algerian intervention which finally bore fruit; both Saddam Hussein, by this time the powerful vice-president of Iraq, and the Shah of Iran were persuaded to attend the OPEC meeting in Algeria in March 1975. They met, embraced and decided on the spot to settle the basic cause of the dispute between the two countries – the river border in the Shatt al-Arab. The Treaty on State Borders and Good Neighbourly Relations, the document embodying the understanding reached, laid down that the frontier in the estuary would follow the thalweg, the median line of the deep-water channel, thus giving Iran control from the centre of the waterway instead of from the eastern bank, as in the past, when Iraq had claimed all tolls and had required ships to fly an Iraqi courtesy flag. Iraq did get a few minor parcels of land to straighten out the border further north, but that was entirely incidental: what mattered was that in return for its concessions in the south, Iraq got a promise that the shah would stop all support for the Kurds in the north and would cut off their supply line, something that would put an immediate end to the rebellion.

As Professor James Bill records, the American CIA chief organizing the supply of American arms to the Kurds saw very well what the effect would be. On 10 March he sent a message to William Colby, the director: 'Is headquarters in touch with Kissinger's office on this? If the US government does not handle this situation deftly in a way which will avoid giving the Kurds the impression that we are abandoning them they are likely to go public. Iran's action has not only shattered their political hopes, it endangers thousands of lives.' There was no response from Langley, from the secretary of state, or from the White House.

US co-operation with the shah had been arranged by Henry Kissinger as a counterweight to growing Soviet influence in the region through Iraq, and approved by the now-deposed Richard Nixon. Their aim had been to weaken Iraq by maintaining the Kurdish rebellion at a constant level, never allowing the Iraqi army to triumph, or the Kurds to succeed, and thus steadily bleeding both, something which particularly pleased the shah, the main American ally in the region, the best customer for arms the world had ever seen, and the designated American surrogate in the Gulf. It was the shah who was directing the course of events, so when he decided to end his quarrel with Iraq, the Americans went along meekly with this betrayal of the Kurds they had originally been brought in to protect – Iran supplied 90 per cent of the hardware the Kurds needed, but it was felt an American involvement would reassure a suspicious Barzani and keep him fighting. If he had to depend on the Iranians alone, Mullah Mustafa would have been more likely to seek an accommodation with Baghdad, knowing from his own experience how quickly Persian policy could change.

In this case the shah kept his promise to Saddam Hussein with a swift and brutal cynicism which, according to Kimche, shocked even the Israelis who were in Iran. Iranian commanders said there was to be a troop rotation, but the units swiftly pulled out were not replaced. Thus on 13 March 1975 the Iraqis knew that the Kurds would be informed of the end of Iran's backing, and would be told of a two-week grace period during which there would be a ceasefire before the border would be closed to them. It was on 12 March that the Iranian forces with the Kurds were pulled out, and the following day, the day when there should have been a ceasefire, the Iraqis began their massive attack just as the Kurdish leaders were told of what was going on.

On 1 April the frontier was sealed, but in those two weeks the Kurds were left on their own to face a merciless onslaught by the whole Iraqi army, which was able to switch maximum force to the north in the reasonable certainty that there would be no attack from Iran anywhere else at that time. Mullah Mustafa, with his sons Idriss and Massoud, fled into Iran with his closest advisers, while in Iraqi Kurdistan the army took the first instalment of its terrible revenge on the people who had defied it for so long. Thousands were massacred, thousands more captured and transplanted to inhospitable and unsuitable places in the hot south of the country, more still forced across the borders into Iran and Turkey.

For once there was in inquest and an epilogue. After Watergate, Congress set up a Select Committee on Intelligence, chaired by the New York Congressman Otis Pike. The committee examined how the CIA had acted in a number of cases during the Nixon administration, its relationship with the State Department, and the conduct of officials. Among the situations which concerned the committee was the way in which arms were supplied to the Kurds of northern Iraq, how that covert operation had been authorized and by whom, and whether America had been in control. It produced a devastating report which became public only because it was leaked to a well-known journalist, and because the *Village Voice*, the radical and anti-establishment newspaper, decided to publish the contents.

The committee neatly summarized what had happened:

In 1972 Dr Kissinger met with the Shah of Iran, who asked the US to aid the Kurds in their rebellion against Iraq, an enemy of the shah. Kissinger later presented the proposal to President Nixon, who approved what would become a $16 million programme. Then John B. Connolly, the former Nixon treasury secretary, was dispatched to Iran to inform the shah, one oilman to another.

The president, Dr Kissinger, and the shah hoped that our clients would not prevail. They preferred instead that the insurgents simply continue a level of hostilities sufficient to sap the resources of our ally's neighbouring country. This policy was not imparted to our clients, who were encouraged to continue fighting. Even in the context of covert operations, ours was a cynical enterprise.

The committee noted that Dr Kissinger had personally ordered the Kurds not to launch an attack on Iraq during the Arab–Israeli war in 1973, when such an attack might have been successful, and he had also concurred in the decision to drop the Kurds once the shah reached his agreement with Iraq.

The committee report noted that when this section of its findings were shown to 'a senior official' – Kissinger – he commented: 'Covert action should not be confused with missionary work.'

The Pike report made it plain that America's supply of arms to the Kurds was done as a favour to Iran.

As our ally's aid dwarfed the US aid package our assistance can be seen as largely symbolic. Documents made available to the committee indicate that the US acted in effect as a guarantor that the insurgent group – the Kurds – would not be summarily dropped by the shah. Notwithstanding these implicit assurances, the Kurds were abruptly cut off by the shah, three years, thousands of deaths, and $16 million later.

It appears that had the US not reinforced the shah's prodding, the Kurds may have reached an accommodation with the central government, thus gaining at least a measure of autonomy while avoiding further bloodshed. Instead, the Kurds fought on, sustaining thousands of casualties and 200,000 refugees.

The Pike report also noted that once the shah reached an agreement with Iraq, he did not even bother to inform 'his junior American partners' that the programme of help to the Kurds was about to be ended.

The Kurds were clearly taken by surprise as well, while the Iraqis, knowing of the impending aid cut-off, launched an all-out search-and-destroy campaign the day after the agreement was signed. The autonomy movement was over and our former clients scattered before the central government's superior forces.

In the event, it proved not to be the end of the Iraqi Kurds' struggle for autonomy, but just one more way station on their

long search for a form of independence. But it was the end for
Mullah Mustafa Barzani. He was forced to go to Iran, to live as
the guest of the man who had betrayed him for the second time
in his life – it was, after all, the shah who had given the *coup de
grâce* to the independent Kurdish republic of Mahabad thirty
years earlier. Mullah Mustafa stayed in Iran until 1977, then
went to spend his last years on the soil of that other state which
had so meanly deserted him, so plainly put great power politics
before the lives of individuals. He died in McLean, Virginia, in
March 1979.

Chapter Seven

THE INCIDENT AT HALABJA

After 16 March 1988 one word came to symbolize the tragedy of the Kurds: Halabja. The events of the day in that Iraqi frontier town did more than any other single incident in seventy years of rebellion against central authority to remind Kurds everywhere of their separate Kurdish identity. Halabja was a turning-point from which many nationalists mark the birth of a national consciousness spanning the borders which divide the Kurdish people.

In the late afternoon of 16 March the first wave of Iraqi planes appeared over the town to drop their bomb-loads of mustard gas, nerve gas and cyanide. Within a few hours as many as 5,000 people were dead and as many again lay burned and gasping for breath from the effects of the chemical attack. The actual death toll was never independently verified, but the aftermath of the attack indicated the scale of the disaster. Bodies littered the streets, as the victims fell where they were standing when the attack came. Men, women and children lay dead with no visible marks of injury, but with faces distorted by asphyxiation. The body of a man lay face down at his doorstep, his arm wrapped around the body of his dead baby in a futile gesture of protection.

The Kurds call Halabja the Kurdish Auschwitz, not because the scale of the massacre was comparable with that of the Nazi death camp, but because the victims were chosen merely because they were Kurds. The dead, overwhelmingly civilian, were killed by Saddam Hussein's forces as a punishment for their assumed collaboration with Iran and the Iranian-backed *peshmerga* who had seized Halabja from Iraqi forces less than forty-eight hours earlier. It was a warning that Baghdad would stop at nothing to eradicate Kurdish 'treachery'.

It was not the first time the Baathist regime had used chemical weapons against the Kurds – Mullah Mustafa Barzani complained to the United Nations as early as 1963 that Baghdad was using chemicals. Nor was it to be the last. In the twelve months leading up to the raid on Halabja there had been chemical attacks against villages, civilians and *peshmerga* units in isolated valleys on twenty-one separate days. After a raid on the Balasan valley in Arbil province on 16 April 1987, 286 injured Kurds made their way to Arbil city for medical attention. They were all captured and killed by the Iraqi army. But Halabja was the most ruthless and deadly operation until then, and had been directed at targets – civilian citizens of Iraq – with no possible military significance.

Despite the scale of the massacre and the fact that Western journalists were on the scene within days, the international reaction to the bombing was muted. Although no one took seriously the attempts of some Iraqi officials to deny responsibility, or, indeed, to blame the Iranians, there appeared to be little appetite within the international community for taking any form of punitive action against Baghdad. The eight-year Iran–Iraq war had entered its end game, and the world powers were unwilling to take action against Iraq for its use of illegal weapons in such a way as to appear to be siding with Iran.

The Arab states stayed firmly on Iraq's side, although they were in no doubt as to what had happened. When a Kurdish delegation appealed to Kuwait to protest against innocent civilians being sprayed with poison gas, they were asked by a Kuwaiti official: 'What did you expect to be sprayed with, rose-water?'

There was greater concern at the time for the safety of shipping in the Gulf than there was for the fate of the Kurdish population on an obscure stretch of the frontline. The US State Department expressed its disgust at the pictures of the massacre coming out of Halabja, but limited itself to condemning the use of chemical weapons by any country, anywhere, and any time, before going on to say that Iran was probably just as guilty.

Six weeks after the attack a report drawn up on behalf of the United Nations by a Spanish military doctor, Colonel Manuel Dominguez Carmona, stated that it was impossible to say for certain whether Iran or Iraq – or both – had been responsible for the use of chemical weapons at Halabja. A resolution subsequently adopted by the Security Council failed to single out Iraq as the culprit or to impose mandatory sanctions against Baghdad. Saddam Hussein had got away with it.

The events at Halabja soon entered Kurdish legend, and became the theme of a song by the leading Kurdish folksinger, Turkish-born Shirwan Pewar, which came to enjoy the status of a national anthem. The needless slaughter of Kurdish civilians had as much of an emotional impact among Kurds in Turkey, the Soviet Union and in the Kurdish diaspora as it did in Iraqi Kurdistan. In Iraq the Kurds knew of events at Halabja only by hearsay. Iraqi censorship meant that they never had an opportunity to see film of the massacre; not, that is, until the spring of 1991, when the Kurdish parties took the film to villages and towns in the liberated zone; those who watched were stunned into silence or wept uncontrollably. Afterwards the nationalists asked themselves whether it had been right to show the film to Kurdish civilians at such a time and whether the shock of seeing for themselves the events at Halabja contributed to the subsequent panic-stricken flight into the mountains in the face of the Iraqi counter-offensive.

It was unlikely that Saddam Hussein would have resorted to chemical weapons in 1991, in view of the likely response of the allies; but such was their power to instil terror among both the *peshmerga* and civilians that he scarcely needed to. The seemingly fearless Kurdish fighters, who went singing into battle against better-armed Iraqi ground forces, would scatter as soon as a helicopter gunship appeared, fearing it might be carrying chemicals.

Although the attack on Halabja represented a prima facie offence by the Iraqis against international law and a violation of the 1925 Geneva Convention, the Kurdish nationalist movement could not entirely escape blame for the scale of the massacre or for the circumstances in which it was carried out.

Although the capture of Halabja in mid-March was later portrayed as an Iranian victory, it was in fact carried out by Kurdish *peshmerga*, principally from Jabal Talabani's PUK, who undertook the operation as the price they had to pay for continued financial and logistical backing from Tehran. The assault on the town was carried out by 500 *peshmerga* led by Shawkat Haji Mushir, a senior PUK official and a native of Halabja. Other guerrillas, from Massoud Barzani's KDP, captured resettlement camps north and south of the town. Everywhere the Iranian forces only entered the town after the chemical bombardment on 16 March. The Kurdish nationalist forces were therefore responsible for the safety of Halabja's civilian population, although it would have been impractical to evacuate the townspeople to protect them from the inevitable Iraqi retaliation.

There was also to be a shameful blot on the Halabja legend. After the chemical bombardment, a number of *peshmerga* proceeded to loot houses in the town.

Whatever the failings of the nationalist movement, the silence of the international community was even less excusable. Apart from a few notable exceptions – the Scandinavian countries, Australia, Canada and (for less altruistic reasons) Israel and Iran – governments failed to condemn outright the Iraqi atrocity, despite the fact that the Kurds had been warning for five years that Saddam Hussein intended to use chemical weapons against them and that the raids of 1987–8, including that on Halabja, represented the first ever military use of nerve gases, substances such as Tabun, which were more deadly, more difficult to counter and harder to detect than simpler compounds. The *peshmerga* were not equipped with gas masks, but they could hope to escape the worst effects of mustard gas by wrapping their faces in wet turbans or lying flat to wait for the gas cloud to pass. Against the fast-killing nerve gas there was no such protection.

The Kurds were aware that the Iraqi forces had used chemical weapons against the Iranians as early as 1982. But in 1984 the discovery of gas masks during a *peshmerga* raid on an Iraqi garrison at Amadiyeh, far from the frontline, appeared to confirm the Kurds' suspicions that the government intended to use chemical weapons against them. Much later the Kurds captured a number of documents which referred to the use of chemical weapons, including a secret telegram from the Zakho military district bordering on Syria and Turkey. It reported that KDP guerrillas in Badinan had managed to obtain 4,000 gas masks and added that 'the saboteurs [*peshmerga*] will wear them when we use chemical materials to attack their concentrations'.

The use of chemical weapons, culminating in the massacre at Halabja, was just one of the instruments of terror and repression employed against the Kurds of Iraq in the 1980s. To understand why Saddam Hussein came to adopt a policy against a section of his own population which verged on genocide, it is necessary to go back to the mid-1970s and the aftermath of the defeat of the Barzani rebellion.

The first task of the Baghdad government after March 1975 was to create an impression that normality had returned to the region with the expulsion of Barzani's 'feudal renegades'. We were among the first group of journalists to be taken to the north in the early summer of 1975 to experience for ourselves the peace and tranquillity which reigned in the cities of Arbil, Kirkuk and Suleimaniyeh, and to see for ourselves how meticulously Kurdish cultural rights were being respected. There was much talk of Arab–Kurdish brotherhood and of the fact that the Kurds of Iraq enjoyed greater autonomy than their brethren in neighbouring countries.

At this time, however, Baghdad had already embarked on a

strategy of Arabization and forced deportations which was consciously aimed at altering the ethnic complexion of Kurdistan. According to Kurdish sources, some 200,00 Kurds were uprooted and sent to live in Arab regions of southern Mesopotamia, the object being to depopulate the regions bordering Turkish and Iranian Kurdistan.

Outside the very limited autonomous zone, Arabic was re-imposed as the language of instruction for Kurdish schoolchildren. Early in 1976 provincial boundaries were redrawn to bring yet more Kurdish territory, principally in the Kirkuk area, into 'Arab' Iraq. A few weeks later Baghdad boasted, in a report to the UN Committee for the Elimination of Racial Discrimination, that it had achieved 'the restoration of peace and national unity following the solution of the Kurdish question in the north of the country'.

After the defeat of Barzani most of the tribal leaders went over to the government side and abandoned further thoughts of rebellion. Saddam Hussein skilfully employed his favoured strategy of carrot and stick to win the loyalty of the *aghas*. For the first time government funds were ploughed into the region to improve the rural infrastucture, and while many thousands of Kurds were deported, others were allowed to return and claim compensation for lost land. These returnees formed a separate peasant class of their own; they were well aware that they owed their belated good fortune to the regime in Baghdad.

The increase in oil revenues in the 1970s spilled over into Kurdistan, bringing with it a construction boom in the cities of the region and greater work opportunities for Kurds. Despite a general regime of repression, physical conditions improved and, as a consequence, support for the defeated nationalist movement declined. This presented the nationalists with a challenge and also prompted a reshaping of the movement away from a tribal-based leadership and towards a more modern party-based structure.

The collapse of the Barzani revolt and the Iraqi regime's strategy of containing Kurdish nationalism by a combination of reward and repression did not signal an end of armed rebellion in the north. As early as May 1976 the *peshmerga* resumed operations against the army, some in the towns of the Badinan – Amadiyah, Dahuk and Zakho – which were strongholds of the Barzani cause. A month later they launched a daring attack designed to prove that Kurdish resistance was still alive by blowing up an arsenal at Kirkuk. This sporadic guerrilla campaign was organized from within Iraq, with little direction from the exiled political leaderships.

The only organization then based inside the country was the Komala, a small urban-based Marxist organization centred on Suleimaniyeh, and, since June 1976, a partner in Jalal Talabani's newly formed PUK. After Barzani's defeat, Talabani had created the PUK as a radical alternative to the old guard, which he denounced as reactionary and anti-revolutionary because of its association with the shah, the CIA and the Israelis.

Talabani's link with the Komala guerrillas inside Iraq gave him a propaganda advantage over his old comrades in the KDP, provoking further rivalry between the two parties. So the KDP began sending its men back into Iraq and, despite talk of inter-party co-operation, the two sides were soon in conflict. In the spring of 1978 Talabani sent 800 men to the Turkish border area, ostensibly to clear a supply route to Turkey, where Kurdish rebel groups had agreed to supply the PUK with logistical support. But this took the PUK *peshmerga* through traditional KDP territory; a large part of the PUK force was wiped out by the KDP *peshmerga* and some 300 were captured by the Iraqi and Turkish armies. Some of the commanders captured by the KDP were later executed.

While they were busily fighting each other, the activity of the *peshmerga* against the Baghdad regime had little military impact. But, by keeping the flame of Kurdish nationalism alive among the civilian population, it constituted a challenge to Baghdad's strategy of pacification.

Saddam Hussein therefore went to Kurdistan at the end of

June, little more than a year after Barzani's defeat, to assure the Kurdish people that the more unpopular measures taken to restore peace, such as forced transfers of people from border zones, had achieved their purpose and were henceforth being suspended.

Once again, Saddam's promises failed to match up to the reality on the ground. Within a month he announced a new policy of establishing a cordon sanitaire in Kurdistan by evacuating the entire population within a 20-km strip along the border zones. Everyone straying into the area was to be shot on sight. These measures were promoted as something designed to protect the Kurds from the depredations of 'separatist renegades'.

Saddam's deal with the shah in 1975 was ostensibly about the dispute involving sovereignty in the Shatt al-Arab. In fact, from Saddam's point of view, it was about maintaining Baghdad's hegemony in Kurdistan. He was later to recall a conversation with Mustafa Barzani's son Idriss, in which he warned:

If we fight, we shall win. Do you know why? . . . You depended on our disagreement with the Shah of Iran. The root of the Iranian conflict is their claim to half the Shatt al-Arab. If we could keep the whole of Iraq with the Shatt al-Arab, we would make no concessions. But, if forced to choose between half of the Shatt al-Arab and the whole of Iraq, then we will give away the Shatt al-Arab, in order to keep the whole of Iraq in the shape we wish it to be.

In 1975 Saddam gave away the Shatt al-Arab to keep Kurdistan. Within five years, however, the Iranian revolution erupted, overturning the power balance in the Gulf and presenting Saddam with what he saw as the opportunity to regain what he had given away.

The shah fled Iran in January 1979 in the face of a wave of popular unrest and Ayatollah Khomeini returned in triumph to put into practice his dream of the establishment of an Islamic republic. Within six months the West's greatest ally in the Gulf turned into its greatest enemy, a shift confirmed by the take-over of the US embassy in Iran by Islamic radicals.

The Kurds of Iran at first allied themselves with the revolution in the hope of winning autonomy, but relations with Tehran broke down, and by the summer of 1979 there was full-scale war between the Kurdish nationalists and Khomeini's forces.

It was against the background of the revolution and the violence in Iranian Kurdistan that the KDP of Iraq held its ninth congress, shortly after Barzani's death in exile in the United States. The congress resolved to step up the offensive against the Baathist regime, taking advantage of the general unrest in the region. In 1979 a *peshmerga* offensive almost succeeded in capturing the Iraqi military base at Haj Omran, the central command post for military operations in the Iranian border zone.

The Iranian revolution presented the Baghdad regime with a number of challenges and opportunites in which the situation in Kurdistan figured high in the list of priorities. The Baathists were happy enough to see the downfall of their former enemy and the weakening of the only regional power capable of containing Saddam's ambitions in the Gulf. The unrest in Iranian Kurdistan, however, was an unwelcome development. The Algiers agreement had reflected an understanding that it was to the mutual benefit of both Iraq and Iran to contain Kurdish nationalism in their respective countries, but the collapse of the shah had altered that delicate balance, and the rebellion among Iran's Kurds against the Khomeini regime threatened to spill over the border into Iraq. Should post-revolutionary Iran break up, an autonomous or independent Iranian Kurdistan could turn into a base for Iraq's rebel Kurds.

Relations between Baghdad and Iran deteriorated rapidly in the first year of Khomeini's rule. Iraq was alarmed by the Ayatollah's threats to export the Islamic revolution and, in particular, by his appeals to the Shia of Iraq. The belief of the Baathists that the revolutionary regime would be ready to tear up the Algiers agreement imposed by the 'imperialist' shah proved to be a delusion. Khomeini was as nationalistic as his royal predecessor when it came to defending Iranian territorial rights, and as dedicated as the shah had been to maintaining Iranian hegemony in the gulf.

The tensions between the two sides almost led to open war in the spring of 1980, with the flashpoints centred on Kurdistan. The Iraqis shelled the Iranian frontier zone from positions near Khaneqin, and the two sides accused each other of violating sovereign air space. Baghdad began deporting tens of thousands of potential domestic opponents – both Shia and Kurds – who were forced across the border in southern Kurdistan, where the Iranian authorities gathered them into tented refugee camps.

Saddam Hussein's final decision to go to war with the Khomeini regime stemmed from his belief that the revolution had brought Iran's armed forces to the point of collapse. He delayed his invasion until later in the year, partly out of concern for the possible response of the superpowers; then on 22 September 1980 he launched a full-scale offensive along a 300-mile front, and within days his forces had moved deep into Iran. The chosen theatre of war was Iran's southern province of Khuzestan along the disputed Shatt al-Arab border.

By the Iraqis' own timetable, the war should have been over within fourteen days: the blitzkrieg was intended to leave Baghdad in control not only of all the major towns of Khuzestan but also of one third of Iranian Kurdistan, specifically the southern provinces of Ilam and Kermanshah.

As it was, the initial offensive became bogged down in a conflict which was to last eight years, most of it fought, after 1982, on Iraqi soil and on the soil of Iraqi Kurdistan. From the start the Iranians and the Iraqi Kurds saw the benefits of a strategic alliance: if the Kurds could pin down regular army troops in the north, this would relieve the pressure on Iranian forces fighting the main campaigns in the south. The Kurds were willing to support the Iranian war effort as long as it appeared likely to lead to the downfall of the Baghdad regime, but they were reluctant to see the main theatre of battle moving to Kurdistan itself. As Iran regained the initiative, however, and pushed the war across the border into Iraq in 1982, this was inevitably what happened.

Contrary to the popular perception that the Iranians paid no regard to the number of their own casualties and that their tactics were based on human wave assaults, the Tehran regime was alarmed by the high price it was paying for pushing the Iraqis out of the occupied zone. This was particularly so after the Iraqis resorted for the first time to using chemicals east of Basra in 1982. Despite the euphoria generated by the expulsion of the invaders from Iranian territory, public knowledge of the frontline death toll made it increasingly difficult to raise volunteer recruits.

Having ousted the invaders, the Iranian war effort moved towards punishing the aggressor, a process Tehran believed would inevitably lead to the downfall of Saddam Hussein. In this phase they altered tactics, extending the war to areas of Kurdistan only marginally affected until then. This had several advantages: it would thin out the Iraqi frontline; it would create logistical problems for the Iraqi army by moving the front into mountainous terrain; it would reduce Iranian casualties; and, above all, it would take the war to a zone where a popular rebellion against Baghdad already existed. The Iraqis would be fighting on hostile territory.

By draining Iraq's military capacity towards the south, the war had, by this time, enabled the Kurdish guerrillas to extend their control over some 10,000 square km of territory along the Iranian border. The Kurdish national movement had encouraged civilians to move back into this liberated zone, previously part of Baghdad's depopulated cordon sanitaire. The danger to the Kurds of a new Iranian front in Kurdistan was that this process of repopulation would be halted and that, in the worst case, the liberated zone might be lost altogether. But by 1982 the Kurds had little choice but to co-operate with their Iranian allies if they were to retain the logistical and base support which they were granted by Tehran.

The so-called Vali-Fajr, or Dawn Offensives, were launched in the spring of 1983 and, on the northern front, were centred on areas of Iraqi Kurdistan north and east of Suleimaniyeh. In Vali-Fajr II, launched on 20 July along a 20-mile front between the Kurdish Iranian towns of Sardasht and Piranshahr, the Iranian forces succeeded in taking the now abandoned base at Haj Omran which the *peshmerga* had failed to capture in 1979. The invaders also took the 9,000-ft Kado mountain range, putting them in a strong position to advance on the Iraqi Kurdish towns of Rawanduz and Qaladiza. The KDP *peshmerga* joined the offensive and were left in control of many of the forty-three villages captured in the area. Kurdistan was now firmly in the war zone.

Vali-Fajr III was launched on 30 July and aimed at clearing the hills around the Iranian Kurdish town of Mehran which the Iraqis had already evacuated. The offensive ended with Iran holding territory on both sides of the border. The Iranian strategy was to neutralize the heights along the border in order to free as many men as possible for an anticipated offensive on the southern front.

In late October the Iranians began a fresh offensive along a 90-mile front east of Suleimaniyeh. This time the aim was to close two mountain routes which the Iraqis were using to supply the guerrillas of the KDP of Iran, who were fighting the Khomeini regime. For just as the KDP of Iraq had thrown in their lot with Tehran, their brethren across the border were taking help from the enemy in Baghdad, and while the Iraqi Kurds had their bases in Iran, so the Iranian Kurds enjoyed a safe haven in Iraq until the Iranian counter-offensive came. The October offensive was partially effective except that, where possible, the Iranian KDP forces returned to their strongholds as soon as the Iranian government forces had moved on.

The Iranian offensive moved south towards Penjwin, where, for the first time, Saddam Hussein's elite Republican Guards were used in a wartime combat role. The Iranians were prevented from taking Penjwin, and the Republican Guards proved to be a focal point in the Iraqi war effort. Previously they had been held in reserve to protect Baghdad and the regime. In 1991, in order to quell the Kurdish revolt, Saddam Hussein would again rely on the Guards to reassert his authority in Kurdistan.

Politically, the Iranians sought to put the captured territory under the authority of the Supreme Council of the Islamic Revolution (SCIRI), an Iranian-created and predominantly Shia front organization which Tehran wanted to put into power once the Baathists were overthrown. The Kurds naturally sought to assert their own authority on their own turf, and had no desire to see the Baathist forces replaced by another group of outsiders.

In practice the Kurds accepted the authority of SCIRI as long as Iranian forces remained in the area. But soon after the October offensive, for instance, *peshmerga* forces took over captured villages, declaring that no foreign power – whether Iraqi or Iranian – had a right to them.

Among the options open to Tehran after a wave of military successes in 1983 and 1984 was a major attack towards Kirkuk and Suleimaniyeh which would have brought the main cities of Kurdistan into the frontline of the war. The object of this option would have been to cut the Iraqi–Turkish pipeline running north from Kirkuk, on which Iraq depended to export its oil. The idea was rejected, however, on the grounds that it would alienate the Turks and, just as importantly, because it would have to rely too heavily on Kurdish co-operation which, in the eyes of the Iranians, was always suspect. Iran's Supreme Defence Council opted instead for a major offensive against Fao in the far south of Iraq, sparing Kurdistan yet more suffering.

As the war progressed, with Iran taking the initiative, the Kurdish parties were less than united about their own war aims. The KDP favoured maintaining pressure against Baghdad on the grounds that this would inevitably hasten the fall of Saddam Hussein, but there were logistical difficulties. Some 120,000 young Kurds were estimated to have fled to the mountains from the cities of the plains rather than face conscription into Saddam's army. They were a burden on the guerrilla infrastructure: the liberated zone was under economic blockade by Baghdad, and food was scarce. There was also a need for more weapons, so the Kurdish movement appealed to Syria and Libya as well as Iran for new arms to fight the war; little was forthcoming except for supplies of light arms, rocket-propelled grenades and light anti-aircraft guns from Colonel Muammar Gaddafi, much of which was confiscated by the Iranians.

A bizarre triangular relationship existed among the Kurdish groups which straddled the Iran–Iraq border. The KDP of Iraq was Tehran's ally in the struggle to defeat Saddam Hussein, while the KDP of Iran based itself inside Iraq in order to pursue its own struggle against the regime of the Ayatollah Khomeini. Jalal Talabani's PUK of Iraq meanwhile controlled the areas in which the Iranian Kurdish rebels were based and was in alliance with them at the same time as opposing Baghdad. While Massoud and Idriss Barzani's KDP forces joined the Iranians for the 1983 offensive in Iraqi Kurdistan, the PUK declared that, on the contrary, it would fight to repel the Iranian invaders.

The Iraqi KDP strongholds were in the Badinan, the Kurmanji-speaking area bordering Turkey, while Jalal Talabani's PUK was based in the Sorani-speaking areas north and east of Suleimaniyeh. While Talabani was allied with the Iranian KDP, the Iraqi KDP frequently took up arms against its Iranian brethren on behalf of Tehran, and in 1981 drove the Iranian Kurdish rebels from areas it controlled.

To further complicate the inter-Kurdish relationships, the PUK was engaged in a struggle with the smaller left-wing parties in order to establish its supremacy within its area of control. This involved violent attacks by PUK *peshmerga* against guerrilla bases of the Communist Party and the Socialist Party of Kurdistan, with which the KDP had been allied since 1980 under the umbrella of the Democratic National Front. In May 1983 the PUK attacked Communist and SPK headquarters, killing many senior members of both parties and in subsequent intermittent clashes hundreds more died. In these battles the left-wingers lost most of their territory to the PUK.

Sources in the KDP continued to insist, long after the event, that the May 1983 attack on its leftist allies at their base in Peshtashan was nothing more nor less than an attempt by Talabani's group to make a goodwill gesture towards Saddam Hussein. The PUK's attitude to the war and to Saddam Hussein was certainly more ambivalent than that of the KDP. Talabani argued that, as Saddam was under such pressure, this was the ideal time to make a favourable deal with him.

With the Iranian Kurdish leader Abdolrahman Qassemlou acting as go-between, the PUK entered into negotiations with Baghdad on the basis that, in exchange for a new autonomy agreement, its guerrillas could help establish security in the border zone, both against the Iranians and against the KDP as well if it should decide to continue the fight. The plan involved forming an alliance of the PUK, Qassemlou's KDP of Iran and Baghdad, to confront the alliance which already existed between the KDP of Iraq, its leftist allies and Tehran.

The KDP, which saw itself as the potential victim of the proposed deal, responded by encouraging violent anti-regime demonstrations in Kurdistan during 1984, ostensibly protesting against the formation of pro-government militia units in Kurdistan but in fact showing to Saddam the limits of PUK control in the north.

Baghdad was happy enough to string the PUK along, as this removed one potential opponent from among the foreign and domestic enemies ranged against it. There was the added advantage that Talabani had agreed to the stationing of army units in areas under his party's control.

But by the mid-1980s, with a lull in the war on the northern front while the Iranians concentrated on their offensives in the south, the circumstances were inauspicious for a Saddam–Talabani deal. The course of the war was still running in Iran's favour, but Saddam was more confident of his position on the diplomatic front. America, fearing an outright Iranian victory, was shifting away from its stated policy of neutrality towards the Iraqi camp; the Russians had resumed arms sales, which were suspended as long as Iraqi troops were on Iranian soil; and the French were fulfilling most of Iraq's other armament needs. The Turks, in addition, were pressing Saddam not to sign an autonomy deal with Talabani that might have a negative impact on their own Kurdish problem.

Saddam was also more confident about his position in Kurdistan. In 1983 he had visited the region to offer a deal to those who had shown their reluctance to fight in his Arab crusade against the Iranians. Instead of being conscripted into regular units, the Kurds were to be allowed to join National Defence units to defend themselves against the Iranians and their rebel *peshmerga* allies. These units would be run by military commanders, but the volunteers would be allowed to serve in their own region and wear Kurdish national dress.

By the end of 1984, when these units were established, Saddam felt he no longer needed a deal with Talabani to safeguard security in the north, and, at the last moment, he declined to sign the proposed autonomy accord. The PUK side broke off the talks and exacted its revenge against Saddam by attacking army units stationed in territory it controlled, a move regarded as an act of treachery by the Baathists in Baghdad.

Having abandoned hope of a deal with Baghdad, the PUK effected a reconciliation with the KDP and pursued efforts to re-establish its understanding with Tehran. The two parties normalized relations at a meeting in Iran in 1987, although the KDP was subsequently to criticize Talabani for entering too wholeheartedly into the Iranian war effort by taking Iranian Revolutionary Guards on operations deep inside Iraq, a charge previously levelled against the KDP by its rival. In 1987, for instance, the PUK accompanied Iranian forces as far as Kirkuk to attack oil installations. PUK policy appeared to be based on proving its credentials to the Iranians after the débâcle of the abortive deal with Saddam.

The Iraqi dictator exacted his revenge by ordering fresh waves of arbitrary arrests, torture and executions at the end of 1985, which principally affected the Suleimaniyeh area, where the PUK was strongest. Amnesty International told the UN Human Rights Commission that some 300 children were rounded up and tortured in Suleimaniyeh in the autumn of 1985 as a punishment against parents alleged to be involved with the *peshmerga*. Additionally, twenty-three people were summarily shot in the city in October of the same year, and eight others were buried alive in the main cemetery. The Iraqis clamped a curfew on the city and shot 200 people during street demonstrations and in summary executions.

The repression continued into the following year, with Amnesty reporting that twenty-one people had been executed in Suleimaniyeh and Arbil in March and April 1986, after an assassination attempt on the governor of Arbil. Six of those summarily executed on the afternoon of 9 April, shot in public outside Suleimaniyeh central prison, were young sympathizers of the PUK under the age of eighteen.

The scale of the repression did not mean that the Kurdish insurgents were in retreat – rather the reverse. In May the *peshmerga* launched a new offensive in which they captured Mangesh, a strategic town near Mosul, and put Dahuk under siege. They claimed to have captured in the process an Iraqi battalion with all its modern weaponry and enough ammunition to hold the area for a year. Foreign intelligence experts estimated that the Kurds were now such a threat to Saddam that they were capable of tying down a quarter of his armed forces.

In August Iran resumed its activity in the north with the Kerbala I offensive directed at an area north of Suleimanyeh. The Iranians captured some strategic heights, but the operation was essentially diversionary, to distract Iraq's attention from more important offensives on the southern front. There were further operations in Kurdistan in September, but the Iranian option of going for Suleimaniyeh itself was never put into effect.

By the spring of 1987 the Kurds were in control of a vast area of northern Iraq. The PUK held most of Suleimaniyeh and Arbil provinces, outside the cities; the KDP controlled the Badinan, including much of Dahuk and Mosul provinces. It had, however, suffered the blow of losing its joint leader, Idriss Barzani, who died of a heart attack in March 1987, although the Iraqis were to claim they had killed him in an air raid on his base in Iran.

With Saddam facing the possible collapse of his frontline east of Basra in the south, it now looked as if the cities of the north might fall to the rebels. The Kurds had acquired a number of SAM-7 surface-to-air missiles via Libya, and this was an important factor in holding the Iraqis at bay; one fixed-wing plane and a number of helicopters were brought down by the *peshmerga*.

Faced with this desperate situation and with the failure of previous efforts to contain the Kurdish nationalist threat, Saddam appointed his cousin Ali Hassan al-Majid as governor of northern Iraq with absolute powers to suppress the Kurdish menace. Majid, a former army officer, was to be given a similar task in 1990 when Saddam appointed him governor of occupied Kuwait. His job in Kurdistan was to suppress the rebel movement with whatever methods he found necessary, and with all the weapons at the regime's disposal, including chemicals.

Majid instituted a system of revenge killings, ordering the public execution of young Kurds each time a member of the regime died at the hands of the *peshmerga*. He ordered the deportation of all civilians from areas which were only partially under government control and had their villages razed to the ground. Within these prohibited areas, no living creature was allowed to survive. 'It is the duty of military forces,' according to a memorandum of 14 June 1987, 'to kill any human being or animal that exists in these areas, which are considered totally forbidden.' In a decree issued by Majid the same month he ordered military commanders to use artillery, helicopters and jets to dislodge anyone defying the order to leave the areas. Those captured were to be interrogated and then executed. Crops, farms, trees and livestock were to be destroyed, and the water supply polluted.

These tactics, aimed at denying so-called 'grey' areas as potential bases for the *peshmerga*, were merely a prelude for the main stage of Majid's strategy – to subjugate the liberated areas and Arabize vast areas of Kurdistan. In the process some 4,000 villages were demolished and some half a million people sent to live in protected camps, several in the very south of the country. A total economic blockade was clamped on the region. On 15 April, less than a month after Majid's appointment, the chemical weapons attacks on the people of Kurdistan began.

The scale of devastation wrought by Majid's pacification programme remained largely unknown to the outside world until the spring of 1991, when, for the first time in four years, Kurds were able to re-enter the areas which been closed to them. Travelling with a KDP *peshmerga* guide at the end of March 1991, we passed scores of ruined villages south of Zakho and in the Badinan which had been bulldozed and dynamited by Majid's forces. In some places the former villages could be made out only from a thin line of stone foundations; in others the rubble had been left in place with no attempt to hide the destruction. At one village the only construction left standing was a concrete plinth bearing the familiar likeness of Saddam Hussein, a monument to his part in the destruction of the region.

On the dirt road between Shaklawa and Amadiyeh, our vehicle became bogged down in the mud beside the ruins of what had obviously been a substantial village, with solid stone foundations which the Iraqi dynamite had failed to dislodge. Some peasants stopped to pull us free with their tractor. They were the first of the vast exodus heading into the mountains to escape the next round of Iraqi repression. They told us that the ruins in front of us were the remains of Barzan, the seat of the Barzanis.

Closer to the plain, south of Zakho, were the open grain fields and strategic hamlets to which the Iraqis had moved Arab settlers as part of their Arabization programme. Every 1 km along the two-lane highway to Baghdad there was a fortified position – a small central blockhouse with six guard posts on the perimeter – behind an earth embankment. Close to the road were grim, one-storey breeze-block terraces of homes, surrounded by barbed-wire fences. Between these artificial settlements were the remains of the Kurdish villages which once peppered the plain. At Somel, once 100 per cent Kurdish before it was totally Arabized, there was a more substantial military command post, with barbed-wire and a minefield to prevent anyone moving to or from the mountains.

The forced Arabization programme, accompanied by the de-portation of Kurdish civilians, the clearing of the 'grey' zones and, above all, the use of chemical weapons constituted a serious crisis for the Kurdish movement. But it was not as grave a threat as the course which the Iran–Iraq war was taking. By early 1988 the hopes of Iran and the KDP that the war would lead to the downfall of Saddam Hussein were fading, as the Iranians moved on to the defensive for the first time in six years. The Kurds had taken part in the operation to seize Halabja at Iran's insistence. The revenge which Saddam exacted was a threat of what would happen if Iraq ever gained ascendancy in the war.

After Halabja the Iranians came to the realization that the war would have to end. Supplies of weapons and ammunition were running low, and replacements were increasingly difficult to find on the international market; Iran had little defence against Iraq's ruthless use of chemical weapons; in the Gulf the American fleet was stepping up its pressure against Iranian forces.

On 17 July 1988 the KDP met at its base at Rajan, inside the Iranian border, to discuss its future tactics. The choices were few: there was little hope of fighting on if the Iranians capitu-lated, and the Kurds could expect massive retaliation by Baghdad once its forces were freed from the burden of fighting Iran; and there was little prospect of a peaceful settlement with Saddam, given the Kurdish role in supporting Iran's bid to overthrow him. Ironically, on the same day, the Iranian leadership was gathered in Tehran for a meeting which would resolve to end the eight-year war. The news of Iran's acceptance of UN Security Council Resolution 598, and therefore of a formal ceasefire, came through to Rajan while the KDP leaders were still meeting. The following day it was announced to the world.

With 15,000 full-time *peshmerga* in the field and 30,000 village militia on stand-by, the KDP decided to mobilize its forces for the defence of Kurdistan. While Iraq fought on for several weeks more, taking last-minute advantage of the Iranian collapse, the situation remained relatively calm in the north. Baghdad sent emissaries to tell the Kurdish rebels that a settlement was possible, and Majid informed the head of the pro-government *jash* in Dahuk that he considered the Kurdish question an internal matter for Kurds to solve. This apparent mood of reconciliation conflicted with intelligence reports gathered by the Kurds that Iraq was massing its forces for an attack on the north. The Kurds concentrated their forces in the triangle where the borders of Iraq, Iran and Turkey meet and awaited the worst.

The expected offensive came as soon as the war with Iran was over, and lasted until 1 September. The Iraqis resorted to the generalized and widespread use of chemical weapons, both because it was the most efficient way of clearing the rebel-held zones, and also because the 60,000 ground forces involved in the operation were considered too demoralized by the prospect of fighting an internal campaign after eight years of war against Iran to be totally reliable.

The Iraqi offensive, spearheaded by the 5th Army and backed by fighter-bombers and helicopter gunships, spread north across the entire 4,000 square miles controlled by the nationalists. Rebel strongholds deep inside the liberated zone suddenly found themselves in the frontline. On 2 August the Iraqis almost succeeded in wiping out Barzani and the KDP leadership in a chemical air raid on Oshnaviyeh, but they hit targets in the wrong part of town. Three weeks later, from 25 August to 1 September, Iraqi planes used chemicals to attack seventy-seven villages, mainly in the Badinan. During this summer offensive the Iraqis destroyed a further 478 villages to add to Majid's existing toll. It was obvious that this unequal fight could lead only to the destruction of the nationalist movement and further suffering for the people of Kurdistan, who even now were being forced to flee to the mountains. The decision was taken to beat an orderly retreat.

In the week from 28 August to 5 September, 50,000 Kurds fled Iraq, their departure precipitated by the 25 August raids. Those who left said that it was the fear of chemical weapons which had forced them out. By the end of the exodus up to 150,000 Kurds had managed to find refuge in Turkey, where they met cold and hunger, and the ill-disguised hostility of the Turks. They were the lucky ones. Others were trapped inside Iraq, driven from their homes by the air raids but with no means of escape. They were rounded up and put into a camp on the open plains outside Arbil to survive the rigours of winter as best they could.

On 4 September the Iraqi foreign minister, Tareq Aziz, was able to assure those gathered in Geneva for the first round of Iran–Iraq peace talks that the Kurdish insurgency was over and the rebels were on the run. He blamed Barzani and Talabani for trying to create publicity for themselves by encouraging women and children to flee Iraq. For the record, he added: 'There is no use of chemical weapons and no necessity of using them.' This conflicted not only with the testimony of the fleeing Kurds but also with that of independent observers who went to assess the situation. Among these were Peter Galbraith and Christopher Van Hollen of the US Senate Foreign Relations Committee, who reported back to Washington that chemical weapons had been used.

Three months after the offensive, a British documentary film-maker, Gwynne Roberts, made a clandestine visit to Iraqi Kurdistan and brought back soil samples which were submitted for independent analysis by a private British firm. The analysts found traces of three compounds indicating the presence of sulphur mustard gas. The British chemical defence establishment at Porton Down reached similar conclusions from the samples, describing them as 'relatively heavily contaminated'.

Roberts also interviewed survivors of an air raid on 28 August against Kurdish civilians sheltering in the Bassay gorge, 20 miles south of the Turkish border. Their accounts left no doubt that chemical weapons had been used. One survivor, Ramazan Mohammad, told him: 'There must have been 3,000 bodies and thousands of animals, all dead. The dead had a film over their eyes and out of their nose and from the sides of their mouth there was a horrible slime coming out. The skin was peeling and bubbling up.'

There was an outcry in the international press against Saddam Hussein's slaughter of the Kurds, which caused greater reverberations at government level than had been the case after the Halabja massacre. The Arab states routinely backed Iraq in the face of what was seen as pro-Zionist and anti-Arab propaganda, while the official Soviet and Eastern bloc media ignored the events in Kurdistan. But the Western Europe allies and the United States reacted more forcefully than before. George Shultz, the US secretary of state, told the Iraqis he had conclusive proof that they had used chemical weapons, and the British Foreign Office said it was equally convinced. President François Mitterrand of France said he saw it as his duty as a friend of Iraq to express his deep disquiet against the methods used to suppress the Kurds.

Despite this international pressure, the Iraqis resisted the dispatch of a UN inquiry team on the grounds that the events in Kurdistan were an internal affair. And despite a standing resolution of the Security Council that any state using chemical weapons would face immediate sanctions, no such action was enforced.

The lure of the anticipated post-war reconstruction boom and a general desire not to create new tensions in the Gulf so soon after the ceasefire were enough to persuade most countries to play down the Kurdish question. Once the uproar over the forced exodus to Turkey had abated, the issue was quietly allowed to die. This softly-softly approach was illustrated in a Foreign Office briefing paper of September 1988, which stated: 'We believe it better to maintain a dialogue with others if we want to influence their actions. Punitive measures such as unilateral sanctions would not be effective in changing Iraq's behaviour over chemical weapons, and would damage British interests to no avail.'

On the basis of the report by the Senate Foreign Relations Committee staffers, Galbraith and Van Hollen, the committee chairman, Claiborne Pell, introduced the Prevention of Genocide Act 1988, which won widespread Congressional support in favour of sanctions against Iraq. In the end the legislation was dropped in the face of White House opposition, and in the rush to wind up Congress before the presidential election.

Perhaps inspired by the weakness of foreign reaction, Saddam Hussein pursued his policy of repression throughout 1989, uprooting Kurdish populations not only from strategic border areas but also from towns and villages well inside Iraq, using the spurious pretext of creating yet another cordon sanitaire. In June the army forcibly evacuated the entire population of Qaladiza – some 100,000 people, according to Kurdish sources – before reducing it to ruins.

For the Kurds it was 1975 all over again. From a position of strength, the nationalist movement had been all but destroyed as a result of events beyond its control. The commitment to an alliance with Iran proved worthless once Iran decided to seek peace with Iraq, just as in 1975 Barzani had been defeated by the Algiers agreement between Saddam Hussein and the shah. And just as they had in 1975 – and were again to do in 1991 – the Kurds headed for the refuge of the mountains, their only constant friends.

Chapter Eight

THE MOUNTAIN 'TURKS'

Forced migrations, collective punishment, beatings, torture, arbitrary arrests, a massive army presence – all the apparatus of repression which made the Iraqi regime notorious could also be found in Turkey. Quietly, behind a screen of official denial, hidden by censorship, the authorities in Ankara managed for years to keep their treatment of the Kurds a secret, with information of the plight of the ten million Kurds living in Turkey, a fifth of the country's population, emerging only through human rights organizations, through the few journalists able to penetrate the eastern provinces, and through the devoted and brave efforts of Turkish Kurds, who risked their freedom to draw attention to the lack of liberty suffered by their compatriots.

In 1991 the situation appeared to change dramatically. Anxious to exploit the situation created by the Gulf war, President Turgut Ozal invited Kurdish representatives to meet him in Ankara, then announced that a ban on the use of the Kurdish language would be lifted and political prisoners freed. The Turkish parliament, the Grand National Assembly, duly passed the new laws the president wanted in a thirteen-hour session, and, for the first time since Mustafa Kemal imposed the ban in 1924, Kurds were able to speak their own language freely in public and in dealings with the authorities. The repeal of the laws against the use of Kurdish, and the ending of a ban on communism, meant that some 43,000 out of 46,000 convicted prisoners in eastern Turkey were freed, and 270 men awaiting the death penalty had their sentences commuted. It seemed a remarkable reversal of the official attitude.

Yet the Turkish moves were less than they seemed. Cynical Turkish diplomats, unusually forthcoming because of their opposition to the conduct of foreign policy by their president, pointed out that the relaxation merely legitimized what was already happening. Hundreds of thousands of Turkish Kurds spoke nothing but Kurdish, so the new act merely stopped them breaking the law each day. It permitted them few new liberties: written Kurdish remained prohibited, so that newspapers could not be published, nor political pamphlets printed. Teaching and broadcasting remained firmly Turkish.

All that happened in practice was that Turgut Ozal saw a chance to improve his country's image in America and the West. It was significant that the decision to change the situation was taken by the president alone and pushed through parliament by compliant parties, rather than having arisen in parliament itself or through the decision of political groups. From the beginning of the Gulf crisis in 1990, Ozal took over the conduct of foreign policy – in the process, bringing about the resignation of three Cabinet ministers and the chief of staff. The president's aim was deceptively simple: given the slim chance of admission into the European Community because of the prejudice of the twelve member states, which were unhappy about accepting a Muslim nation into the community and feared the effect on their own economies of Turkish migrant workers, President Ozal determined to carve out for his country a special relationship with the United States, the one remaining world power. Ozal wanted to emulate the relationship which the Shah of Iran had had with Washington at the height of Tehran's modern power – to be an American surrogate policeman and, in that role, to receive most favoured treatment in all his dealings with the United States, as well as emerging as the dominant power in an area stretching from the Balkans to the Gulf.

The early beneficiaries of the Turkish change of tack were the ordinary people of eastern Turkey, the Kurds of the eight provinces along the frontiers who overnight achieved some of what they had been seeking for generations. For the authorities too there was an early gain: the same laws which allowed Kurdish to be spoken hardened the penalties against those waging war against the state, in this case, the PKK, that extremist and violent Marxist group. By allowing the basic right of people to express themselves in their own tongue, the government swept away one of the most fundamental causes of unrest in the Kurdish areas and deepened still further the growing rift between the guerrillas of the PKK and the people among whom they operated.

The PKK was the latest in a long line of insurgent groups which had tried over the years to obtain basic human rights for the Kurds of Turkey, a group officially described until 1991 as 'mountain Turks who have forgotten their own language'. The movement was based in Syria until an improvement in relations between Damascus and Ankara caused it to be diplomatically moved to the Bekaa valley of Lebanon – but still under Syrian control. Led by Abdullah Ocalan, the PKK was one of the most violent of all Kurdish organizations. At times backed by the Soviet Union, on other occasions by Iran, the PKK was as ruthless in its treatment of Kurdish 'collaborators' as it was in its attacks on the Turkish military. The village guards, armed by the authorities, became prime targets, as well as landlords, officials and any deemed to be supporting the state, whether they were Turks or Kurds.

This ruthlessness reflected the attitude of Ocalan, a charismatic figure, a smiling, fast-talking and quick-thinking man. Known to his followers by the nickname Apo, he is rarely seen by outsiders, spending most of his time at his headquarters and at the Masoum Korkmaz training base in the Bekaa valley, and still occasionally leading fighting patrols into Turkey. He was prominent in the underground Turkish Communist Party before joining the PKK, and still follows an old Stalinist style of thinking, applying Marxist principles to all problems – no *glasnost* or *perestroika* for Apo.

Like most 'freedom fighters', he is also given to exaggeration:

he claims to be the leader of twenty million Kurds in Turkey, though the total in the country is certainly no more than twelve million at the most, and the majority are opposed to his brand of extreme communism, still preferring to put their hopes in the more Westernized and democratic Kurdish parties. He is bitter at the lack of recognition, as he sees it, of the war going on in eastern Turkey. 'The newspapers are full of news about the freedom of the Lithuanians, or about the situation in Albania. They discover minorities in Bulgaria and Greece, and talk about violation of human rights. But Kurdistan is forgotten; we are not treated like people.' Like many communists, Ocalan believes that he and his party alone have the truth: for him, Barzani is a Turkish stooge, Talabani an agent of Iraq.

So what has the PKK achieved so far? For once there is a pause, perhaps as memories of the casualties occur – more than 3,000 on both sides. Then the answer comes, significantly, almost the same as the one Yasser Arafat gives to similar questions: 'The most important thing is that we have awakened the national consciousness of an entire people. Our aim is not to change frontiers, but to change the political, economic and social situation. We demand the independence of Kurdistan, and that will not fragment the Middle East, but will be a guarantee of the freedom and autonomy of all the peoples of the region.'

Ocalan believes Turkish moves during the war with Iraq, the stationing of 100,000 Turkish soldiers on the border and the opening of the country to allied air forces, had more to do with the Kurdish uprising, and with Turgut Ozal's ambitions, than with any desire to help the allies against Iraq. He was unimpressed by Ozal's decision to allow the Kurds of eastern Turkey to use their own language:

There has been no liberalization. It is a humiliation to be 'allowed' to speak our own language. Not even animals can be forbidden to speak their own language, and you can't sew people's mouths up. Never before in human history have people been forbidden to speak their own language. And don't forget that even after this, we are forbidden to read or write our own language, and the question of teaching in schools in Kurdish simply is not mentioned. There is no freedom for the Kurds.

As we found, Turkish officials agree with Ocalan that the much vaunted decree allowing Kurds to speak Kurdish actually has little meaning; the move was no more than part of a public relations campaign aimed at the United States, the West and the Kurds of other countries, who might one day be persuaded to opt for autonomy under Turkish dominion, something which such leaders as Jalal Talabani say they would at least consider.

The uncompromising tactics adopted by both sides in what became one of the most violent of guerrilla wars was partly made possible by the lack of information on what was happening. With increasingly tough methods used by the army and the brutality of the PKK, the civilians in eastern Turkey were caught in a dreadful pincer movement. 'We either offer the guerrillas food and face military persecution or deny them any help and get killed,' said Yusuf Acu, headman of Toptepe village. A Turkish MP, Cuneyt Canver, noted: 'East and south-east Anatolia have been transformed into a vast penal camp. Everyone is afraid of everyone else. The people cannot speak, still less criticize. When the villagers, out of fear, give the terrorists food, the security forces come later and call them to account for such actions.'

The daily bloodshed in eastern Turkey from 1986 onwards may have been nothing new, but it was the worst and most prolonged of all the struggles between Kurdish separatists and the central government, which had been going on for well over a hundred years. In its modern form Kurdish nationalism in Turkey was the direct consequence of a decision by the founder of modern Turkey, Mustafa Kemal, to make his country a homogeneous whole. His apparently harsh edicts may have had their origins in the vengeful attitude of the victorious allies at the end of World War I. The aim of France and Britain, in particular, was not only to break up the Ottoman empire as a means of punishing it for siding with Germany in the war, but also to carve out their own spheres of interest and control, many of which had been decided years earlier.

President Woodrow Wilson, with his idealistic Fourteen Points Declaration, was quite useful to the cynical British and French leaders, who thought they could shape his concern for minorities to create buffer zones and weaken potential enemies: by giving or withholding backing, they also believed they could ensure the continued support of friends.

The response of Mustafa Kemal and the Turkish nationalists to this colonialist carve-up was to launch their own war of independence, during which the fledgeling Armenian Republic was quickly snuffed out, and a Kurdish state was prevented from coming into existence. The Greeks were defeated and expelled, and, on 29 October 1923, just three months after the signing of the Treaty of Lausanne, the Turkish Republic was proclaimed, with Mustafa Kemal as president – a post he was to hold for the next twenty-five years – and with the Republican People's Party which he founded the dominant group in parliament. Turkey adopted a parliamentary constitution, but for all practical purposes it was ruled by one man for the next quarter of a century.

Mustafa Kemal, more than most who suddenly come to power, was faced with a maze of problems. For decades Turkey had been known as 'the sick man of Europe', its economy unable to keep pace with modern life, its empire contracting, its technology behind those of its competitors. If it was to join the twentieth century, massive changes were needed, and these Mustafa Kemal was ready to bring about. The internal situation had to be addressed first, and, with the troubles caused by minorities within his country fresh in his memory, Mustafa Kemal was determined to avoid such problems in the future, not merely discouraging minority groups, but laying it down that they broke the law if they tried to maintain their separate

identities. So as a first step towards the modern Turkey which
was his vision, he promulgated a new constitution, just one year
after the Treaty of Lausanne had laid down careful safeguards
for minority groups. The largest of these, the Kurds, occupied
about a third of the land mass of the new state of Turkey and
made up about one fifth of the population. The Treaty of Lausanne, signed so soon after the bloody massacres of Armenians
and the bitter war between Turks and Greeks, had stipulated
that

no restriction shall be placed on the free use of any language by a
Turkish national, neither in private relations nor in commerce, nor in
matters of religion, press or publications, nor in public meetings.
Notwithstanding the existence of an official language, Turkish
nationals whose language is not Turkish will be given the right to oral
use of their language before the tribunals.

Even when Mustafa Kemal had taken over in all but name,
Turkey had agreed that this clause, and others like it protecting
the rights of minorities, should become part of the fundamental
law of the country, so that subsequent laws, regulations or
decrees could not supersede them. With hands metaphorically on
their hearts, the Turkish negotiators asked how they might be
suspected of wanting to tamper with such laws; after all, there
were seventy-five Kurdish MPs in the Grand National Assembly
in Ankara, a clear indication that they spoke for the whole
country. Certainly the provisions guaranteeing the right of free
speech to minorities would be upheld.

That was in 1923. On 3 March 1924, having dissolved the
Grand National Assembly, Mustafa Kemal issued a decree prohib-
iting the use of the Kurdish language, banning education in that
language, and making illegal all publications in Kurdish. His aim
was clearly to unify his country, to set all the peoples of Turkey
on an even footing as they set off on their new modern adventure
– secularization of the state, with the mystical dervish orders
banned, the Latin alphabet replacing Arabic script, the fez and

the veil, those symbols of submission to Islam, eliminated, the privileges of European states abolished, and pragmatic economic policies adopted. It was a recipe which proved hugely successful in transforming Turkey from the ailing heartland of a bankrupt empire into a modern state able to compete with its European neighbours; at the same time, by ignoring its largest minority group it laid the seeds of the trouble which today erupts in violence and bloodshed in the villages of the eastern provinces.

The Kurds became, overnight, second-class citizens in their own country. Living in the poorest regions of Turkey, they were still forced into additional expense each time they had to deal with authority: banned from using their own tongue, they had to have intermediaries to speak for them in all dealings with the state. They became ready recruits for the Turkish army, not always because they were poor and needed a living; sometimes too because young men were persuaded that it would be useful to learn the skills of their enemies, how to handle weapons, where to plant bombs. In the army those Kurds who joined at the instigation of separatists and nationalists had their prejudices reinforced: they had to put up with plenty of abuse, just as they did when they left their homeland for the cities of the west. Recruiting sergeants would ask them for the numbers of their caves when they took their addresses, and they had a hard time on the parade ground or ranges until they learnt enough Turkish to respond quickly to orders. The Turkish army was always the guardian and inheritor of Mustafa Kemal's ideas, the protector of his values; but in that army the Kurds were inferior beings, rarely rising to senior level unless they had become assimilated into the Turkish mainstream.

Over the years the simmering discontent remained. There were minor revolts easily put down by an increasingly brutal Turkish army, there was subversion, and exiles kept the flame alive abroad. But no one leader emerged to unify the rival factions, still based, as they were in the other areas of Kurdistan, on family, clan and tribe. The vast majority sought to live peaceful lives, putting up with authority, getting round regulations, keeping to their own areas. Poverty and the lack of development until the 1980s drove hundreds of thousands away, and the presence of large Kurdish communities in Ankara, Istanbul, Izmir and other Turkish towns played a part in the government decision to develop the east of the country. The South-eastern Anatolian Project began as a small irrigation and energy development in the 1960s aimed merely at improving conditions for peasant farmers, but under the influence of Turgut Ozal, a visionary economist as well as a clever politician, it turned into a massive programme to transform the whole of eastern Turkey. Even so, the presence of large Kurdish communities in the Turkish cities affected the attitude of ordinary Turks to these Kurds in their midst: following the example of the government, they always regarded the Kurds as potential members of a fifth column. And in the violent 1970s the Kurds lived up to that reputation, many siding with the revolutionary left which brought the country close to civil war, until the military stepped in to end the bickering of the politicians and imposed their own peace.

By 1970 the Kurds made up 5 per cent of the population of non-Kurdish areas, and far from being 'mountain Turks who had forgotten their own language', many had actually forgotten Kurdish. At least half the Kurds living outside the east of the country then and now speak only Turkish, and are fully assimilated into the Turkish life of Turkey.

Yet through all the long years of repression, the Kurds in Turkey have still managed to retain their national identity and their separate culture, and to keep alive the hope of autonomy, at least, for their eight provinces. In recent years the very harshness of their environment and the economic deprivation they have suffered, allied to the geography of the region, have played a part in the upsurge of nationalism which has its violent expression in the bloody war being waged by the PKK.

Because it is relatively easy for them to travel, between 1950 and 1980 more than a million Kurds sought work outside Turkey, according to Christiane More's 1984 estimate. Some 300,000 went to West Germany alone and, in the way of migrants, tended to form their own communities, quite isolated from the host country and separate from other colonies of migrant workers, including Turks. In Germany, and among the groups in other Western countries, the Kurds found the freedom to do the things denied them at home – not only could they speak Kurdish publicly, they could also teach their children in their own tongue, publish magazines and political tracts, perform traditional Kurdish dances, and attend presentations of Kurdish folklore. All these things were banned in Turkey, where it was held that even traditional Kurdish songs could be subversive, with their age-old themes of heroic resistance to oppression, epic battles and doomed love stories.

The migration of Kurds within Turkey played a part too. Because of the underdevelopment of the eastern provinces, bright and ambitious young men – and a few women – were forced to go to the Turkish cities for their education. Among them were some of the sons and daughters of the local *aghas*, better able to afford it. In the schools and universities they saw the freedom and prosperity of the Turkish cities, and contrasted them with the repression and poverty of the Kurdish areas. Many of them absorbed the ideas of the Turkish left, the biggest grouping and most eloquent creed during the years of weak government in the 1960s and 1970s. The result was that at the lowest level the Kurds who returned to their villages as the local schoolmasters and administrators began quietly passing on to a new generation their own observations about the inequality of life in Turkey, and inculcating a modern nationalism in their audiences.

The sons of the *aghas* rebelled against their expected role as props of the feudal structure into which they had been born. A few of them tried to educate their own tenants in the new ways they had themselves been taught, only to find economic pressures forcing them back to the old ways. There were attempts to form branches of the Turkish revolutionary groups in the

Kurdish provinces, but organizations like Dev Genc and Dev Yol – Revolutionary Youth and the Revolutionary Way – were urban creations and did not transplant to the rural provinces, where life still demanded loyalty to the clan and the tribe, and where the village was the centre of society. Underground activity and communist organizations could never take root in such a society, and nothing could be kept secret.

The army was a useful educator too, not only in the military arts which could later be used against the state which taught them, but also in giving elementary skills to those too poor even to attend a school – many families in the remotest regions still could not spare sons needed to tend animals and help in the fields, and in such places the idea of education for girls was not even considered. In the army, for all its harshness, young men were taught to read and write, and those with any aptitude became drivers and mechanics. After their service they would not go back to being shepherds and rural labourers, and, if they did not join the exodus to the west, drifted into the towns, always more difficult to control than the countryside.

Eventually, when the Turkish military stepped in again in 1980 to end the fratricidal struggle between left and right which was tearing Turkey apart, that other classic training ground of revolutionaries came into its own: prison. A former inmate recalled the governor's address to a new batch of prisoners:

You are not Kurds, but Turks, and we are going to make you see that. You will not speak Kurdish. Only Turkish will be allowed, and if you cannot speak Turkish, then you will not be allowed to speak at all.

You are enemies of the state, and should be destroyed, but instead, the state has decided to educate you, to make you good Turks and good Kemalists. We will fit you for society.

It was an empty boast. Rather than fitting Kurds for Turkish society, Diyarbakir prison became the university of Kurdish nationalism. It was a brutal place, but once a man had graduated from it, he was sure of the respect of his own people. He would be one of the new leaders, passing on the ideas of nationalism, autonomy or independence which were constantly discussed.

Bulent Ecevit's Republican People's Party (RPP), though it was the inheritor of the Kemalist tradition, should have been a natural home for the Kurds in the 1970s, as it had moved to the left under popular pressure and in response to Suleiman Demirel's rightist ideas which he imposed on the other main political group, the Justice Party (JP). The JP was the party of the land-lords and *aghas*, and when in power actively encouraged such men to act as intermediaries between the state and the people, just as in the feudal times of the Ottoman empire.

Some Kurds did join the RPP, but both in the Kurdish pro-vinces and in the cities of Turkey they soon found that the RPP was no more inclined than any other party to make concessions. This was a factor in turning the urban youth towards the revolu-tionary groups which eventually spawned the PKK, while in the country the small farmers and peasants found the KDP of Turkey more attractive. Based on the old tribal structure, the KDP in Turkey was closely linked to Mullah Mustafa's group in Iraq, and there was a good deal of interchange across the border near Hakkari until the Turkish army sealed the frontier. Even now, though, the Kurds of Iraq, Turkey and Iran all carry on a well-organized and useful smuggling business, and in the process learn of political developments taking place in each country.

Today the excesses of the PKK are driving the Kurds in Turkey towards more moderate groups, with Turgut Ozal's Motherland Party making headway in the eastern provinces. Many of the growing number of intellectuals among the Kurds oppose this trend, arguing – as they did in the magazine *Rizgari* ('Liberation') before it was closed down in 1979 – that the people of an occupied country should not concern themselves with the politics of the oppressor but concentrate on obtaining their own freedom.

With Kurdish political life still banned, the activists are forced to join the extremists or to abandon any further role in the continuing drive for autonomy, or at least for an improvement in conditions in the Kurdish areas. This lassitude, this opting out, is becoming more marked as the South-east Anatolia Project gradually improves the economy of the region, creates more jobs and increases agricultural output. Yet in the celebrations at village weddings, in the coffee shops, and in the clandestine activity of those graduates of Diyarbakir prison, the dream is still kept alive. As Shivan, the great Kurdish singer, said when told his songs were censored in Turkey: 'Music moves like the wind. Can they stop the wind?'

Kurds charge that the Turkish government is again applying old methods, using the excuse of the need for land for the vast new irrigation programme to remove whole villages and, in the process, transfer the people to more manageable places – an adaptation of the Iraqi policy. It was used earlier in Turkey: in the immediate wake of Mustafa Kemal's take-over, there was a deliberate programme of removing Kurds from whole areas, of wiping villages off the map, as a means of containing and eradicating the resistance to the government, and of smothering Kurdish anger at the breaking of the international promises of statehood and the Turkish assurances of cultural autonomy.

As early as 1925 the first serious revolt broke out, uniting Kurds in Syria with those in south-eastern Turkey. Militias were formed, villagers and townspeople ejected or murdered all representatives of the state, and foreign aid was sought – and denied. The Turkish army, confident after the successes of its struggle against the Greeks, was able to suppress the ill-organized uprising, though more than 35,000 troops and a squadron of planes were needed to do so. The modest and confused aims of this early revolt were shown by its declaration that the goal was an independent Kurdistan under Turkish protection, and the restoration of the sultanate. In the end fifty-three leaders were sentenced to death; as Jawaharlal Nehru wrote: 'The Turks, who had only recently been fighting for their own freedom, crushed the Kurds, who sought theirs. It is strange how a defensive nationalism develops into an aggressive one, and a fight for freedom becomes one for dominion over others.'

A Turkish newspaper saw it another way. 'There is no Kurdish problem where a Turkish bayonet appears,' one wrote. The government in Ankara seemed to take the same view: there was no attempt at reconciliation, no sop to Kurdish nationalism. Instead the authorities used the 1925 revolt to crack down on communists, trades unions and other minorities as well as the Kurds. There were mass arrests, deportations from one part of the country to another, and harsh application of the laws discriminating against the Kurds.

Inside Turkey the result of all this was a sullen acceptance, an understanding that for the moment nothing could be done. But as usual those outside the country were eager to keep the flame of revolution alight, and at last managed to unite most Kurdish nationalist movements, and to form an alliance with the Armenians. Known as the Khoibun, this alliance managed to hold a congress at Bhamdoun in Lebanon, and began contacts with the outside powers who, for mutually conflicting reasons of self-interest, were unhappy at the way things were developing in Turkey – notably Britain, France and the Soviet Union. This time some clandestine help was forthcoming, and a new revolt began in 1930 around Mount Ararat – Buyuk Agri – in the northern part of Turkish Kurdistan on the border of the area regarded as Armenia. The choice of place for the uprising reflected in part the need for the Kurds to carry their Armenian comrades with them, but was also seen as an attempt by the Armenians to take over the leadership of the fragmented Kurdish movement, to try to use the Kurds as their foot-soldiers. There was also the tactical hope of using Iranian territory as a base, but this was quickly dashed when Iran gave the Turks permission to cross the border in their fight against the rebels. Once again the uprising was soon put down.

Now the situation of the Turkish Kurds was worse than ever, with the world recession of 1930 adding poverty and hardship to the repression of the government. Crushed under the weight of taxation and living under the watchful eye of the Turkish gendarmerie, the Kurds could do little, but occasionally, pushed too far, whole communities erupted in anger. When that happened, punishment quickly followed: local leaders were executed, others imprisoned on trumped-up charges, families moved to Turkish areas, and crops destroyed. The League of Nations in 1937 received a letter from the people of Dersim – now Tunceli – in which they sought help against the brutalities of the Ankara government, 'which closes Kurdish schools, prohibits the use of the Kurdish language, removes the words "Kurd" and "Kurdistan" from serious works, uses barbarous methods when forcing the Kurds, including women and girls, to work on military projects in Anatolia, and deports the Kurds in groups of ten people into Turkey'. Later evidence showed that those deportations of groups of ten had finally resulted in more than a million people being moved out of Turkish Kurdistan, defined as the eight south-eastern provinces.

According to Kurdish historians, hundreds of thousands died in the revolts which went on all through the 1920s and 1930s, not only in the fighting but also in mass executions carried out by the Turkish army. But as another Kurdish memorandum noted – this time to the United Nations:

As a result of the deep-rooted feelings of frustration and deprivation they experienced for not having their own national state, the Kurdish people in all parts of Kurdistan never ceased to revolt. Once the occupiers temporarily crushed a revolt in the eastern part of Kurdistan, another revolt would emerge in the western, southern or northern part of Kurdistan. This does not indicate that the Kurds are a war-like people, but it does indicate their total refusal to submit to slavery.

In Turkey the disaffection remained, but the situation grew too difficult for the Kurds constantly to take up arms. During the years of World War II, local autonomy movements of all kinds had to take second place to the wider struggle going on, and the Kurds, like others, remained quiet. Later the military in Turkey emerged more and more strongly as the most powerful organ of the state, intervening directly in government whenever it felt that the ideals of Kemalism were being betrayed. In the 1960s Kurdish activity was apparently minimal, but it was in this decade that the Kurds forced from their homes were absorbing the more radical ideas of those among whom they found themselves. Those Kurds who chose to become part of Turkey had no problems, as government policy was to accept all Kurds who declared themselves Turks, who gave up their language and their customs, and joined the mainstream, as the Turks would express it. Those who stubbornly maintained their Kurdishness could find understanding, sympathy and support only among the radicals, which in Turkey in the 1970s increasingly meant the activists of the far left, the young revolutionaries of Dev Yol, the Turkish People's Revolutionary Party, the Revolutionary Army and many more splinter groups of the far left, based usually in the universities, with activists drawn mainly from the trades unions.

Even some of the official parties allowed by the Turkish constitution began speaking of the need to protect the rights of minorities, and there was a growing move towards recognition, at least, that there was a Kurdish problem. The result was that from university discussion groups and the violent activities of the terrorist fringe, Kurdish activists began to take a public role in the eastern provinces, as anarchy gradually spread throughout the rest of the country, making it more difficult for the authorities to concentrate their power in the eight Kurdish provinces.

In 1977 a Kurdish socialist and avowed separatist, Mehdi Zana, was elected mayor of Diyarbakir, the unofficial capital of Turkish Kurdistan. While the rest of the country erupted into fratricidal strife, as the army and police tried to contain the onslaught of militant Marxism matched by the fascism of Alparslan Turkes's Grey Wolves (see p. 226), Diyarbakir had a brief spell of liberalism. It was not to last. As the situation deteriorated, martial law was proclaimed in the eastern provinces, and when one of the present authors visited Diyarbakir in 1979, it was like visiting a town under occupation. The elite Turkish paratroop regiment patrolled the town in pairs, fingers on the triggers of their rifles, reinforcements always close at hand, armoured cars and tanks strategically placed. Kurdish was still being used in the streets and in people's homes, but the locals would fall silent as police or military came by. Cassettes of Kurdish music could be bought under the counter in some shops, though we were told of Turkish troops using their rifle butts to smash tape recorders used to play them. Almost anyone was willing to talk to a foreigner about hopes of independence, the struggle to come, and the harshness of the authorities.

In a long interview, arranged with representatives outside Turkey and conducted in secret and at some risk for all concerned after a series of cut-out meetings, a leader of the banned Turkish KDP claimed that a new People's Army was being raised, and that the final struggle to liberate Turkish Kurdistan was not far off.

It was not to be. In 1980 the Turkish army finally lost patience with the quarrelling Ankara politicians, whose wrangling was preventing any solution to the country's growing chaos. In a bloodless coup the army took over, extended martial law from Kurdistan to all parts of the country, and, to the surprise of most, swiftly established peace and order, a reflection more of the Turkish people's weariness with strife than the army's ideological expertise.

With all political parties banned and with stern, direct and visible military power in control of every aspect of life, Kurdish insurgency appeared to have come to an end. One factor was that as well as maintaining internal order, the army for the first time for many years exercised strict surveillance of the frontiers, patrolling borders and so preventing the casual toing and froing which the Kurds of Turkey, Iran, Iraq and Syria all used to enjoy, something which in the past had greatly helped the insurrections in the various regions of Kurdistan. Now the way was barred, so that the Kurds of Turkey found themselves virtually cut off from what was going on in other countries. The outbreak of the Iran–Iraq war in 1980 made things even worse, though before that both the Kurds of Iran and Iraq had been more concerned with what was going on in the countries in which they lived than with issues of a wider Kurdistan.

But dissent was stifled, not ended, and the lull which followed the military take-over of 1980 was short-lived. In the crack-down which followed the coup, many left-wing radicals were rounded up, particularly among the trades unions, but a considerable number managed to get away. One of those was Abdullah Ocalan, then a student in the faculty of political science in Ankara University, who had joined the so-called Ankara Democratic Patriotic Association for Higher Education, founded in 1974 to seek recognition of Kurdish culture and the Kurdish language. By 1978, when Ocalan became active, the association had spawned the PKK, a much more radical offshoot which mixed nationalism and Marxism, and had close contacts with various Turkish revolutionary groups. One of the original Turkish members of the association, Baki Karer, broke with the PKK in 1985 after seeing the violence of its methods, and has since frequently denounced Ocalan and those who still support him.

Ocalan and his closest associates went to Syria, where they had contacts among the Kurds there. They determined to continue their activities from abroad, and were soon spotted as likely material by the ever-watchful Syrian intelligence apparatus. Damascus was already playing host to a number of other Turkish extremists as a way of undermining the pro-Western Ankara government.

For four years Ocalan and his lieutenants trained and organized, welcoming activists fleeing from Turkey, extricating others who got into trouble there, and encouraging militant Kurds to join them in Syria. The Syrians themselves gave the

Kurds weapons, uniforms and enough money to keep going, trained them in techniques of guerrilla warfare, and imbued them with their own violent philosophy of war without quarter. The Syrians saw not only an opportunity to use the group against the Turks, but also against American targets in Turkey, and against Iraq. Syria was by now actively supporting Tehran in its war with Baghdad, so a new motive was added to its desire to embarrass its traditional enemy.

By 1984 the PKK was ready, and Ocalan ordered his men into action. At that time he probably had no more than 500 all told, but what they lacked in numbers they made up in ruthlessness, not only against their enemy but against any suspected of siding with the Turks. To maintain discipline within its own ranks, the PKK warned its cadres that the penalty for defection was death. One of those who was sentenced to death after leaving the movement in disgust at its excesses was the Kurdish folk-singer Shirwan Pewar. His life was spared only after the direct intervention of Massoud Barzani, head of the Iraqi KDP.

The first two PKK attacks in Turkey were in August 1984, in the villages of Eruh and Semdinli, near the Iraqi border, perhaps in a Syrian-inspired attempt to make the Turkish government believe the new insurgency was directed at them by Baghdad alone. Police stations, gendarmerie posts and military convoys were among the first targets, but the PKK quickly showed how it meant to conduct its campaign: food, shelter and all kinds of help was demanded from the people of the remote villages of the mountains in the Kurdish heartland, where Turkey, Iraq and Syria all meet. Any refusal was met with the execution of the headman, or even worse, the murder of the families of the village leaders. At other times peasants were taken prisoner, and young men were forced to join the PKK; the local *aghas* were compelled to donate money, food and weapons; and there were many cases of rape.

As the years went on, so the incidents multiplied, sometimes with pitched battles between the guerrillas and military patrols.

The insurgency became an everyday fact of life, a secret *intifada*, as some Turks called it. Government estimates of the numbers involved varied greatly, from the initial figure of no more than 500 active 'terrorists' to almost 4,000 fighters operating inside Turkey. So great was the pressure that the Turkish government was forced to negotiate two agreements with its neighbours: the first, soon after the military took over in Ankara, was officially said to permit the Turkish army the right of hot pursuit into northern Iraq, that is, empowering the Turks to cross the border if they were in contact with a rebel group, rather than having to break off an engagement at the frontier. Through secret clauses the agreement went much further than that, virtually giving the Turkish army a free hand against Kurds in northern Iraq in return for a promise of Turkish assistance if Iran should threaten either the area or the vital oil pipeline passing through Turkey from Kirkuk to the Mediterranean. An early indication of the scope of the pact came when the Turkish air force bombed rebel bases well inside Iraq, then in 1983 sent ground forces into the country without even the pretence that they were in hot pursuit of raiders.

The second agreement was with Syria; it was less ambitious than the treaty with Iraq, providing merely for improved relations, the development of trade and the exchange of information. The Turks publicly attached considerable significance to it, perhaps to persuade the Kurds that the PKK had lost important support, but Syria did little to back the Turkish line. Instead it let it be known that Abdullah Ocalan and his men had merely been required to leave Damascus, and that they were still operating from Syrian-held territory, the Bekaa valley of eastern Lebanon.

One of the most potent weapons in the hands of the Turkish government was the rivalry between the PKK and the few other Kurdish groups operating. The ruthlessness with which the PKK operated, their policy of revenge killings, not only against those who opposed them but also against those who merely failed to help, did much to alienate the local people. Foolishly, the Turkish authorities chose to ignore the potential of the divisions within opposition ranks, and instead themselves embarked on a course of total repression which at least matched the brutalities of the PKK. Typical was a round-up of PKK suspects which resulted in a mass trial in Diyarbakir of some 500 people, lasting on and off for five years. In the end, twenty-three of the defendants were sentenced to death, but, during the course of the trial, thirty-two young men had died in prison as a result of torture, hunger strikes or suicide.

Matching unnecessary violence with unreasoning repression, the PKK at its third congress vowed to 'eliminate all enemies', plainly meaning rival Kurdish groups as well as the Turkish police and military. This was soon followed by a wave of crimes across Europe, where the PKK has most of its outside representation. In Holland and Germany, Kurdish activists were killed, to be denounced – sometimes even before their assassinations – as traitors by the PKK journal, *Serxwebun* ('Independence'). So extreme did the reputation of the PKK become that they were immediately the prime suspects when Olof Palme, the Swedish prime minister, was murdered in 1986. The motive was thought to be no more than a Swedish police determination that the PKK was a terrorist organization, and that as a result a visa had been refused for Ocalan to visit the country, which has a large and growing Kurdish minority.

In 1991 Turkish secret police and intelligence agents began adopting the same methods: a number of Kurdish activists and reputed members of far-left groups were shot dead in public. Most were killed with a single bullet through the back of the head, sure sign of an 'execution' by government death squads.

The reasons for PKK success, if that is what it is, can be found in the make-up of the organization. Almost all recruits are young and from the poorest groups in society. Usually between fifteen and twenty-two, they are easily indoctrinated, and can be made fiercely loyal to their group and to its ideas and ideology.

Another factor is that, like the Israeli army, the PKK has a tradition of leading from the front: the commanders and commissars do not stay back at base camps, but go in with their men to face the Turkish army. The result is that at least five central committee members have been killed, and, according to the legends, Ocalan himself has only narrowly escaped death or capture on many occasions.

Poised uneasily between East and West, Turkey has always had to walk a careful tightrope, and during the eight years of the war between Iran and Iraq this balancing trick became even more difficult. By keeping the Iraqi oil pipeline open, indeed, protecting it, Turkey enabled Iraq to earn enough revenue to prosecute the war. To balance that, the Turks made sure that the land route into Iran was also kept open, allowing arms, munitions and other vital goods to be taken to Tehran.

In dealing with the Kurds at this time, the aim of the Turks was to keep things quiet inside their own territory, caring little what happened in neighbouring countries, unless it impinged on the eastern provinces. For years it was a policy which worked, even after 1984 when the PKK began its campaign. Punitive raids were made into Iraq following the agreement with that country, but no action was taken in Syria, which would not have permitted any cross-border incursions, or in Iran. Inside Turkey, rigorous military control, even after the army handed power back to the civilians in 1982, kept an effective lid on things and ensured that the uprising was confined to south-eastern Anatolia.

Only at the end of the Iran–Iraq war in 1988 did things get out of hand. In the panic exodus caused by Saddam Hussein's use of chemical weapons in his post-war offensive against the Iraqi Kurds, 100,000 people fled to Turkey and Iran. In Turkey there was no welcome. The army feared that among the refugees would be 'trouble-makers', activists who would organize and further politicize the Turkish Kurds if they were allowed freely into the country. The army set up refugee camps in inhospitable and remote areas, and gave only minimal co-operation to international aid agencies, or to those seeking to establish beyond doubt that the Iraqis had in fact used gas against a civilian population – Turkey had no wish to antagonize Iraq, still powerful at the end of the war. Nor did many others; Britain and the US carefully looked the other way, unwilling to offend a country they had decided was to be not only an important trading partner but also a continuing bastion against revolutionary Islam, and an addition to the moderate bloc in the Middle East.

Conditions in the camps on the Turkish border remained bad, and when Saddam announced an amnesty for Kurds wishing to go home, many did so: of those who returned, hundreds immediately disappeared. More went to Iran, either voluntarily or at Turkish instigation, and the Iranians had little choice but to accept them.

Three years later, when the Kurds of Iraq were once more forced to flee into Turkey, President Ozal had a clear concept of where his country's interests lay. As a Turkish commentator, Altemur Kilic, wrote:

The implications for Turkey of the tragedy on her borders include more than just administrative, economic and financial difficulties. The very integrity and future of Turkey depends on resolution of the problem. If one million Iraqi Kurds settle in Turkey, its balance and security will be significantly upset.

Kilic claimed that the Kurdish issue in Turkey was quite different from the Kurdish problems in Iran or Iraq, as in those countries Kurds had been given 'minority status' from time to time, while in Turkey they had always been 'part of the Turkish national mosaic'. He went on:

Any hint of Kurdish autonomy or Kurdish secession, or even the possibility of a buffer region evolving into an independent Kurdistan which might eventually incorporate parts of Turkey, is abhorrent to the Turkish government and to other Turks. This is the main reason why President Ozal has been against both the dismembering of Iraq and the creation of an independent Kurdistan or Shia state. Another equally important apprehension is that an independent Kurdistan would swallow some three million ethnic Turks of Iraq, who constitute the majority in the oil-rich Kirkuk region.

As well as trying to ingratiate his country with the Americans, Ozal wanted to ensure Turkey was well-placed in the event of a break-up of Iraq, which at times seemed quite possible. He spoke on several occasions as if he were ready to revive the Mosul question, and to seek restitution of that area to Turkey sixty years after the issue was settled by international arbitration. Equally, he was determined to position himself in such a way that if by ill-fortune a Kurdish state did emerge, then Turkey would be the one power to exercise decisive control over it.

Chapter Nine

MURDER IN VIENNA

The Vienna policemen who were called to No. 5 Linkebahngasse on the evening of 13 July 1989 found the door to the fifth-floor apartment open. The flat was in complete disorder as if a fierce struggle had taken place. In the living room at the end of the corridor, slumped in an armchair and with his shirt soaked in blood, they discovered the lifeless body of Abdolrahman Qassemlou, the leader of the KDP in Iran and the intellectual mentor of a generation of Kurdish nationalists.

On the floor beside him lay the bodies of Abdullah Ghaderi-Azar, his party's representative in Europe, and Fadhil Rassoul, a Kurdish researcher at Vienna University and a prominent journalist. All three men had been shot through the head in the manner of an execution. The door had not been forced, leading the Austrian police to conclude that the victims had known their assailants.

Dr Qassemlou had arrived in Vienna two days previously for what he hoped would be the successful conclusion of a series of secret negotiations with representatives of the Tehran regime aimed at a peaceful settlement of the Kurdish question in Iran.

As secretary-general of the KDP of Iran and the commander of its guerrilla forces, Qassemlou had been at war with the ayatollahs for a decade. The Islamic republic's campaign to suppress Kurdish separatism had begun soon after the triumph of Khomeini's revolution in 1979, pushing the Kurds into open rebellion against Tehran. From the start of the Gulf war the following year, the Iranian *peshmerga* managed to tie down as many as 200,000 Iranian government troops along the Iraq border

just as, on the other side of the frontier, the Iraqi Kurds harassed
the forces of Saddam Hussein.

Although Qassemlou had consistently called for an end to the
Iran–Iraq war, the ceasefire between the protagonists in the
summer of 1988 presented as much of a threat to his movement
as it did to the Kurds of Iraq. The Iranian Kurds were spared the
chemical weapons attacks and the forced exodus which afflicted
their Iraqi brethren, but the ending of the war nevertheless gave
Tehran an opportunity to reassert its authority in the north-
western provinces. Qassemlou, although a vigorous and successful military commander, had always preferred a peaceful solution
of the Kurdish question, and once the war was over he saw little
alternative but to negotiate. It was this moderate, conciliatory
outlook that had estranged him from the hardline People's Mujahedin, the underground Iranian opposition group with whom he
had previously co-operated under the umbrella of the National
Council of Resistance.

The middleman in the process of attempted reconciliation that
was to follow was Jalal Talabani of the Iraqi PUK, a man who
was based in Tehran and had influence with the Iranian side,
given his party's role in fighting Baghdad during the war, and
who also enjoyed a long-standing friendship with Qassemlou.
Through Talabani, the Iranians put forward the possibility of a
settlement with the rebel Kurds, a proposition which the PUK
leader put to Qassemlou at a meeting in Paris in the autumn of
1988. True to his stated principles that negotiation rather than
war was the only way to solve the Kurdish question, Qassemlou
accepted the offer and embarked on a series of meetings with
Iranian representatives in December 1988 and January 1989
under the auspices and protection of Talabani's PUK.

The first contacts took place in Vienna in the final week of
1988, with further meetings in the second half of January 1989.
On each occasion Qassemlou was accompanied by Ghaderi-Azar,
with Talabani in attendance as the man whom both sides had
agreed should be responsible for the organization and security of

the negotiations. Each encounter took place in a different location, chosen by Talabani and watched over by armed members
of his PUK. The bodyguard of the Iranian contingent, Amir
Mansour Bozorgian, who knew Vienna well, was usually in
charge of fetching food for the participants but was never
allowed out of sight of the meeting place unless he was accompanied by a PUK minder. The Iranians at the meeting came
as the representatives of the future president, Ali Akbar Hashemi
Rafsanjani, who was already effectively running day-to-day
affairs in Iran during the closing months of Ayatollah Khomeini's
life.

In the first series of talks the Iranians were represented by
Mohammed Jaafar Sahraroudi, alias 'Rahimi', and his number
two, Hadji Moustafawi. The former was an intelligence officer
in the Revolutionary Guard Corps charged with contacts with
the Iraqi Kurdish groups, second-in-command of the corps' 15th
Division in Kurdistan and a reputed expert on Kurdish affairs.
The latter was a senior government official in the information
bureau and head of the secret service in the Kurdish areas of
West Azerbaijan province. The two men arrived in Vienna on
diplomatic passports. Bozorgian, who had an Iranian service
passport, was there as Sahraroudi's bodyguard.

The Vienna talks that winter appeared to make considerable
progress. Qassemlou argued for Kurdish autonomy within a
democratic Iran, for Kurdish cultural rights and for the right of
the *peshmerga* to maintain security in the region. The Iranians
appeared to concede the principle of autonomy, so all that
remained to be settled in future negotiations were the modalities.

In the meantime the Iranians were annoyed that word of the
secret contacts had got out, and blamed the talkative and occasionally indiscreet Talabani. On these grounds they proceeded
to cut Talabani out of the negotiations, and at the beginning of
July contacted Fadhil Rassoul, an Iraqi-born Kurd, to act as the
new go-between. Rassoul protested that, as a simple academic
and journalist, he did not have the status to mediate in such an

important encounter, and proposed instead the former Algerian president, Ahmed Ben Bella, his colleague in the Arabic-language magazine *al-Hiwar*.

Both the Iranians and Ben Bella accepted the proposal, and on the eve of the July talks Qassemlou, Rassoul and the Algerian met in Vienna to discuss the arrangements. Because of the Iranian demand that the encounter should be kept totally secret, neither Talabani nor Qassemlou's closest collaborators in the KDP of Iran knew of the arrangements. The Kurds even bowed to the Iranians' demand that Ben Bella should not be allowed to attend the talks in person. As a result, unlike the talks the previous winter, the July meeting took place without any security guarantees for Qassemlou and his colleagues in the unguarded apartment of a sympathizer. Even his trusted Vienna contact, Azad, who was due to collect him at the nearby Hilton Hotel at 7.15 on the evening of 13 July, was kept in the dark about the exact nature and venue of the discussions.

On that evening the Kurdish team of Qassemlou and Ghaderi-Azar was joined by Rassoul; the Iranian side was represented, as before, by Sahraroudi and Moustafawi, with Bozorgian acting as bodyguard. The first hint among Qassemlou's associates that anything was amiss was his failure to make the 7.15 rendezvous with Azad. What Azad did not know was that at almost that precise moment, just a few hundred yards away, neighbours were alerting police to the presence of a man, bleeding heavily from a head wound, near the doorway of No. 5 Linkebahngasse. The wounded man was Sahraroudi, the Iranian negotiator, and the police arrived in time to see a second man, Bozorgian, take a package from him which was later found to contain documents and $9,000 in cash. Sahraroudi was taken to hospital for an emergency operation, Bozorgian to police headquarters, where he told investigators that he had left the meeting to buy food and had no knowledge of what had happened in the apartment.

When Sahraroudi recovered from his operation two days later, he gave an account of events to the police which they refused to make public. Leaks from the investigation, however, suggested that Sahraroudi had claimed that one or possibly two armed men had entered the apartment and opened fire. Because of his own injuries, he was unable to say what happened next.

A number of circumstantial theories arose from the Qassemlou murder: on the one hand, he and his colleagues may have been the victims of a death squad dispatched by the People's Mujahedin, angered by his decision to make a deal with Tehran, or by the Iraqis, fearful of a *rapprochement* between the ayatollahs and the rebel Kurds; alternatively Qassemlou's killers may have been working for a hardline faction within the Tehran regime, out to embarrass Rafsanjani. In this scenario it was assumed that Sahraroudi was a sincere negotiator, acting for Rafsanjani, while Moustafawi was an agent in the employ of the radical information minister and head of Iranian intelligence, Mohammad Reyshari. Another theory was that the assassinations were ordered by Rafsanjani himself, and that the negotiations had merely been designed to lure Qassemlou into a trap. The Iranians themselves promoted the theories of Iraqi or Mujahedin involvement and even suggested that dissidents within Dr Qassemlou's own movement were responsible. There had indeed been a split in the KDP of Iran between those who supported Qassemlou's moderate negotiating strategy and others who believed the armed struggle should continue in partnership with other Iranian opposition groups.

At a press conference in Tehran later that year, we asked Rafsanjani what information he could give towards identifying the killers. All the resources of the state, he told us, had been committed to solving the case. But it remained, as yet, a mystery.

The Austrians, publicly at least, were equally unable to come up with a solution to the crime. Although warrants were subsequently issued for their arrest, the Iranians had by that time left the country. No one was ever put on trial for the killings, but the overwhelming evidence pointed to Iran, although at what level the killings were ordered was never established.

The total secrecy surrounding the July meeting made it unlikely that any outside agency could have mounted the operation. Sahraroudi's injuries – he was hit in the forearm by a bullet which ricocheted into his jaw – may have been caused either by a stray bullet or else one aimed deliberately at him, as someone who was not party to the murder plot.

Moustafawi disappeared on the evening of 13 July, and Bozorgian fled into the Iranian embassy as soon as he was released from police custody within twenty-four hours of the killings. Moustafawi was never located. Bozorgian was allowed to return home in exchange for leaving the embassy to give further evidence. Sahraroudi was discharged from hospital on 22 July and returned directly to Tehran.

Kurdish sources alleged that the Austrian authorities were less than diligent in their pursuit of the killers, as a result of threats by the Iranians to seize Austrian hostages or attack Austrian interests in the Middle East. At the time the government in Vienna was also facing embarrasing courtroom revelations about the Noricom affair, in which senior officials and employees of the state armaments company were accused of supplying arms to the Gulf war combatants.

Within hours of the killing the Vienna police had discovered a blood-stained anorak in a station dustbin, along with three weapons used in the murders – an Uzi sub-machine gun and two pistols fitted with silencers. They also found the sales invoice for a Suzuki motorcycle, the purchaser of which was later identified as Sahraroudi. The Suzuki may have been used by the killers or as a getaway vehicle for Moustafawi, although he was later identified as the passenger of a taxi which he hired to take him to Vienna airport before diverting to the Iranian embassy.

On 28 July Kurdish demonstrators gathered at the airport to protest against the departure of a fourth man believed to be implicated in the assassination plot. He was identified as Magaby, or Mozafar, a frequent companion of the three Iranians in the days before the 13 July meeting. The Austrian police had been tipped off about Magaby and, indeed, had picked him up for interrogation. He was held for forty-eight hours before being put on the flight to Tehran.

Dr Qassemlou had broken all the rules in his quest for peace with Tehran. In what must have been a calculated risk, he put his faith in the sincerity of those who for a decade had sought his annihilation in order to establish a basis of trust with his former enemies. Perhaps he should have pondered the fate of Simko, the great Iranian Kurdish war-lord of the 1920s, of whom he had written: 'On the 21st of June 1930, Simko was invited to attend negotiations with the Iranian military at Ushnu, where he was assassinated.'

Qassemlou was a unique figure in the Kurdish national movement. He spoke eight Middle Eastern and European languages; he taught Kurdish and economics at the universities of Paris and Prague, he led armed uprisings against both the shah and Khomeini at the same time as preaching a peaceful solution of the Kurdish question. He denounced terrorism at every opportunity and conceded that: 'They don't speak enough about the Kurds, because we have never taken any hostages, never hijacked a plane. But I am proud of this.'

He was a fervent nationalist who combined political pragmatism towards his enemies with a chronic annoyance with his Kurdish allies, because their failure to unite weakened the nationalist movement. Looking back on the defeat of the Kurdish insurrection in Iraq in the early 1970s, he wrote: 'The sad end of the movement led by Barzani in Iraq shows how dangerous and even tragic it is to adopt Machiavellism as one's political credo and to sacrifice the very principles of national liberation for ephemeral tactical advantages.'

Qassemlou was born into a landowning family near the Iranian town of Orumiyeh in 1930 and was still a schoolboy during the brief and turbulent Mahabad Republic which ended with the execution of Qazi Mohammed in 1947. He moved to Iraq, and then to Prague and Paris, before returning to Iranian Kurdistan to take part in, and eventually to lead, the fight for autonomy against Tehran.

The struggle for Kurdish national rights in Iran was intimately linked with a similar struggle in neighbouring Iraq, but the constant competition between the two countries for regional supremacy led each one to seek temporary allies among the dissident Kurdish communities on the other's side of the border. Just as in the sixteenth century Kurds had fought each other on behalf of the rival Ottoman and Persian empires, so in the 1980s they took opposite sides in the war between Iraq and Iran. It was not a situation which pleased Dr Qassemlou, who frequently spoke out against the stupidity of the Gulf war. Nevertheless he accepted Iraqi help in order to maintain his rebellion against Khomeini even as the war was going on.

As leader of the KDP of Iran, Qassemlou inherited the leadership of a Kurdish nationalist movement which had grown up outside the former borders of the Ottoman empire. The battle of Chaldiran in 1514 had led to a division of Kurdistan between the Ottoman and Persian empires which was formalized in 1639 in a treaty between Shah Abbas and Sultan Murad. As in Ottoman Kurdistan, local princes retained their autonomous rights over the region until the centralizing policies of the nineteenth century brought their territories under government control. The attempts of the shah's officials to bring the Kurds into line provoked a number of rebellions, as did similar attempts by the Ottomans, culminating in Sheikh Ubaidullah's revolt, the first rebellion aimed towards the unification and independence of Kurdistan.

World War I and the break-up of the Ottoman empire had repercussions in Iranian Kurdistan, where Simko, the chief of the Shikak tribe, launched his revolt in 1920 and captured the whole of Iranian Kurdistan east of Orumiyeh in pursuit of his demands for an independent state.

The war brought massacre and devastation to Iranian Kurdistan and in particular to the area around Orumiyeh. Russia occupied the surrounding region in 1912, and Orumiyeh itself in

1915 after major Russian–Ottoman encounters in the first year of the war. Both sides then set about wooing the tribes, both Kurdish and Christian, in an attempt to win local allies. The Christians were divided into the impoverished serfs of Kurdish feudal lords and independent warrior tribesmen who competed with their Kurdish neighbours for local supremacy – both of which were relationships which fed the constant antagonism and conflict between the two communities.

The Assyrian patriarch Mar Shimoun Benjamin, who gloried in the title of Patriarch of the Orient and India, received emissaries from both Petrograd and Constantinople, and, despite better terms from the Ottomans, opted to give his support to Tsarist Russia. On 10 May 1915 he formally declared war on the Ottoman empire and ordered a general mobilization of Christian forces, but the Russians failed to live up to their promises to send supplies and reinforcements to their Christian allies, and the Assyrians were soon under attack by Ottoman and Kurdish forces.

The Russian revolution of 1917 prompted a withdrawal of Russian forces from the Ottoman front, so that there was an urgent need among the remaining allies to raise local forces to prevent the advance of the Turks into Mesopotamia. The French, the British and the White Russians, who were all competing for influence over the local minorites, nominated the Assyrians to hold the Orumiyeh region. The harsh occupation of the Russians, which had alienated the local Muslim population and created ill-feeling against all Christians, was nothing compared to the reign of terror instituted by the local Christians, above all the Nestorian tribes known in Iran as the Jelos. The Christian levies were nominally under the command of White Russian officers, but in practice they acted as they liked, unrestrained by Mar Shimoun and increasingly under the control of a former confidence-trickster Agha Petros, who had once been gaoled in Canada for fraud before moving to Rome, where he received a Vatican medal for services to Catholicism. This unlikely war-lord supervised the creation of bloodthirsty tribal militias which spent most of their time pillaging the villages of the Muslim Kurds and Azeris, while some Christians who had emigrated to the United States took advantage of the situation to return and settle old scores with their former Muslim neighbours. To add to the chaos, famine and epidemics spread to Orumiyeh, where starving bands of Kurdish refugees came to seek some protection from their Christian oppressors.

In February 1918 the Muslim population of the town took the disastrous decision to go on the offensive against the Christians, who had set up four Russian-manned artillery pieces on the outskirts. When the Muslim forces attacked, thousands of Christian tribesmen abandoned their depredations in the surrounding countryside and flocked to the town, where they easily overcame the Muslim resistance. Although a ceasefire was arranged by the allies, the Christians entered the town and slaughtered men, women and children where they stood.

Although the Kurds had suffered at the hands of the Christians, the principal targets of the Jelos militias were Persians and Azerbaijanis. The Kurds generally took advantage of the reign of disorder to steal what the Christians had overlooked. Simko, who seemed inclined to accept the persuasion of the British to join the allied cause, even expressed sympathy for the Assyrians and sought a pact with them.

Mar Shimoun, whose supremacy was under threat from Agha Petros, decided to accept Simko's invitation to discuss an Assyrian–Kurdish alliance against the Ottomans. He travelled to Simko's headquarters with an escort of fifty horsemen, and during a welcoming feast reached agreement with the Kurdish chief over future co-operation. Then, as the feast ended, two of Simko's men opened fire, killing the patriarch and most of his bodyguards.

The motives for Simko's treachery remain unclear, though it was known that he carried out the assassination at the behest of the Persian authorities at Tabriz, where there wash general rejoicing at the news of Mar Shimoun's death. As a result, money and volunteers were raised in the city on behalf of Simko, and he may actually have been paid in advance to commit the murder. But it achieved no other positive results. Rather, it provoked an immediate anti-Kurdish pogrom in Orumiyeh, where the Christians slaughtered 500 refugees. Agha Petros set off at the head of two Christian columns in pursuit of Simko and almost succeeded in capturing him. To compensate for failing to trap the chief, the Christians burned Kurdish villages and slaughtered their inhabitants.

The allied consuls based at Orumiyeh often complained of having to take responsibility for the excesses of their Christian allies, despite the considerable success of the latter in combating the Ottoman forces. The Turks nevertheless advanced into Persian territory, encircling Orumiyeh. The Christians attacked the Ottoman forces on 12 June in the hope of joining up with Armenian forces heading south towards Persian territory, but a week later their offensive crumbled in the face of a detachment of Ottoman Kurdish cavalry near Salmas. On 18 July the Ottoman forces entered Orumiyeh, and the Christians in the city fled to the safety of the British lines at Hamadan, but not before many had been massacred by their Muslim fellow citizens. Those who escaped without food or supplies ran the gauntlet of Kurdish tribes through whose territory they passed. Of 80,000 refugees who left Orumiyeh that summer, only 60,000 reached Hamadan. It was the end of the Christian domination of the area.

After the war was over, Simko organized the Kurdish tribes for the abortive attempt to create an independent Kurdistan which ended with his assassination.

The events in wartime Orumiyeh show that tribalism and brigandage were far from being the exclusive preserve of the Kurds; they were but one community seeking to stake its claim in a hostile and disorderly frontier environment, and they were as often as not the victims as much as the oppressors of their neighbours. They were also the victims of religious antagonisms fanned by outside powers which hoped to dominate the area themselves.

After Simko's death, tribal revolts continued in the far north-west, inspired by the Kurdish uprisings in neighbouring Turkey and Iraq. Unable to subdue the rebels by force, Reza Shah entered into negotiations with them and finally reached an agreement under which the Kurds would lay down their arms. The day they did so, Kurdish bases were bombed by the Iranian air force.

Reza Shah saw his role as one of centralizing control in Iran and creating a modern state from the decayed ruins of an empire which had changed little since the Middle Ages and which was constantly threatened by the machinations of outside powers. This modernizing trend met its nemesis with Reza Shah's son, Mohammad Pahlavi, whose headlong rush to turn Iran into a Westernized, though autocratic, world power provoked the resentment of the conservative, religious forces which were to join in unseating him.

The policies of both men involved the suppression of tribalism, and not just of Kurdish tribalism. Unlike modern Turkey or Iraq, Iran is a multinational rather than a bi-national state. The Persians are outnumbered by the combined total of other ethnic groups – Kurds, Azerbaijanis, Arabs, Baluchis and Turkomans. All except the Azerbaijanis were tribally based communities, and even among the Persians there were important nomadic and semi-nomadic tribes who were often prepared to rise against the central authority in order to preserve their tribal rights.

One of the tactics of the Pahlavi shahs in building their modern state was therefore to try to eliminate these ethnic and cultural distinctions, and to assert the Persian character of the Iranian state.

After the fall of the Mahabad Republic, the monarchy instituted a regime of repression in Kurdistan that was to last almost unbroken until the Islamic revolution, with only the brief interlude of the Mossadeq government in the 1950s, during which it seemed that democracy might be achieved. In a national referendum in 1953, in which Iranians were allowed to vote on limiting the shah's powers, only two people out of 5,000 voters in Mahabad were in favour of the monarchy.

Even after Mossadeq was deposed in a CIA-organized coup, pockets of resistance continued to exist in Kurdistan. The Juanro tribe, based in the inaccessible mountains north of Kermanshah, near the Iraq border, continued to hold out against the Iranian military well into the 1950s. The Juanro, like many Kurdish insurgents before and since, eventually fell victim to one of those occasional periods of co-operation among the states of the region. In February 1955 Iran, Iraq, Turkey and Pakistan formed the Baghdad Pact, an alliance sponsored by Britain – which later joined in itself – as a defence against communist penetration in the Middle East. A year later, confident of the backing of his new allies, the shah launched an all-out offensive, using tanks and planes to subdue the Juanro. Thousands of Kurds were killed or wounded, the tribe was forced to flee its villages and move to the mountains, and its stronghold, the Juanro fortress, was reduced to rubble.

The Iraqi revolution of 1958 killed off both the Baghdad Pact and the era of co-operation between Tehran and Baghdad. With its promises of emancipation for the Kurds of Iraq, it also served as an inspiration to the Kurds of Iran, so that there was a consequent growth in nationalist activity to which the shah again responded with repression. The region was heavily militarized and put under tight surveillance by the shah's secret police, Savak, and the movement of Kurds from village to village was restricted. Kurdish was forbidden as the language of study, and schoolchildren were forced to learn Persian as part of the shah's attempts to deny the separate identity of the Kurds.

The process of detribalization had begun under the shah's father, who forcibly settled the nomads and deported whole tribes to other parts of Iran to be replaced by Persians and Azerbaijanis – policies also adopted in Iraq and Turkey. The international frontiers, which in many cases divided individual tribes, were closely guarded to end the traditional pattern of tribal movement. The result was that, by the second half of the twentieth century, the nomadic and semi-nomadic life-style of many Iranian Kurds was all but extinct.

Despite the repression and the attempts to undermine the structures of Kurdish society, the monarchy never succeeded in eradicating the nationalist aspirations of the Kurds. When the Iraqi Kurds launched their insurrection against the Qassem regime in 1961, many Iranian Kurds crossed the border to join the ranks of Barzani's *peshmerga*, and many more helped to smuggle supplies of food and ammunition into Iraqi Kurdistan.

These gestures of solidarity were not reciprocated. As Barzani fell deeper under the patronage and influence of the shah, he was obliged to bow to Iranian pressure to restrain the activities of the Iranian Kurds. The Iraqi Kurds persuaded the nationalist movement as a whole to put a freeze on all activities by the KDP of Iran, given the importance of ensuring the success of the rebellion in Iraqi Kurdistan. Henceforward any serious hostile act against the shah was to be considered an attack on the Kurdish revolution. The shah's policy of supporting the Iraqi Kurds was designed, in part, to neutralize the Kurds in his own country; by threatening to withdraw aid to Barzani if rebel activity continued within Iran, he temporarily succeeded in this aim.

Some KDP of Iran militants refused to accept the ruling and returned from exile in Iraq to organize a new peasant-based uprising in the winter of 1967 which was to last for eighteen months. With no outside bases – Kurdish-controlled areas of Iraq were barred to them – the rebellion had little hope of success. The leaders were either killed in battle or rounded up by Barzani's men and handed over to the Iranians.

The Pahlavi dynasty came to an end at the beginning of 1979, after a year of popular unrest and street demonstrations which the repressive organs of the state were unable to contain. The demonstrators marched under the banner of Islam, inspired by the exhortations of Ayatollah Khomeini, smuggled on tape from abroad, to overthrow the corrupt regime. But many who took part in the unrest of 1978 were left-wingers and liberals who saw the movement as a progressive and fundamentally secular uprising against an autocratic monarch. Qassemlou and the KDP of Iran were very much part of this secular camp, and the Kurdish population as a whole, although devout, saw little attraction in Khomeini's plans for Islamic government, given that he was a Shia and they were predominantly Sunni.

The Kurds, like other ethnic minorities, nevertheless saw the revolutionary movement as an opportunity for securing the autonomy which had been denied to them under the shah. Qassemlou returned to Kurdistan from exile in France five months before the February revolution and began organizing party cells throughout the provinces of Kurdistan, West Azerbaijan and Kermanshah. During the closing stage of the uprising, in which predominantly leftist guerrilla groups in Tehran seized the capital from the armed forces, troops and officers based at Mahabad declared for the revolution, and Qassemlou's followers captured large quantities of arms from garrisons and police posts in the north. The whole of the north-west was soon under the control of the *peshmerga*, with day-to-day administration run, as elsewhere in the country, by revolutionary committees.

The KDP of Iran met in Mahabad on 3 March and, before a crowd of 200,000 in the square where the leaders of the Mahabad Republic had been executed in 1947, it declared its own legalization after more than three decades underground. The party resolved to obtain Tehran's recognition of the de facto Kurdish autonomy which already existed in the region since the fall of the shah. The first formal contact with the provisional government of Khomeini's prime minister, Mehdi Bazargan, came in the first days of the new regime when a delegation travelled up from Tehran to Mahabad to listen to the Kurds' demands for 'Kurdish autonomy within a democratic Iran'.

It was soon apparent that the new regime was not going to be any more willing than its predecessor to recognize minority rights. At a meeting in Qom on 28 March, three days before a referendum which formally abolished the monarchy and established an Islamic republic, Khomeini told a Kurdish delegation, headed by the Kurdish spiritual leader Sheikh Ezzedin Hussein, that the demand for autonomy was unacceptable. 'I want calm in Kurdistan. No problems,' he told Sheikh Ezzedin, to which the Kurd replied, 'I want autonomy.' The two men stood up and Khomeini grasped the Kurd by the collar of his robe and angrily repeated that he wanted no problems in Kurdistan, to which Sheikh Ezzedin replied, 'I want autonomy.'

In Kurdistan more than three quarters of the electorate boycotted the referendum. Left-wing and liberal groups, although not the People's Mujahedin, joined the Kurds in supporting the boycott, on the grounds that the referendum left no option for the creation of a secular democratic state.

The autonomy demands of the Kurds also had an influence on the other ethnic minorities, and in the early months of the revolution the Arabs, Baluchis, Turkomans and Azerbaijanis all began campaigning for their national rights. Khomeini, intent on holding post-revolutionary Iran together, replied to those such as Qassemlou who sought autonomy that in the Islamic republic all were equal and all Muslims were brothers, so that there was no need for any special status for the minorities.

As the first summer of the revolution progressed, more and more of the regime's forces were dispatched from the Persian heartland to put down unrest in the provinces. The first trouble broke out in Kurdistan on 18 and 19 March, involving violent clashes between the *peshmerga* and forces loyal to Khomeini. Ayatollah Mahmud Taleghani, the religious mentor of the People's Mujahedin and a frequent mediator in the disputes which erupted in the first months of the revolution, was dispatched north to arrange a ceasefire. He reached agreement with the Kurds by promising that the regime would grant autonomous status to the ethnic minorities.

A month later, however, in the Kurdish town of Naghadeh, the regime showed its true colours. On 20 April the KDP of Iran organized a mass demonstration at which shooting broke out, and the town erupted in a battle in which the Kurds fought the local Azeri forces, while both sides opposed the intervention of an army unit sent in from Orumiyeh. The fighting spread to neighbouring towns and villages such as Paveh, Saqqez and Maha-bad, and lasted throughout the summer.

While Ayatollah Taleghani and a number of political leaders continued to hold out the prospect of autonomy, a campaign was launched to portray the Kurds as counter-revolutionaries, enemies of Islam and the agents of communism, Zionism and imperialism. On 17 August Khomeini declared a holy war against the Kurdish insurgents, and the forces of the former shah's army were sent north to suppress the rebellion. It was an all-out offensive involving tanks and planes, and the ferocity of the attack took the Kurdish movement by surprise. By 5 September the regime's forces had succeeded in occupying the main towns of Kurdistan, which the Kurdish movement had held and administered since the triumph of the revolution. Qassemlou and his *peshmerga* once more headed for the mountains.

Commanding the regime's forces was Colonel Seyyed Shirazi, one of many military leaders over the years to earn the epithet 'The Butcher of Kurdistan', who was promoted to commander of ground forces in recognition of his victory over the Kurds. It was a victory won at the cost of villages destroyed, towns shelled and bombed to rubble, and hundreds killed.

Travelling in the rearguard of Shirazi's advancing army came Hojatoleslam Sadeq Khalkhali, the head of Khomeini's Islamic tribunals. He proceeded to reimpose Tehran's authority on the recalcitrant Kurds with a brutality which would have impressed the shah. Within a few days he sentenced 200 people to death in the conquered towns of Kurdistan. Many were lined up in groups and summarily shot with assault rifles by the Revolutionary Guards who accompanied him. The executions were carried out after the briefest of trials; suspects would be brought to Khal-khali, and, after one or two questions and on the basis of no more than his personal whim, he would declare them guilty or inno-cent. Nothing was done to disguise the nature of the repression in Kurdistan. Foreign journalists were allowed into the region, and the Tehran press carried daily photographs of the summary executions, grainy pictures of men in blindfolds wearing Kurdish national dress, awaiting death at the hands of the Revolutionary Guard firing squads.

As the military campaign headed into winter, Tehran sought a respite and, after the appointment by Khomeini of a four-man ministerial committee to seek a negotiated settlement of the crisis, the Kurdish leaders announced a ceasefire on 3 November. The following day pro-clergy radicals seized the US embassy in Tehran and took its diplomatic staff hostage, an event which was to dominate international coverage of events in Iran for months to come, and which took attention away from the plight of the Kurds. The secular-led government fell and was replaced by a Revolutionary Council dominated by the hardline clergy. The following month the Soviet intervention in neighbouring Afghanistan presented the world with yet another grave crisis in the region. The Kurdish problem, which early in the year had threatened to tear apart post-revolutionary Iran, was all but for-gotten.

Under the terms of the ceasefire the *peshmerga* began returning to the towns of Kurdistan to resume their control, but isolated clashes continued through the winter. The continuing unrest allowed the regime to postpone parliamentary elections in the region.

In elections to the constituent assembly in 1979, Qassemlou had been overwhelmingly elected to represent Kurdistan, but he declined to come to Tehran out of obvious concern that he would not be allowed to leave again. On hearing this, Khomeini declared: 'What a shame. We could have had him arrested and shot.'

In the spring of 1980 the newly elected president, Abolhassan Bani-Sadr, once more decided to resolve the problem by force, and in April he ordered a new offensive against the Kurds. Sanandaj was besieged by four divisions and attacked by land and air over a period of twenty-five days. Saqqez, Baneh and Marivan were also attacked and subdued, and Mahabad was shelled for two weeks, even though the *peshmerga* had already left the city.

Given the tensions arising from the American hostage crisis and a general paranoia within the regime about foreign-inspired plots to unseat it, Bani-Sadr's worries about the continuing unrest in the north-west had some justification. There had been a revolt in Tabriz among Azerbaijani followers of Ayatollah Kazem Shariat-Madari, who opposed Khomeini's constitutional plans, and tensions were growing with neighbouring Iraq, where Iranian royalist exiles had based themselves to launch an intended counter-revolution. Bani-Sadr's fears appeared to be borne out in June when a plot was uncovered at the army base of Piranshahr in Kurdistan. Several hundred officers and other ranks were arrested and a number executed, while some 200 were spared a similar fate when they were rescued by Qassemlou's *peshmerga*.

The events in Iranian Kurdistan had a considerable impact on Saddam Hussein's policy towards Iran. He was content enough to see Iran weakened by the revolution, its army reduced from its former glory by internal dissent and purges, but he was alarmed at the unrest on the Iranian side of the border and the possibility of Qassemlou's *peshmerga* joining up with his own Kurdish rebels. At least the shah had stuck to his 1975 commitment to preserve security along the frontier; now, however, Khomeini's regime appeared incapable of holding down the Kurds. One of his motives in deciding to go to war in September 1980 – aside from an opportunistic desire to wipe away the ignominy of the 1975 Algiers treaty – was to protect his Kurdish flank. As the war progressed, he adopted the policy of supporting Qassemlou's movement, a tactic which kept the Kurdish movement divided, given Iran's support for Barzani in Iraq.

The war gave the Iranian Kurds the opportunity to reassert control, at least over the countryside, and to pin down large numbers of Iranian forces which would otherwise have been available to fight on the southern front. After 1984 Qassemlou's 12,000 *peshmerga* reverted to hit-and-run guerrilla tactics, avoiding the head-on confrontations in which they had suffered heavy casualties in the first years of the war. The region became increasingly difficult to hold once Iran had ousted the occupying Iraqi forces from its territory in 1982, and Kurdistan became a focus for operations in the next stage of the Iran–Iraq war. But the *peshmerga* were still capable of taking towns almost at will, although not of holding them for any length of time: Mahabad was attacked in 1982, Baneh in 1985. Based for the most part in the caves and valleys of the inaccessible no man's land along the border, the *peshmerga* would move down at night into the towns and villages which, by day, were controlled by Khomeini's Revolutionary Guards. Tens of thousands of Iranian conscripts, dispatched to the border in the belief they would be fighting the Iraqis, ended up the victims of *peshmerga* raiding parties. Up to 1986 the KDP estimated its own side had lost 3,000 *peshmerga* in the war.

But the KDP of Iran was not the only movement active in the north-west. Members of the now outlawed People's Mujahedin, with whom Qassemlou was allied until 1985, sought refuge in Kurdistan in order to continue their struggle against Khomeini. In addition there was the Komala, the Kurdish Marxist organization active within KDP territory which preached self-reliance and denounced both the policies espoused by its Kurdish rivals and the pragmatic alliances into which they had entered. The split led to open conflict between the two parties, and, at a time when they might have united in their shared opposition to the Tehran regime, the KDP and the Komala became engaged in an all-out war for local supremacy until an uneasy truce was established in the mid-1980s.

By early 1988 it was clear to the Kurds of Iran, just as it was

to those of Iraq, that the war was destined to end, probably in a
stalemate, and that the Kurdish populations of both countries
would be the first to suffer. At its eighth congress in January the
KDP of Iran gallantly adopted a resolution condemning the war
and calling for acceptance of UN Security Council Resolution
598 in the certain knowledge that the sudden ending of the eight-
year conflict would pose grave problems for its own position in
Kurdistan.

It was the ending of the war and the subsequent Iranian
counter-offensive in Kurdistan that pushed Qassemlou towards
the path of negotiation and ultimately to his death. In the months
after the ceasefire the Tehran regime ordered a wave of executions, including those of political prisoners serving gaol terms, as
an act of revenge against the People's Mujahedin, which had
staged an abortive invasion of western Iran at the end of the
war. Kurdish militants, although they had opposed the Mujahedin invasion, inevitably fell victim to the general repression.

With the assassination of Qassemlou, the Kurdish movement
lost one of its most moderate and eloquent spokesmen. He was a
proven democrat and one of the few Kurdish leaders at ease in
the outside world. For all that, he was relatively little known on
the international stage, and his persistent pleas for moderation
and his visceral opposition to any form of terrorism attracted
little of the attention enjoyed by leaders of other national liberation movements who espoused more ruthless means to publicize
their cause. It was an irony which he himself recognized. 'By
taking hostages and placing bombs, any tiny group can gain
notoriety, while liberation groups which do not practise terrorism
are ignored,' he once said. In his youth he had been a communist,
but he broke definitively with the party and with the Eastern
bloc in 1968 when he spoke out in support of Alexander Dubček's
short-lived Prague Spring. The Soviet intervention forced him to
leave Czechoslovakia for a new exile in France.

His political philosophy with regard to the Kurdish question
was based on relying upon armed struggle where no other means

were available, but to seek, whenever possible, peaceful negotiations with the central power, leading to autonomy within existing national borders.

Soon after the death of Khomeini on 3 June 1989, and a month before his own death, Qassemlou expressed cautious optimism that the Ayatollah's successors might prove more conciliatory in their approach to the Kurdish problem, though he saw little hope of the early downfall of the regime in the absence of any real organized opposition. He spoke for the majority of Iranians, not only Kurds, when he said, 'They are neither for a monarchy nor the Islamic republic. They want a republic with democratic institutions. They want peace and security.'

It was during the Iran–Iraq war that there were simultaneous uprisings among the Kurds of Iraq, Iran and Turkey, an upsurge in the armed struggle which helped to revive the notion of a Kurdish national identity among Kurds throughout the Middle East and in the diaspora. But there were two states with Kurdish populations where political circumstances and the relative weakness of the national movement made it impossible for the community to rise up – Syria and the Soviet Union.

Kurds probably make up about one in ten of Syria's seven and a half million population, although reliable statistics are hard to come by in President Hafez al-Assad's tightly controlled Baathist state. Of these perhaps a third live in the capital, Damascus, with the remainder divided between the Kurd Dagh and the Jezireh. A smaller Kurdish enclave exists in the Ain-Arab region, north-east of Aleppo.

The Kurd Dagh, the westernmost part of Kurdistan, with a climate temperate enough to grow olives, was a Kurdish stronghold from medieval times. A rich agricultural land overlooking Antioch and close to the Mediterranean, it was the most important region of medieval Kurdistan. From there Kurdish lords held sway over their Arab vassals. It was a period in which Saladin and his Kurdish generals controlled the destiny of the Muslim population of the Levant in the struggle to oust the Christian crusaders.

The Jezireh was an area traditionally shared by Kurds living in settled villages and nomadic Arab tribes; there were also semi-nomadic Kurdish tribes who wintered their flocks there. After the defeat of the Kurdish rebellions in Turkey, other Kurds moved there in the 1920s and helped to turn the area into an important grain-growing region, its green fields rising into the uplands after the sparse scrubland west of the Euphrates.

Although these three areas constitute an integral part of Kurdistan, they are divided from each other by Arab territory. They are in fact an extension of Turkish Kurdistan, although the people of the Jezireh also have close affinities with the Kurds of the Sinjar region of Iraqi Kurdistan. The post-World War I map-makers took little interest in the ethnic make-up of the Levant when they drew the border between the new state of Turkey and French-mandated Syria. Under the terms of the 1921 London Agreement, the three Kurdish enclaves went to Syria, while a number of Arab communities found themselves on the Turkish side of the border.

In the first decades of post-independence Syria, the Kurds were treated with some tolerance and were accorded a measure of cultural freedom in the predominantly Arab state. In 1957 the KDP of Syria was formed on the lines of the Iraqi KDP, but it was an organization of intellectuals dedicated to the wider democratic movement within Syria and posed no threat to the state.

With the rise of Arab nationalism in the region and even before the coming to power, in both Syria and Iraq, of chauvinistic Baathist regimes, the Kurds became a target of state repression. From 1961 it was the rebellion of the Iraqi Kurds, which was regarded in Arab nationalist terms as an attack on Arabism, which was the source and justification of this shift in policy. The Kurds of Syria came to be seen as a potential fifth column whose loyalties lay with their fellow Kurds in Iraq who were attacking a brother Arab state. In the Jezireh 120,000 Kurds were summarily declared to be non-Syrians and were stripped of their citizen's rights.

The situation worsened after 1963 with the coming to power of the Baath Party of Michel Aflaq, an extreme nationalist and the ideological mentor of Saddam Hussein. The Kurdish writer Mustafa Nazdar quotes a report of the time by the Jezireh police chief Mohamed Talab Hilal, in which he seeks to undermine the status of the Kurds within the Syrian state. Hilal argued that the Kurds did not constitute a nation and that 'the Kurdish people are a people without history or civilization or language or even definite ethnic origin of their own. Their only characteristics are those shaped by force, destructive power and violence, characteristics which are, by the way, inherent in all mountain populations.'

Previous governments had already proposed the expulsion of the Kurds from the Turkish border areas. Hilal now put forward a plan not only to disperse them but also to deprive them of education and employment. They were to be displaced by armed Arab settlers grouped in state-run collective farms. Although the Kurds were spared some of the worst elements of the Hilal programme by the intervention of the 1967 war with Israel, the Arabization programme went ahead and continued until 1976 with the construction of model farms and model villages inhabited by Arab immigrants from west of the Euphrates. Kurdish culture was banned, and Kurdish towns were given Arab names.

Despite these measures, the Jezireh and its capital, Qamishli, remain unmistakably Kurdish in character. The Syrian Kurds were spared from total dispersal and annihilation by the pragmatism and *realpolitik* of the Baathist regime. After the split between the Syrian and the Iraqi Baath in 1968, the Syrians had no reason to assist their rivals in Iraq in putting down the Kurds. In 1963 the Syrian Baath had sent planes and troops to help the first Iraqi Baathist regime combat Barzani's insurgency; in later years, however, Assad actively supported the Iraqi Kurds against Baghdad.

A second motive for Assad's relatively benign approach towards the Kurds was that, as a member of the Alawite sect, he himself came from a minority within predominantly Sunni Syria. By the early 1980s the main challenge to his secular regime came from the Sunni Muslim Brotherhood. It was a challenge which he put down with the utmost brutality, culminating in the destruction of the city of Hama in February 1983. At the same time he instituted a policy of relative tolerance towards the minorities, including the Kurds; although they were also Sunni, they had no affinity with the Arab-based Brotherhood. Within the limitations of the severe control which touched all members of Syrian society, the Kurds were allowed to live their own lives.

This did not prevent a serious outbreak of unrest in 1986 after Syria signed a number of co-operation accords with Turkey, which had already begun its guerrilla war against the PKK. These arrangements included a border security agreement which threatened to restrict significantly the relative freedom of Syria's Kurds.

On 21 March, the Kurdish new year festival of Newruz, 4,000 Kurds assembled in the Ghotah district of Damascus for annual celebrations which had, until then, been tolerated by the regime. They were told, however, that this year the celebrations had been banned and were ordered to disperse. This led to clashes in which the security forces opened fire, killing one person and injuring several others. A Kurdish delegation which asked to see the president was beaten up and a hundred people were held. Similar incidents occurred at Afrin, north of Aleppo, where eight people were killed, and at Qamishli, where the bazaar shut down as a protest at the killings.

Five years later to the day, there were armed Kurds on the streets of Qamishli, discreetly patrolling under the watchful eye of the Syrian Mukhabarat. They were not Syrian Kurds but Iraqis, members of the KDP and PUK, exercising a right to bear arms which was denied to their Syrian counterparts. For, across the border in Iraq, the Kurdish revolt against Saddam Hussein was at its height, and the ever-pragmatic Assad had decided to support the insurgents against his Arab rival. The aid was limited: Assad allowed the Kurds to use a river crossing-point to ferry supplies to the Iraqi side and permitted wounded *peshmerga* to be evacuated in the opposite direction. Guerrilla commanders were allowed across to assess the military situation from the Syrian shore and to discuss tactics with Syrian commanders. But the aid was never sufficient to permit the Kurds to sustain their rebellion and to defeat Saddam. Instead, once again, they found themselves being used as cat's-paws in the rivalry between neighbouring states.

One of the most moving moments for Kurds who attended a Paris conference in October 1989 on Kurdish human rights was a speech by Nadir Nadirov, a representative of a community which had been cut off from its roots for seven decades – that of the Soviet Kurds. Nadirov, speaking in Kurdish, described how in 1932 he was deported from Armenia with his widowed mother and her nine children to the central Asian republic of Kazakhstan as part of Stalin's campaign to split the Kurdish and other ethnic minorities. Stalin feared the presence of the Muslim Kurds so near to the sensitive southern borders of the Soviet Union so much that he had them dispersed among nine Soviet republics, and to areas thousands of miles from their traditional homes.

The journey of the Nadirov family took one and a half months. For the next twenty years they were restricted to their Kazakh village, where Nadir finished his schooling, banned from travelling even to the next settlement. Frustrated at not being able to continue his studies in that isolated backwater, Nadirov took the bold step of writing directly to Stalin to appeal for his help. As a result he was allowed to move to Moscow to complete his education and was later appointed to the Academy of Sciences at Alma-Ata in central Asia.

Nadirov's visit to Paris was a small but significant element of the *glasnost* policies of the 1980s. It enabled other Kurds to learn about the fate of this forgotten community and also to hear from Nadirov that it was much larger than had previously been thought. Under Soviet rule, statistics on the Kurdish population had varied wildly from census to census. The general belief was that they probably numbered around 300,000. Nadirov revealed, however, that latest figures showed the population to be more than a million, as large as the Kurdish minority in Syria.

The fate of the Soviet Kurds varied according to the vagaries of Soviet nationality policy. Sometimes Kurdish culture and institutions were banned, at other times they were encouraged. Many had lost their language and traditions, while others, such as the Nadirov family, had preserved their way of life in exile.

The Kurds of the Soviet Union are not a homogeneous unit. Some are descended from tribes who moved into Armenia and the Caucasus from the eighteenth century onwards, either as nomadic herdsmen or as mercenaries in the Russian–Ottoman wars. Others were descended from Kurdish tribes which had been transferred to the north-eastern fringes of the Persian empire to defend its frontiers. Others still were Yazidis, who had fled to the safety of Tsarist Russia to escape persecution by their Muslim neighbours, both Kurds and non-Kurds. After the Russian revolution an Autonomous Republic of Kurdistan was set up, but the rivalry of more powerful local minorities led to its assimilation.

During a visit to the Soviet Union in the 1970s, the Kurdish historian Kendal Nezar discovered that many Kurds still jealously preserved their national identity and closely followed events in other parts of Kurdistan. He saw portraits of Mullah Mustafa Barzani in many homes, including those of Communist Party members.

Such expressions of nationalist feeling were tolerated by the state. But even under Mikhail Gorbachev the scattered Kurdish communities were not allowed to return home from exile to gather in a single territory which they could call their own.

Chapter Ten

THE TRIBE AND THE NATION

The Kurds are a disputatious people, and both their ancient and modern history demonstrates the truth that unity is strength – 'one hand washes the other; two, the face' as the Kurdish proverb puts it – and that division is fatal to national aspirations.

These divisions, coupled with the overall lack of the political sophistication needed to promote their cause, have meant that until recent years their plight has gone largely unheeded and their appeals for help unheard. In some respects the suffering of the Kurds has been as great as that of any oppressed people since World War II. They are the only community ever to have suffered bombing by nerve agents since those banned weapons were invented. The Iraqi secret police have used poison to liquidate specific Kurdish opponents both at home and abroad, and even in the camps where ordinary Kurds have sought refuge. They have lost thousands at the hands of the armies of the states in which they live as well as in inter-Kurdish civil wars, which as often as not have been propagated by those who seek to keep the Kurdish nation subjugated.

In 1983 the Barzani clan alone lost 8,000 men at a stroke – an act of vengeance by Saddam Hussein which has few parallels in modern history and yet which passed virtually unnoticed by the outside world.

In mid-July of that year, at the height of the war between Iraq and Iran, the Iranians advanced into enemy territory in Iraqi Kurdistan. Saddam Hussein blamed the Kurds, not only for participating in the offensive but for having guided in the Iranian troops.

So, on 30 July, he sent his forces to surround the Qushtapa and Diyana refugee camps near Arbil. They had orders to round up every man wearing a red turban, a sign of membership of the Barzani clan. All males between the ages of twelve and eighty, whether sick or well, fit or handicapped, were seized, loaded on to trucks and driven in convoy towards Baghdad. Later they were transferred to southern Iraq and finally to desert camps near the Jordanian border. They were never seen again. Some weeks later the regime arrested and executed three of Mullah Mustafa Barzani's sons. All supplies to the families of the 8,000 were cut off, and they were left to fend for themselves, without ever being told what had happened to the menfolk.

The fate of the 8,000 was never revealed. Jalal Talabani, during his abortive peace negotiations with Baghdad, raised the matter with Saddam and was asked why a Talabani should bother about what happened to a Barzani. He replied that, despite their differences, they were both Kurds. It seems beyond doubt that the Barzanis were murdered soon after their capture. In Kurdistan we were told that they had been buried in mass graves, some with limbs left exposed to mark the burial places.

If the massacre was meant to end the Kurdish rebellion, then it failed. For all the iniquities visited upon the Kurds, they persist in returning to the fray, despite the apparent hopelessness of the cause. Even today they appear no nearer the ultimate goal of a nation-state than they ever were. In Iraq the majority of Kurds would be happy to settle for autonomy, at least in the short term, not independence, in spite of all that has happened; in Iran too Kurdish nationalist feeling would be satisfied by greater recognition from the government; only in Turkey are the PKK guerrillas intent on setting up their own state, and they are opposed by as many of their own people as they are by Turks.

Kurdish attitudes to statehood are partly a result of geographical isolation: the country is land-locked, mountainous and has been historically dominated by hostile neighbours. There has never been a consistently friendly country to act as the patron of an emergent Kurdish state; Kurdish history is one of exploitation by occupiers and by rival empires which used the Kurds as their border police, or as trip-wires to give warning of invasion. In the earliest records of the Kurds references are always to tribes or principalities, never to the Kurds as a nation or ethnic group, or even to what would now be considered the whole of Kurdistan.

Although the Kurds are clearly a separate nation by all the usual criteria of shared language, culture and way of life, it frequently appears that the fact of being different from their neighbours is the main thing which unites them. Only in recent years have the first tentative steps been taken towards creating a pan-Kurdish under-standing – 'movement' would be too strong a word – and this only took place because of the impetus given by the disasters visited upon Iraqi Kurdistan in 1988–9. The International Conference on the Kurds held in Paris in October 1989 was the first occasion in modern times on which Kurds from all five states and from the diaspora were represented. The meeting, held under the auspices of Madame Danielle Mitterrand's France-Libertés organization, was principally aimed at examining the human rights situation in the various regions of Kurdistan, and in discussing ways of publicizing the plight of the Kurds. Its political content was virtually non-existent; while many spoke in the conference hall in favour of greater co-operation among Kurds of different states, PKK militants stood outside and condemned the 'petit bourgeois reformists' inside for limiting their demands to cultural autonomy.

Yet, for allowing this modest gathering to take place on its soil, the French government brought down the wrath of three powerful states upon its head. Turkey accused the French of trying to destabilize a friendly country and banned left-wing MPs from travelling to the conference; Iran referred to France's 'hostile action'; and Iraq summoned up all the resources of the powerful pro-Iraqi lobby in France to try to have the conference suspended because it represented 'a Zionist and imperialist plot against Baghdad'. If a meeting of 200 Kurds can pose such a threat, what might the Kurdish nation not do if it were united?

These extreme reactions to the Paris conference provide a snapshot of the chronic dilemma faced by the Kurds when they try to get together: they always face a united response from those who claim to be their protectors. If there is one policy which is shared by the governments of Iran, Iraq, Turkey and, to a lesser extent, Syria, it is one of maintaining the Kurdish population in a state of cultural, political and, at times, physical subjugation. Another facet of the dilemma is that outside powers, when faced with the choice of supporting the Kurds or risking alienating a regional power, invariably opt for maintaining good relations with the regional power. Thus, when Turkey and Iraq protested at Jalal Talabani's April 1988 visit to the State Department, the United States bowed to the pressure by ordering the 'no contacts' policy which was to remain in force long after the invasion of Kuwait.

Because the responses to even the most tentative steps towards Kurdish unity have been so harsh, the Kurds have generally gone out of their way to make clear that, in each state, they are fighting separate campaigns against different enemies. This has often brought the nationalist movement into conflict with itself, as in the late 1960s, when Mullah Mustafa Barzani's forces in Iraq helped to strangle the Kurdish peasant rebellion in Iran on behalf of the shah. Similarly, in the 1990s the Kurds of Iraq sought to improve relations with Turkey, at the same time as their fellow Kurds in the PKK were waging a violent guerrilla war against the Ankara government.

At the height of the 1991 rebellion against Saddam Hussein, the Iraqi Kurdish leadership was at pains to stress that theirs was a movement towards autonomy, not independence. This assurance was given, not for the benefit of the government of Iraq but rather for that of the governments of neighbouring states, which feared the uprising might spill over the frontiers into their territories. Even before the rebellion began, the KDP of Iraq took the precaution of warning Turkey's PKK not to disturb the peace along the Turkish border near KDP territory.

If results are anything to go by, then this self-imposed demarcation within the Kurdish nationalist movement has not served the wider Kurdish cause. Rather, it has given the regional powers the opportunity to play off one community of Kurds against the other; at the same time Kurds in one state have shown themselves only too willing to ignore the rights of their people in other states in order to pursue their own local struggle.

The Kurds have been kept divided by outsiders but have also kept themselves divided. As a consequence, and in contrast to the experience of other national liberation struggles, no pan-Kurdish political movement has evolved. The Iraqi Kurds have often sought to portray themselves as a model for Kurds elsewhere, because of their occasional successes and the part they have played in keeping the nationalist movement alive; but this is a long way from claiming to be a pan-Kurdish movement. The PKK has aspired to be the vanguard party of all Kurds by claiming to fight for the complete independence of Kurdistan, but it is essentially a Turkish-based movement which opportunistically saw in the defeat of the Kurdish rebellions in Iraq a chance to extend its own influence.

By a narrow definition of the concept of nationhood – that of a community sharing a common outlook and purpose – the Kurds probably fail, and are condemned for ever to exist uneasily as minorities within the frontiers of more advanced nations. Yet the virulence and persistence of their struggles against central authority appear to show that there is a sense of common purpose lurking in the Kurdish consciousness, if only the political structures were there to bring it to the fore.

One of the problems is that despite their shared cultural heritage, the Kurds have been driven apart by historical trends which have tended to accentuate their differences. As a consequence of this, no cross-border culture has emerged, which in turn has helped to perpetuate the differences between the separate groups. Probably the single greatest drawback to Kurdish nationhood is the lack of a commonly accepted script for written Kurdish. The

Iraqi, Syrian and Iranian Kurds still write in Arabic script, while in Turkey the modified Roman script introduced by Ataturk for modern Turkish is used by the Kurds.

Ironically, it was the Kurdish intellectual class that emerged in the final years of the Ottoman empire which helped to create this linguistic divide. Though the early Kurdish nationalist publications were printed in Constantinople from the turn of the century, when the Young Turk movement provided a reformist climate, they were published in Turkish, so that even if it had been possible, nothing would have been achieved by taking the pamphlets into Kurdistan. The very first Kurdish journal, called simply *Kurdistan*, appeared in Cairo in 1898 and was subsequently published – such were the vagaries of Ottoman politics – in Geneva and Folkestone before finally moving to Constantinople after the Young Turks' coup.

The appeal of the Kurdish politicians was always in the towns, where clandestine writing could be circulated, and where there was an educated elite capable of reading it. Illiteracy has been higher among the Kurds than the generality of the country in which they live, due to the inhospitable geography of the region they inhabit and to the fact that what little schooling they get is usually in a foreign language – Arabic, Persian or Turkish. So, even if problems of distribution and surveillance could have been overcome, there would have been little point in circulating political tracts inside any part of Kurdistan.

Yet there has always been a respect for learning among the Kurds, and although Kurdistan was on the outer, tribal-dominated fringes of the Ottoman empire, an intellectual class emerged among the families of the elite in the late nineteenth century, just as similar movements emerged among the Arab and Christian subjects of the Sublime Porte. Kurds, Albanians and others were prominent in the modernizing political movements within the empire in partnership with those reformist Turks who were ultimately to move towards pan-Turkish nationalism. Young Kurds, particularly in the reign of Abdul Hamid II, were enrolled in military academies and tribal schools which were specifically set up to integrate the Kurds into the new reformist Ottoman structures. As a result, by the outbreak of World War I Kurds held important posts in both army and state.

Like most of the politico-intellectual groups within the empire, the Kurdish organizations took their lead from Europe – for the subjects of the sultan, Europe was equated with both civilization and progress. They adopted Western dress and Western culture, and campaigned for the introduction of the Latin script to replace Arabic writing. After the revolution of 1908 Kurdish and other ethnically based movements were relatively free to organize within the empire, and the first Kurdish political organization, Taali we Terrakii Kurdistan, or Renewal and Progress of Kurdistan, was established in Constantinople by a descendant of Bedir Khan. The city-based intellectuals tried to spread their message of political and cultural nationalism to Kurdistan itself by setting up Kurdish clubs in the main cities there, but the Ottoman authorities proved less permissive in the countryside than in the capital, and Kurdish nationalism remained a force confined essentially to Constantinople.

In any event the period of liberalization lasted only as long as it took for the Young Turks to establish themselves, and to set out on the course of pan-Turkish expansion which had always been at the root of their movement, and which excluded the interests of the non-Turkish populations of the empire. Some Kurdish activists were gaoled, while others – members of the Bedir Khan clan in particular – sought refuge in Europe.

Back in the mountains, political developments in the Ottoman capital were of little consequence. At the very moment when the Kurdish intellectuals were excited by the false dawn in Constantinople, the Barzanis and others were in a state of revolt against the continuing interference of the Ottoman authorities in tribal affairs.

Religion has always been another divisive factor, despite the fact that the majority of Kurds are Sunni Muslims. The differences are less important now than in the past, when the declaration of a *jihad* by the sultan influenced the Kurds to fight with the Turks and Germans against the allies, or when religious intolerance inspired the Kurds to take part in the pogroms against the Armenians. But religion does remain a factor in the continuing divisions within Kurdish society, which includes many sects that are, in Sunni Islamic terms, heretical. These religious differences also have class overtones, with the dispossessed minorities within Kurdish society tending to be associated with the more esoteric and unorthodox sects. And, although the leadership of the Kurdish revolts from the nineteenth century onwards has tended to fall to the Sunni tribal aristocracy, the religious minorities have generally proved to be the most fervently rebellious sections of Kurdish society.

Centuries after they converted from Zoroastrianism, some of the customs of the old religion, such as Newruz, with its emphasis on fire, linger on. Those who converted to Islam followed the liberal Shafite school of Sunnism, which distinguishes them from their Turkish and Arab neighbours, who predominantly follow the Hanafite school. In the southernmost Kurdish provinces of Iran, however, the Muslim Kurds are predominantly Shia, sharing the religion of their Persian neighbours.

There were Christian converts in the first centuries after Christ – there is a record of the conversion of a tribe which worshipped trees and deified a copper idol – and there are still important Christian communities, particularly around the Iraqi towns of Zakho and Amadiyeh in northern Iraq, Kurdish cities at the centre of ancient caravan ways, the confluence of old roads and migrations. The Christians of these towns have always been the first to join new uprisings against repressive governments and are noted for their nationalist fervour.

One of the most important minority groups which is exclusively Kurdish is the Yazidi sect. The beliefs of the Yazidis owe something to all the main religions of the area, Zoroastrianism, Islam, Christianity, Judaism and Manichaeism. They were once a million strong in what is now Iraq, but their numbers were reduced to 70,000, mainly in the Mosul region, through systematic massacres by the Sunni Ottomans. The Yazidis, whose holy book, which no outsider may see, is said to be written in Kurdish, deny the existence of evil and believe in the dualism of God and Malak Taus, or Satan, whom they believe to be the agent of the divine will. For this reason, and as a result of the propaganda of more orthodox neighbours, these highly moral people have been persecuted as devil-worshippers.

A much larger minority community is that of the Alevis, an extreme offshoot of Shiism. The three million Alevis in Turkey are the descendants of the tribes, both Kurdish and Turkoman, which fought on the side of the Shia Persian empire against the Ottomans in the sixteenth century. When the Ottomans drove the Persians out of eastern Anatolia at the beginning of the sixteenth century, the Alevis found their homeland incorporated into the Sunni caliphate. They resisted the Ottomans, but they were crushed – 40,000 Alevis were massacred in 1514 by the victorious Ottomans.

As outcasts within Sunni society, following a religion which had elements of non-Islamic faiths, the Alevis were little understood, and there began to attach to them all the libels which in another era were spread about the Jews. Their Sunni neighbours called them 'extinguishers of light' and alleged that they took part in nocturnal orgies. Anyone from eastern Anatolia is assumed by Turks to be an Alevi and treated with suspicion, and sometimes contempt. Even other Kurds distance themselves from the Alevis, who speak a separate dialect, Zaza, which exists alongside the more generally used Kurmanji. They are also notable for their rejection of the usual Islamic practices. Their women go unveiled, they do not observe the Five Pillars of Islam – the statement of belief, prayer five times daily, almsgiving, fasting and pilgrimage – and do not use mosques. Instead trees often become objects of veneration in Alevi areas and may be seen with votive pieces of cloth tied to the branches.

The Alevis in Turkey are objects of political as well as religious dislike, rather in the same way that the Shia in many parts of the Middle East are regarded. Thus, because they have always been a deprived class outside the mainstream, they have tended to drift towards extremist politics and to identify with other disaffected groups. The anti-Kemalist revolts of the 1920s invariably erupted in the Zaza-speaking Alevi regions. In the 1970s many of them took part in left-wing activities, and as a result there was a nasty series of attacks by the Grey Wolves, the right-wing militia run by Alparslan Turkes. There were many killings, as the Grey Wolves were well-armed, while the Alevis were mainly village people with nothing more than knives to defend themselves. Only after several hundred were killed in Karamanmaras did the government send troops to the area to try to restore order.

The eclectic nature of much of Kurdish religion may be a historical reflection of the resistance to conversion during the early Islamic period. Isolated in their mountain fastnesses, the Kurds were not only slow to adopt the new faith, they also adapted it to fit in with the old pagan and Zoroastrian beliefs. In some cases their religions show a mischievous pragmatism whereby some sects pay lip-service to Islam while avoiding its more rigorous restrictions. The Ahli Haq of Iran, for instance, fast for only three days a year rather than throughout the month of Ramadan. Their folklore explains that the Prophet Mohamed was slightly deaf, and when God – evidently a Kurdish-speaker – told him that the faithful should fast for *se ruz* ('three days'), Mohamed misheard it as *si ruz* ('thirty days'). Fortunately, the correct message was relayed to the Ahli Haq by the Shia saint, Ali, and they are therefore spared the need to observe the month-long fast. Again, this heretical religion is the faith of the poor and dispossessed peasantry, a fact reflected in their belief that on the Day of Judgement the rich and the powerful will be punished.

Although the overwhelming majority of Kurds are Sunni Muslims, they follow their religion in an undemonstrative way –

travellers over the years have reported that many Kurds are as happy saying their prayers in Christian chapels as in mosques. The Sufi branch of Islam is also important, with the Qaderi and Naqshabandi dervish orders being most numerous. The mosque of Sheikh Abdul-Qadr al Gailani in Baghdad is at the centre of a Kurdish quarter, and is always well-maintained by government grants as an easy way of buying off dissidence. The dervish brotherhoods were once an important factor in the nationalist movement, acting as a kind of freemasonry which united various areas of Kurdistan. The power of the Barzanis in the Badinan is based firmly on their position as hereditary religious leaders rather than as great landowners.

Even among the Sunni Kurds, there are traces of an earlier, pagan and orgiastic faith which occasionally surfaces and which sets them apart from their fellow Muslims. In the countryside there is a residual belief in djinns and demons and elements of animal worship; until relatively recent times mullahs would act much as village witch-doctors, performing ceremonies and reciting incantations to drive out madness or to cure the sick. This paganistic approach to orthodox religion reached its height with Sheikh Nebi, a nineteenth-century divine who, in order to curb arrogance among his people and exalt humiliation towards God, recommended pornographic formulas to accompany prayer. Sodomy and coprophagy were encouraged, because the depth of the fall was said to reflect the sincerity of repentance. Nebi had forty wives, which did not prevent him, during his travels, from deflowering virgins offered to him by parents in expiation of seven generations of fire in hell.

The Kurds' liberal interpretation of Islam is reflected in their attitude towards women. The veil is practically unknown in many parts of Kurdistan, and it is not unusual for women to attain distinction or high office – in British mandate times a woman took on the leadership of a tribe after her husband was killed, retained the loyalty of the people, and was recognized by the British as being in control of the tribal area. Now, if a Kurdish woman achieves particular fame, her children will adopt her name rather than that of their father.

The religious patchwork of Kurdistan is less rich and vital than it was even two or three generations ago. Up to 1948, for instance, there was a substantial community of Jews in Kurdistan, who shared with the Armenians the craftwork of the souks, making gold and silver jewellery and operating as money changers. Estimates were that as many as 18,000 Jews lived in Kurdistan, but the vast majority moved to Israel once the state was established. The Christian communities have also been on the wane since World War I.

The encroachments of the modern world and the movement of Kurds out of their homeland have caused many of the old traditions to die away. But religious differences are still of more than just anthropological interest; religion is still high in the Kurdish hierarchy of loyalties, and for many, particularly those who have been persecuted for their minority beliefs, their faith is still more important than the much less easily definable concept of pan-Kurdish nationalism.

Despite the divisive factors of language and religion, and the barriers of international borders, the Kurds have all been striving in modern times for some form of separation from the countries in which they find themselves, some identification as a people, even if they cannot achieve nationhood. Although the best hope for the Kurds came at the end of World War I, the state they were promised at the time might well not have survived; just as Mustafa Kemal extinguished the Armenian Republic, he would probably have destroyed a Kurdish entity as well. Yet the precedent alone would have been valuable in asserting present Kurdish claims. As it was, the state was never created, mainly as a result of colonialist geopolitics but also, as most Kurds would now admit, because of a lack of sophisticated leadership.

That too has been a Kurdish failing. The great national leaders they have produced have always come from the tribes – Sheikh Mahmoud, Sheikh Said, Simko, and above all, Mullah Mustafa.

In modern times the educated urban elite have tended to look down on such figures, and to believe they were not capable of providing a focus for all Kurds, or even all Kurds in a particular country. In the same way the tribesmen who provided the backing and the muscle for the nationalists' struggle were contemptuous of the urban politicians, whom they dismissed as talkers, not doers. Qazi Mohammed of Mahabad may have been the one exception to this rule, but the Mahabad Republic was little more than a village state, attracting support only from its immediate environs. Even the idea of this first Kurdish state failed to enthuse the Kurds across the border, who made their attitude plain by setting up their own organization, with the disastrous results which have been seen.

Latterly, the esoteric quarrels between different Kurdish groups have led to fragmentation, to a plethora of separate organizations, and to jockeying among the leaders for what little power there was on offer. The Kurdistan Front established by Massoud Barzani and Jalal Talabani and the rest at the end of the Iran–Iraq war was the first time so many disparate groups had come together.

In Turkey and Iran government repression ensured that no powerful movement grew up. In Iran the effect was to turn the Kurds in on themselves, concentrating on their own affairs and having little truck with cross-border co-operation. In Turkey the harshness of successive governments in Ankara inexorably produced tougher and more militant reaction, culminating in today's bitter struggle by the PKK, which falsely claims to speak for others besides the Turkish Kurds – very few in Iran or Iraq would acknowledge this Marxist group as their representatives.

The model for the Kurds might have been the PLO, which, though it has not yet succeeded in freeing a single inch of Palestinian territory, has kept the Palestinian cause firmly at the forefront of international attention. The parallels between the plight of the Palestinians and that of the Kurds should not be too closely drawn. The Kurds at least have the benefit of living on their own land, even if it is subject to the encroachments caused by policies of Arabization and Turkification. The majority of Palestinians, by contrast, live in exile, having fled their homes when Israel was established in 1948. The Kurdish leaders are keenly aware of the example of the Palestinian exodus, which accounts for the fact that they invariably encourage their people, despite all the dangers, to return to their homes each time they are driven away, lest the land be lost for ever.

The success of the PLO has depended on a number of factors: the existence of a single enemy with a political, geographic, ethnic and religious character; the backing of powerful regional states; a highly educated, articulate and sophisticated base; and a leader capable of holding together individuals and groups with contrasting and often conflicting aims, ideals and methods. By making the PLO an organization which can accommodate such wildly different leaders as the Marxist George Habash and the right-wing Khaled Hassan, and represent both the bourgeois notables of the West Bank and the dispossessed in the Gaza Strip, Yasser Arafat has done more than anyone else to keep Palestine on the international agenda. The PLO has provided the umbrella under which Palestinians of all views can gather to pursue their own goals in their own way.

Arafat himself has time after time lost the political advantage he had gained, notably in the aftermath of the Israeli invasion of Lebanon, or at the time of the Gulf war. Yet he has always managed to hold together almost all the Palestinians – enough, at least, to continue to be heard.

The Kurds have had no such chairman. Mullah Mustafa was the nearest the Kurds ever came to having an Arafat, but he lacked the Palestinian's keen political sense, his single-mindedness, or his ability to tailor his own views as the situation demanded. Mullah Mustafa was a national hero to the Kurds, a legend, but he was no diplomat, or even a very good politician, and there was no one around him who could help. Mullah Mustafa could rally the tribes, but he could never appeal to the increasingly important and vocal Kurds who had drifted to the cities. His method was to demand the maximum when he felt he was in a strong position, and to compromise when the Iraqis were getting the better of him.

Mullah Mustafa understood the tribal politics of northern Iraq, but not the interplay of personalities and interests which governed things in Baghdad, and made no attempt to play off one group against another, to woo the army or to exploit Baath Party weakness. He was an old-style leader, an all-or-nothing man who finished up with nothing. Mullah Mustafa, basically a country gentleman whose youthful interest in politics led others to push him into a role he did not really want, looks better, more charismatic, more adroit, in retrospect than he did at the time.

Mullah Mustafa was, however, a bridge between the traditional and modernizing elements in Kurdish society – a tribal leader who, in modern terms, became a leader of a national liberation struggle. These twin elements are still apparent among the Kurds but over the years there has been a steady increase in the influence of the educated, town-based intelligensia within the nationalist movement. The KDP of Iraq, for example, although it is identified with Mullah Mustafa and his family, is in fact a party run on modern lines by a non-tribal and predominantly urban leadership.

The ascendancy of the educated non-tribals has only been possible, however, because of a strong and distinct tribal tradition which has kept the idea of Kurdishness alive when the Kurds might otherwise have been absorbed into the societies of the states in which they live. It was the town-based nationalists, particularly in Iraq, who succeeded in harnessing the energy of the tribal movement and directing it away from sectarian disputes towards a national goal. The urban intelligensia has not only been active on the political front; it has also been important in creating a Kurdish culture in the fields of literature, poetry and cinema which has helped to establish the cultural framework of a modern, rather than a purely traditionalist nation.

But, despite the gradual emergence of a pan-Kurdish culture, nationalist politics remain firmly confined within the national borders of the regional states. The need to deal with the enemy at home, as represented by the central authority – Saddam Hussein in the case of Iraq – has meant that no pan-Kurdish political movement has emerged. This is an understandable failing: because of the absence of reliable allies, the Kurds have had to fight a piecemeal struggle against their oppressors. When their rebellions fail, as in Iraqi Kurdistan in 1991, they cannot look outside for support and are forced to negotiate and compromise with the state. But this unavoidable weakness has engendered a further political weakness: that of the tendency of the Kurdish nationalists to see their own political future in terms of the non-Kurdish state in which they live. Thus, the political leaders in Iraqi Kurdistan are always as much interested in staking a claim to governmental power in Baghdad – reflected in their demands that certain Cabinet posts be reserved for Kurds – as they are in pursuing demands for autonomy.

By rejecting the concept of outright independence, for perfectly sensible and pragmatic reasons, the nationalist leaders are nevertheless accepting that Kurds will, for the foreseeable future, remain a minority within their host states, whereas, united and independent, they would form a state larger than most of its neighbours.

It is an outlook which the Kurds have been forced to adopt from bitter experience. In earlier times the Ottomans, the Safavids, the Arabs, and the British all used the Kurds, turning them off and on like a tap in one country after another, as a rebellion was needed here, a tribal conflict there, urban unrest in another place. The Kurds sometimes believed the assurances of conquerors and occupiers, and were hurt and distressed when they were betrayed – as they always were.

Because of the international reaction to the plight of the Kurds who fled Saddam Hussein in the spring of 1991, it is unlikely that they will ever again be so mercilessly attacked, or fall victim to the kind of horror which the world carefully avoided seeing at Halabja. It is equally unlikely that the United States and its allies will again mount the sort of operation which set up the safe havens in northern Iraq and prevented the Iraqi army from exercising its authority in its own country. Saddam Hussein may not need the Republican Guard to subdue the Kurds a second time: selective assassination, detention, harassment and economic discrimination can be just as effective as battalions of troops – and much less likely to provoke outside interference or even to excite attention. As the Kurds asked when the allies were giving them assurances of continued protection as they pulled out of Iraq in July 1991, what would it take to make the allies launch their deterrent force from Silopi? One murder? A dozen? One village taken over by Arabs? Two? Of course there was no answer, nor could there be. The Kurds realized that very well, and understood too that only an agreement with Saddam Hussein, an agreement with guarantees, could ensure them a safe future.

The allied war against Saddam brought little benefit to the Kurds, whether in Iraq or elsewhere. In Turkey the situation was made worse by the allied presence. There were allegations from the PKK that the allied forces were helping the Turks, and though there was no evidence of that, the mere presence of the allies naturally sealed off certain areas to the guerrillas and made their operations more difficult to mount. There were again questions about President Ozal's motives too, as he made a bid to have Turkish troops included in the rapid reaction force; the Turkish leader, still running things on his own despite waning political popularity, seemed intent on putting his country in a position from which it could expand its influence into northern Iraq, just as he did at the beginning of the crisis.

Rebuffed for the second time by the allies, Ozal took a leaf from the Israeli book and announced that he was establishing 'a security zone' along the border – on the Iraqi side, of course. Such an extra defence will make things a little more difficult for the PKK guerrillas, but it will no more solve the problem than the Israeli buffer zone in southern Lebanon has prevented Palestinian attacks on Israel. The one thing it seems certain to do is to create a problem for the future: the Iraqis will not for long remain a cowed, subjugated and disarmed nation. An independent and economically viable Iraq will not tolerate the occupation of even a small part of its land by Turkey. This small step by President Ozal may well prove a major problem in the future.

In Iran, at the end of the war, the Islamic regime remained determined to do all it could to embarrass the Iraqis and to whittle away that country's remaining strength so that it could never again pose a danger to Tehran. As a result there was some cross-border co-operation with Iraqi Kurds, but, in the main, the Iranians concentrated on causing trouble in southern Iraq and giving help to the Shia there – about 30,000 were left in the marshes at the end of the rebellion.

From Syria, characteristically, there was silence. After spending frustrating years as a client state of the Soviet Union, President Assad picked his moment to change horses and sided wholeheartedly with the Americans against his old enemy, Iraq. For a few weeks, as the allies encouraged help to the Kurds in Iraq, their brothers in Syria were allowed to give them moral and material support, helping them with their difficult lines of communication, sending in supplies, and playing host to all the Kurdish leaders who went into their homeland via Syria. It was a brief springtime, but any thoughts that the Syrian Kurds might have had of aspiring to some kind of autonomy for themselves were quickly extinguished once the emergency was over; there was no violence, for by this stage in President Assad's long rule, the examples had already been given; it was enough to warn the Syrian Kurds against causing any unrest, against making problems. They heard and understood, and nothing happened.

It was another example of the difficulties faced by the Kurds because of their dispersal over five countries; if they were all concentrated into one state, they might by now have achieved independence. But in the eyes of the majority of the people in all the countries they inhabit, they are second-class citizens: in Turkey because they are regarded as backward, coming from a remote, barren region; in Iran as an integral part of the Iranian nation; and in Iraq and Syria for the worst crime of all – not being Arabs. For all the injunctions about tolerance in the Koran, non-Arab people in Arab lands have never been considered the equal of the indigenous population.

The Arab nationalism which began to emerge in the Ottoman empire after the Young Turks' coup has evolved into an exclusive doctrine, which tends to ignore the rights of non-Arab minorities in the Middle East. In the peculiar doctrine of Baathism, the most extreme form of Arab nationalism, the Kurdish territories of Iraq and Syria are deemed to be Arab land, despite the fact that they have no history of Arab settlement or culture. Ironically, the world powers have tended to share this Arabo-centric view of the region, looking upon it as an Arab preserve in which other nations, regardless of their size, have the status of alien minorities in their own land. It has meant that the Palestinians, for all their undoubted claims to be treated with justice, have dominated the international agenda on the Middle East to the detriment of non-Arab communities such as the Kurds.

The Arab nationalists also tend to gloss over the role played by non-Arabs in their history and culture, whether they be great leaders such as Saladin or the great medieval biographer and historian Ibn-Khillikan, also a Kurd. In more recent times Kurds have also been prominent in the mainstream of the Middle East. The first coup in the modern Arab world was staged in Iraq in 1936 by a Kurd, Bakr Sidqi. Some of the great landowning families of Syria were Kurdish well into the twentieth century and one, the Barrazis, provided two prime ministers for the newly independent state. In Lebanon the great Druse dynasty of the Jumblatts is said to be Kurdish in origin.

In the light of all that has gone on, the remarkable thing is that the Kurds have never adopted the modern weapons of guerrilla warfare – hijacking, hostage-taking, bombing. It has certainly not been for lack of knowledge or opportunity; by including the Kurds in their conscripted armies, all the states concerned ensured a pool of well-trained potential fighters, many expert in the use of explosives. In modern times it has certainly been partly a policy decision: the Kurdish leaders, despite their political differences, understood very well that they would forfeit the goodwill of the world if they took to terrorism – even the grudging, belated rescue operation mounted by the Americans would have been unthinkable if the Kurds were identified with hijacking and kidnappings. But it also has something to do with the Kurdish psyche; their history has always been of facing their enemies in pitched battle, of open warfare, not clandestine operations among civilians.

If there were to be a change – which is possible – then there would be no shortage of volunteers, for the cause would take precedence over in-built reluctance to use such methods. But dozens of Kurds we have talked to told us they would be deeply saddened if such a development took place. They would understand, but they would be unhappy, and, as a result, the politicians and leaders have been doing all they can to avoid a situation in which, out of desperation, a younger generation might decide that only direct action on the Palestinian model could have any results.

Perhaps one of the most significant developments for the Kurds is the upsurge of nationalism which has accompanied the liberation of eastern Europe and the subsequent break-up of the Soviet Union. Long-forgotten and unheard-of minorities are now claiming their right to independence on seemingly more slender grounds than those on which the Kurds base their demands for autonomy. As it is, the Kurds do not even enjoy observer status at the UN, a right accorded to the much smaller Palestinian nation. As the previous subjects of the Soviet empire take their seats at the United Nations, Kurds are perhaps entitled to ask: if an independent Kazakhstan or an independent Azerbaijan, why not an independent Kurdistan? Ironically, many Kurds in the Soviet Union have been forced to flee Armenia and Uzbekistan to seek refuge in the Russian Republic as a result of oppression by local nationalists. Even as others have sought to promote their own claims to statehood, so the Kurds have suffered.

Perhaps in the turmoil of the Soviet Union, there is a chance to re-establish the Kurdish autonomous region of Lechin, which survived for six years after it was set up by Lenin. It might serve as a model for the Kurdish movement elsewhere, although its re-creation remains a distant dream.

For while the rest of the world might be able to come to terms with the death of the Soviet Union and its replacement by a disparate group of greater or lesser independent states, it is much harder to acknowledge the possibility of a united, independent Kurdistan. Iraq, weakened but not destroyed, would counter any such move as a threat to its national survival; Turkey, more powerful and allied to the West, has its own interests intimately tied up with the changes in the Soviet Union, with the dream of a Turkish-speaking Turanian state, stretching from the Hellespont to central Asia, no longer as far-fetched as it might once have been. The Kurds would have no part in such a scheme; they would continue to be an embarrassment and an inconvenience, a non-Turkish heartland in a vast Turkish federation.

The one source of optimism for the Kurds is that, at last, their case is reaching the outside world, principally because of the sufferings inflicted upon them after the war in Kuwait. Military defeat has been outweighed to some extent by a shift in international perceptions towards the Kurdish cause. There is now a large sophisticated and urbanized diaspora – with Kurdish societies in the United States, western Europe and elsewhere – which is gradually learning the techniques of bringing the nation's claims to world attention.

Some days after the death of Stalin, the exiled Mullah Mustafa Barzani, who had been shunted off during his exile to work as a fruit-weigher on a state farm, travelled to Moscow. He went to the permit office at the gates of the Kremlin and hammered on the door. When a guard asked him what he wanted, he replied: 'This is not I but the Kurdish revolution knocking at the Kremlin door.' The Kurds are still knocking on the door, but their knock is louder now.

Index